MASTERING
FINANCIAL ACCOUNTING

ANDY SIMMONDS

**MACMILLAN
EDUCATION**

First published 1986

Published by
MACMILLAN EDUCATION LTD
Houndmills, Basingstoke, Hampshire RG21 2XS
and London
Companies and representatives
throughout the world

Printed in Great Britain by
Anchor Brendon Ltd,
Tiptree, Essex

British Library Cataloguing in Publication Data
Simmonds, A. K. J.
Mastering financial accounting. — (Macmillan
master series)
1. Accounting
I. Title
657'.48   HF5635
ISBN 0-333-38290-0
ISBN 0-333-37650-1 Pbk
ISBN 0-333-37651-X Pbk export

MASTERING

FINANCIAL ACCOUNTING

MACMILLAN MASTER SERIES

Banking
Basic Management
Biology
British Politics
Business Communication
Business Microcomputing
Chemistry
COBOL Programming
Commerce
Computer Programming
Computers
Data Processing
Economics
Electronics
English Grammar
English Language
English Literature
Financial Accounting
French
French 2
German

Hairdressing
Italian
Keyboarding
Marketing
Mathematics
Modern British History
Modern World History
Nutrition
Office Practice
Pascal Programming
Physics
Principles of Accounts
Social Welfare
Sociology
Spanish
Spanish 2
Statistics
Statistics with Your Microcomputer
Study Skills
Typewriting Skills
Word Processing

To Janet

*without whose love, encouragement
and support this book would not
have been written*

CONTENTS

vii

CONTENTS

CONTENTS

CONTENTS

PREFACE

In the years that I have spent both as an accountancy student and as a lecturer to accountancy students, I have consulted a good many accountancy textbooks. Unfortunately, no single textbook has ever met my specific requirement, which is to summarise concisely the subject of financial accounting within a reasonable space. My opportunity to remedy this situation has now arrived! The technique that I have adopted as far as possible is to summarise the objective of each technique covered, set out the special accounts required and the purpose of each, summarise the double entry of normal transactions involved, and provide a worked example to bring the whole together. In order to make the information most easily assimilated, I have used charts to set out the purpose of special accounts and summarise the double entry.

The text takes into account the Companies Act 1985, and at the time of writing SSAP 23 is the most recent Accounting Standard. I have deliberately excluded those areas that I consider to be advanced financial accounting such as merger accounting, inflation and current cost accounting, deferred tax, and the details of earnings per share. At the other extreme, the text commences with a consideration of book-keeping techniques so far as the examination student is concerned; it is not intended to be a full treatise on the subject of book-keeping in practice.

I trust that the final work will prove invaluable to examination students at all levels, as well as enlightening to those to whom accountancy is a mystery! Finally, I wish to acknowledge the assistance of my former colleagues Steve Lumby, in getting the project off the ground, and Peter Bruff, in teaching me the greater part of what I know; also to thank Ellen and Sophia for their secretarial abilities.

London   A. K. J. S.

GLOSSARY

GLOSSARY

ACCOUNT PAYABLE – an alternative term for 'creditor'.

ACCOUNT RECEIVABLE – an alternative term for 'debtor'.

ACCRUAL – an amount recognised in the Profit and loss account of a period which differs from the period in which the item is settled.

ALLOTMENT – the assignment of shares to particular holders. At this stage the holder acquires the unconditional right to be entered in the register of members.

AMORTISATION – depreciation of an asset with a definite useful life, e.g. a lease.

ASSET – an item of property or a resource that is expected to confer an economic benefit.

AUTHORISED SHARE CAPITAL – the term usually used to describe the maximum number of shares at nominal value which a company may issue, as stated in its Memorandum of Association.

BAD DEBT – a debt which, it is assumed, will never be paid.

BASIC RESEARCH – an alternative term for 'pure research'.

BONUS ISSUE – an issue of bonus shares, normally to existing shareholders and in proportion to their existing holdings.

BOOK VALUE – the amount at which an item is stated in accounts.

CALL – a demand by a company for the payment of part or all of unpaid nominal share capital.

CALLED-UP SHARE CAPITAL – the nominal value of shares allotted by a company, including the amount of any calls made but not yet paid.

CAPITAL EMPLOYED – a general term used to describe funds invested in a business. Alternatives include shareholders' capital employed (i.e. share capital and reserves) and total capital employed (i.e. shareholders' capital employed plus long-term loans).

CAPITAL EXPENDITURE – expenditure to acquire or add to fixed assets, or which increases the capacity, efficiency or useful life of an existing fixed asset.

CAPITALISATION ISSUE – an alternative term for 'bonus issue'.

CARRYING AMOUNT – an alternative term for 'book value'.

CONSERVATISM – an alternative term for 'prudence'.

CONTINGENCY – a condition which exists, the outcome of which depends upon an uncertain future event. The key element of a contingency is that it may or may not happen.

CONTRA – the process of netting two equal and opposite entries or balances.

CURRENT ASSET – an asset which is not intended for use on a continuing basis. Such an asset is expected to be sold or consumed in the ordinary course of business and within one year.

CURRENT LIABILITY – a financial obligation or liability falling due for payment within one year.

DEFALCATION – the misappropriation of property by a person entrusted with that property. The term normally extends to false accounting entries made to cover the loss.

DELINQUENT ACCOUNT RECEIVABLE – an alternative American term for a bad or overdue account.

DISTRIBUTABLE PROFITS – profits or reserves which are available to a company for the payment of dividends.

DOUBTFUL DEBT – an alternative term for 'bad debt'.

EQUITY – the residue left after subtracting liabilities of a business from assets. Equity capital is that contributed in return for a share in any distribution, either by way of dividend or on a winding-up, and normally carries votes.

EXTENDED TRIAL BALANCE – a Trial balance to which additional columns are added to allow for adjustments, and the preparation of Profit and loss account and Balance sheet.

FAIR VALUE – the amount at which an asset could be exchanged in an arm's-length transaction.

FIXED ASSET – an asset intended for use on a continuing basis in a business's activities.

FOLIO – two facing pages of an account book, normally given the same reference number.

HISTORIC COST – the actual cost of acquiring or producing an asset.

INTANGIBLE ASSET – an asset in action (as opposed to a physical asset), e.g. know-how, goodwill, right to the use of a process.

INVENTORY – an alternative term for 'stocks and work-in-progress'.

LIABILITY – an obligation or claim against a business which will be settled by the transfer of assets.

MONETARY – an asset or liability whose value is dependent on the unit of currency in which it is measured, rather than upon any future purchase or selling prices.

NET WORKING CAPITAL – the excess of current assets over current liabilities. In the context of a funds statement it may exclude cash.

PAID-UP SHARE CAPITAL – the amount of allotted and called-up share capital for which payment has been made.

PROVISION – the estimate of a liability where the exact amount or timing of payment is uncertain. The term is also used in relation to periodic charges such as depreciation or bad debts.

RECOVERABLE AMOUNT – the amount which is recovered from an asset; it is the higher of the asset's net realisable value and the value arising from its use (or economic value).

RESERVE – profits or surpluses set aside by a company in excess of its known liabilities and which have not been distributed to shareholders.

REVENUE EXPENDITURE – expenditure which is expected to benefit only the current period.

SCRIP ISSUE – an alternative term for 'bonus issue'.

TANGIBLE ASSET – a physical asset.

WORKING CAPITAL – a general term describing stocks, debtors, cash and creditors, i.e. those items used to conduct the day-to-day operations of a business.

PART I

BOOK-KEEPING

ACCOUNTING OBJECTIVES

1.1 BUSINESS STRUCTURES

So! You think you're interested in accountancy! You should be warned at this early stage that your interest may have two serious consequences. The first is that you may end up earning a living from it. The second is that people may class you as the Brain of Britain. This latter effect stems from the public at large refusing to have anything whatsoever to do with adding up (let alone taking away!). It was something they could not understand at school, and assumed it could be avoided thereafter. Accountancy appears to them as a closed book. Unfortunately the day does arrive when the closed book is needed, together with an interpreter (and come to that an author as well!).

This is where the accountant finds his enviable role in society, earning a living from doing something that the general public have told themselves they cannot possibly do!

What, in a nutshell, does an accountant do?

This book is concerned with *financial* accounting. This in essence is the *preparation* of accounts for various classes of business. All courses in accountancy will have some element of financial accounting, although it may be referred to as 'bookkeeping' or simply 'accounts'. We can identify three distinct areas of study. These are:

1 Preparation and maintenance of accounting records;
2 Preparation of final accounts; and
3 Interpretation of the final accounts.

This last area is often overlooked by students, as well as in practice. Since the accountant is the person who prepares the accounts, he or she is in the unique position to understand what they mean. Without the explanation, the figures themselves are rather pointless.

Thus, the accountant's task extends well beyond how to add up and take away. It must start with an understanding of the business with which he or she is dealing.

This is to be our starting-point. This chapter examines the different kinds of business structures commonly encountered as a foundation upon which to understand their accounts.

1.1.1 Sole trader

The simplest type of business structure. A single private individual decides to set up a business. There are no legal formalities to set up, carry on or terminate the business. The name used may be that of the proprietor or some other name. Legally there is no distinction between the proprietor and the business, and an aggrieved customer claiming 'I'll take you for every penny you've got' could certainly try. One outside interested party would be H. M. Inspector of Taxes, who would maintain a more than healthy interest in any profit that the business made. Such profit would be part of the proprietor's personal taxable income.

1.1.2 Partnership

Two or more private individuals join together in business, e.g. solicitors. The partners must agree the management and financial arrangements between themselves, and this is normally written down in case of disagreement. An Act of Parliament does exist (The Partnership Act 1890), but is applied only when the partners have failed to cover some point in their written agreement, so that subject to their own agreement the partners may set up, carry on and terminate their business without legal formalities. The name of the business may be the names of all the partners strung together, e.g. Smith, Smith, Jones and Smith, or some other name, e.g. The School of Accountancy. As with a sole trader there is no legal distinction between the business and the partners, any of whom are privately liable for the business debts. H. M. Inspector of Taxes will wish to know of any profit earned in order to tax it, and will share the burden of tax between the partners.

1.1.3 Limited companies

A limited company, or more properly limited liability company, is a separate legal person in its own right. There is a wealth of legislation, contained in the various Companies Acts, governing the formation, continuation and termination of a company. The 'owners' of the company are the shareholders, whose personal liability for the debts of the company is limited to the shares they have purchased, hence the term 'limited liability company'. An aggrieved customer could sue the company, but could not sue the shareholders. The shareholders may be directly involved in the company's management; this is more likely if the company is small. However, in a larger company the shareholders will take no part in day-to-day management. This is delegated to the directors, who are paid fees and possibly a salary. The company's name will always include the word 'limited', e.g. J. Smith (Butcher) Limited, Marks & Spencer Plc. Plc stands for 'public limited company'. The distinction between 'limited' and 'Plc' is dealt with in Chapter 8.

As regards taxation the company is dealt with as a separate taxable person, liable to pay tax (called corporation tax) on its profits. The shareholders receive a dividend each year, and it is that on which they will account for personal income tax.

1.2 PURPOSE OF ACCOUNTS

Once we have identified the people interested in each business we can identify why they are interested and, more particularly, why they are interested in financial information.

Business structure	Interested person	Reason
Sole trader	Proprietor	Has a profit or a loss been made? How much can be withdrawn? What is the business worth?
	H. M. Inspector of Taxes	How much tax must be paid?
	Bank manager	Is the business a safe risk for lending money?
Partnership	Partners	Has a profit or a loss been made? How is it to be shared out between the partners? How much can each partner withdraw? What is the business worth?
	H. M. Inspector of Taxes	How much tax must be paid? How is it to be shared out between the partners?
	Bank manager	Is the business a safe risk for lending money?
Limited company	Directors	How are we managing the company? Have our decisions resulted in a profit or loss? How much dividend do we recommend to the shareholders? What is the company worth?

Business structure	Interested person	Reason
	Shareholders	How are the directors managing the company? Is our investment secure? Does our investment show a good return?
	H. M. Inspector of Taxes	How much tax must be paid?
	General public	Who is responsible for the company's actions?
	Bank manager (and other lenders of money)	Is the company a safe risk for lending money?
	Employees/unions	Can the company afford to give us a pay rise?

In the case of the sole trader and the partnership accounts are not generally available to the public. However, in the case of a limited company accounts are placed on public file at Companies House, and may be viewed by the public.

1.3 TYPES OF FINANCIAL STATEMENT

The term 'financial statement' covers any statement of financial information. Various forms have been developed to answer the questions raised in the previous section. At this stage we are particularly interested in two forms of statement. These are the Profit and loss account, and the Balance sheet. Once these have been grasped, other forms will be considered.

Financial statement	Structure	Supplementary statements
Profit and loss a/c	List of revenues and expenses in order to show the net profit or loss in a specified period of time	Trading a/c Manufacturing a/c Appropriation a/c
Balance sheet	List of assets and liabilities in order to show the net value of the business at a specific point in time, and to identify the claims of any outside parties on those assets.	

It can be seen that the first statement, the Profit and loss account, covers a period of time which is called the 'accounting period'; it shows whether the business has been a financial success or failure. The second statement, the Balance sheet, shows the position at one specific point in time, normally the last day of the accounting period; it is rather like a financial photograph.

These two financial statements form the basis of a 'set of accounts'. In the next two chapters we will consider the preparation of Profit and loss accounts and Balance sheets of sole traders.

CHAPTER 2

DOUBLE-ENTRY
BOOK KEEPING

2.1 THE ACCOUNTING EQUATION

2.1.1 The basic equation

For the past 500 years a system called 'double entry' has been in operation. All modern accounts use this system. It recognises that each transaction has two aspects. Let's start at the beginning of a business. At the
outset of a business the proprietor introduces cash (say £1,000). The
business now has an ASSET (the £1,000 cash); and the proprietor has
introduced CAPITAL (of £1,000). The two are equal. Thus we can say:

ASSETS	=	CAPITAL
Cash £1,000	=	Capital introduced £1,000

Suppose now that £600 of the cash is used to buy a van. The business
now has two assets. One asset has decreased; cash decreases to £400.
Another asset increases; the van is worth £600. The equation still stands.

ASSETS		CAPITAL
Cash £400 + Van £600	=	Capital introduced £1,000
Total £1,000		

Suppose now that the proprietor borrows £300 from the bank. An asset
is increased; cash increases by £300 to £700. However, the business now
owes the bank £300. This £300 owed to the bank is called a LIABILITY,
and enters our equation thus:

ASSETS		CAPITAL + LIABILITIES
Cash £700 + Van £600	=	Capital introduced Loan owed £1,000 + to bank £300
Total £1,300		Total £1,300

Alternatively, we could write the equation

ASSETS – LIABILITIES		CAPITAL
Cash £700 + Van £600 –		Capital introduced £1,000
Loan owed to bank £300	=	
Total £1,000		

It is in this form that the equation is normally written.

To increase an asset we can   *   increase capital
                   or   *   increase a liability
                   or   *   reduce another asset
To reduce an asset we can   *   reduce capital
                   or   *   reduce a liability
                   or   *   increase another asset

Provided we do the same thing to both sides of the equation, or equal and opposite things to the same side, it will continue to balance.

2.1.2 Debit and credit

For convenience we will adopt a convention in order to tell more easily what individual changes are doing. Any item which appears positive on the left side of the equation, i.e. assets, are deemed DEBIT items. Any item which appears negative on the left side of the equation, i.e. liabilities, are deemed CREDIT items. Any item which appears positive on the right side of the equation, i.e. capital, is deemed a CREDIT item.

> DEBIT appears on the LEFT as a POSITIVE
> or the RIGHT as a NEGATIVE
>
> CREDIT appears on the RIGHT as a POSITIVE
> or the LEFT as a NEGATIVE

Now if we wish to increase or decrease any item we can simply refer to the item affected, and by stating whether the change is a debit or credit change we will know whether it was an increase or a decrease.

Item	Change	Debit or credit?
Asset	Increase	Debit
	Decrease	Credit
Liability	Increase	Credit
	Decrease	Debit
Capital	Increase	Credit
	Decrease	Debit

2.2 CASH TRANSACTIONS

2.2.1 The cash account

In Section 2.1.1 we took a simple example involving:

Capital introduced	£1,000
Purchase of van	£ 600
Loan from bank	£ 300

Each item affected cash. In order to keep a running total of cash at any instant we use a two-sided account. Since cash is an asset, debits (increases) will appear on the left. Credits (decreases) to cash appear on the right. The amount by which the debits exceed the credits represents the excess of cash received over cash paid, or the amount of cash now held by the business. In financial terms we call this cash the BALANCE. The account appears thus:

Cash account

(*Debits*)	£	(*Credits*)	£
Capital introduced	1,000	Purchase of motor-van	600
Loan from bank	300		

The account can then be 'closed off' and the balance identified. This is done by inserting the total of the largest side on both sides of the account and inserting the balancing figure on the small side thus:

Cash account

	£		£
Capital introduced	1,000	Purchase of motor-van	600
Loan from bank	300	Balance carried forward (c/f)	700
	£1,300		£1,300

Balanced brought forward (b/f)£700

This £700 balance is a debit balance. It is carried forward from the credit side and brought forward in the next period to the debit side.

This type of account is called a 'T account' because of its appearance.

The use of T accounts can be applied to any jtem whether asset, liability or capital.

2.2.2 Revenue and expenses

So far we have only considered increasing capital by introducing cash. Consider the following example:

Capital introduced	£1,000
Purchase stock for	£1,000
Sell all stock for	£1,200

The Cash account will appear thus:

Cash account

(*Debits*)	£	(*Credits*)	£
Capital introduced	1,000	Purchase of stock	1,000
Sale of stock	1,200		
		Balance carried forward (c/f)	1,200
	£2,200		£2,200
Balance brought forward (b/f)	1,200		

The only asset now held by the business is cash of £1,200. There are no liabilities. The equation must still balance. The answer is that capital has increased to £1,200. The increase of £200 is attributable to PROFIT on selling the stock, and is an increase (credit entry) to the Capital account. The profit is made up of a sales item of £1,200, which would appear initially in a Sales account less a purchase item of £1,000, which would appear initially in a Purchases account. The sale is referred to as revenue; the purchase is an expense.

The Sales account and Purchases account are netted off to find the profit, and this is added to the Capital account.

2.2.3 Recording the entries

Example 1

Joe decided to set up a grocery business on 1 January. The following transactions relate to the month of January.

1 Jan	Joe paid £1,000 into the business
2 Jan	Purchased goods for resale (stock) for £400
3 Jan	Purchased a delivery van for £350
4 Jan	Borrowed £200 from the bank
10 Jan	Sold all stock for £550
12 Jan	Purchased more stock for £425
14 Jan	Paid motor expenses of £20
15 Jan	Paid rates of £60
17 Jan	Paid rent of £30
20 Jan	Sold all stock for £580
26 Jan	Paid motor expenses of £15

The transactions can be recorded in the accounts. Note that each entry indicates where the balancing entry appears. The word 'account' is abbreviated to a/c.

Capital account

	£			£
		1 Jan	Cash a/c capital introduced	1,000

Cash account

		£			£
1 Jan	Capital a/c – cash introduced	1,000	2 Jan	Purchases a/c – goods purchased	400
4 Jan	Loan a/c – bank loan	200	3 Jan	Van a/c – purchase of delivery van	350
10 Jan	Sales a/c – goods sold	550	12 Jan	Purchases a/c – goods	425

20 Jan	Sales a/c – goods sold	580	14 Jan	Motor expenses a/c expenses	20
			15 Jan	Rates a/c – rates	60
			17 Jan	Rent a/c – rent	30
			26 Jan	Motor expenses a/c – expenses	15

Purchases account

		£			£
2 Jan	Cash a/c – goods purchases	400			
12 Jan	Cash a/c – goods purchased	425			

Van account

		£			£
3 Jan	Cash a/c – purchase of delivery van	350			

Loan account

	£			£
		4 Jan	Cash a/c – bank loan	200

Sales account

	£			£
		10 Jan	Cash a/c – goods sold	550
		20 Jan	Cash a/c – goods sold	580

Motor expenses account

		£		£
14 Jan	Cash a/c – expenses	20		
26 Jan	Cash a/c – expenses	15		

Rates account

		£		£
15 Jan	Cash a/c – rates	60		

Rent account

		£		£
17 Jan	Cash a/c – rent	30		

2.3 TRIAL BALANCE

After all entries are safely recorded the next stage is to identify the balance on each account. Once this is done we will list all the debit and credit balances together. This is called a TRIAL BALANCE. It serves two functions. First, we can check that the debits equal the credits. Second, it is a useful summary from which to proceed to the next stage. The following rules are important:

Assets and liabilities	Balances carried forward are included in the Trial balance and brought forward in the next period.
Revenues and expenses	Balances included in the Trial balance are not carried forward, but will eventually be included in capital.
Capital	Balance is included in Trial balance, but is adjusted later for any profit, loss or drawings.

Cash account   (ASSET)

		£			£
1 Jan	Capital a/c – cash introduced	1,000	2 Jan	Purchases a/c – goods purchased	400
4 Jan	Loan a/c – bank loan	200	3 Jan	Van a/c – delivery van	350
10 Jan	Sales a/c – goods sold	550	12 Jan	Purchases a/c – goods purchased	425
20 Jan	Sales a/c – goods sold	580	14 Jan	Motor expenses a/c – expenses	20
			15 Jan	Rates a/c – rates	60
			17 Jan	Rent a/c – rent	30
			26 Jan	Motor expenses a/c – expenses	15
			31 Jan	Balance c/f	1,030
		£2,330			£2,330
1 Feb	Balance b/f	1,030			

Purchases account   (EXPENSE)

		£			£
2 Jan	Cash a/c – goods purchased	400			
12 Jan	Cash a/c – goods Purchased	425			
			31 Jan	Balanced transferred	825
		£825			£825

Van account   (ASSET)

		£			£
3 Jan	Cash a/c – purchase of van	350	31 Jan	Balance c/f	350
		£350			£350
1 Feb	Balance b/f	350			

Loan account   (LIABILITY)

		£			£
31 Jan	Balance c/f	200	4 Jan	Cash a/c – bank loan	200
		£200			£200
			1 Feb	Balance b/f	200

Sales account   (REVENUE)

		£			£
			10 Jan	Cash a/c – goods sold	550
			20 Jan	Cash a/c – goods sold	580
31 Jan	Balance transferred	1,130			
		£1,130			£1,130

Motor expenses account   (EXPENSE)

					£
14 Jan	Cash a/c – expenses	20			
26 Jan	Cash a/c – expenses	15			
			31 Jan	Balance transferred	35
		£35			£35

Rates account   (EXPENSE)

	£			£
15 Jan Cash a/c – rates	60			
		31 Jan Balance transferred		60
	60			60

Rent account   (EXPENSE)

	£			£
17 Jan Cash a/c – rent	30			
		31 Jan Balance transferred		30
	£30			£30

TRIAL BALANCE at 31 January

	Debit balances £	Credit balances £
Capital a/c	–	1,000
Cash a/c	1,030	–
Purchases a/c	825	–
Van a/c	350	–
Loan a/c	–	200
Sales a/c	–	1,130
Motor expenses a/c	35	–
Rates a/c	60	–
Rent a/c	30	–
	£2,330	£2,330

2.4   TRADING, PROFIT AND LOSS ACCOUNT

This is the first stage in preparing the final accounts. From the Trial balance we identify all the revenue and expense items. In our example these are purchases, sales, motor expenses, rates and rent.

First we compare sales and purchases, the result being GROSS PROFIT.

	£
Sales	1,130
Purchases	(825)
Gross profit	£305

This is called the TRADING ACCOUNT. Below gross profit the remaining expense items are listed, subtotalled and deducted from gross profit; the result is called the NET PROFIT.

		£
Sales		1,130
Purchases		(825)
Gross profit		£305
	£	
Motor expenses	(35)	
Rates	(60)	
Rent	(30)	
		(125)
Net profit		£180

The section from gross profit to net profit is called the PROFIT AND LOSS ACCOUNT.

The whole financial statement is called the TRADING, PROFIT AND LOSS ACCOUNT.

Note that revenue items appear positive, and expense items negative.

2.5 BALANCE SHEET

This is the second stage in preparing the final accounts. The Balance sheet is prepared in two sections. The first lists assets, and deducts liabilities.

	£
Assets:	
Van	350
Cash	1,030
	1,380
Liabilities:	
Loan from bank	(200)
Total assets *less* liabilities	£1,180

Note that assets appear positive, and liabilities negative.

The second section deals with capital.

	£
Capital introduced	1,000
Net profit	180
Capital at 31 January	£1,180

There are two methods of presentation:

VERTICAL PRESENTATION

	£
Assets:	
Van	350
Cash	1,030
	1,380
Liabilities:	
Loan from bank	(200)
Total assets *less* liabilities	£1,180

	£
Representing:	
Capital introduced	1,000
Net profit	180
Total capital	£1,180

HORIZONTAL PRESENTATION

	£		£
Van	350	Capital introduced	1,000
Cash	1,030	Net profit	180
			1,180
		Loan from bank	200
	£1,380		£1,380

The vertical presentation is preferred since it is most widely used in practice, and will be used throughout this book.

The Capital account can now be closed off after the net profit has been entered.

Capital account

		£			£
31 Jan	Balance c/f	1,180	1 Jan	Cash a/c – capital introduced	1,000
			31 Jan	Net profit for period	180
		£1,180			£1,180
			1 Feb	Balance b/f	1,180

2.6 DRAWINGS

If a proprietor takes cash or goods out of the business for private use, we call the value taken out DRAWINGS. A Drawings account is opened, and the entries are as follows:

Type of drawings	Debit entry	Credit entry
Cash	Drawings a/c	Cash a/c (reducing the cash balance)
Goods	Drawings a/c	Purchases a/c (reducing the amount taken into the Trading a/c)

The final balance on the Drawings account (*debit balance*) is transferred to the Capital account, reducing the balance on the Capital account.

N.B. Drawings never appear in the Profit and loss account, and are never included in sales, since a trader cannot 'sell' to himself. The treatment of drawings is illustrated in the example in the next section.

2.7 STOCK ADJUSTMENTS

In the previous example all the goods purchased were sold before the end of the accounting period. Where there is STOCK which has been purchased but remains unsold at the end of the period, an adjustment is necessary.

Adjustment	Reason
TRADING ACCOUNT – the COST of stock unsold appears as a DEDUCTION from PURCHASES	Purchases less the stock unsold now represents the COST of stock which has been sold
BALANCE SHEET – the cost of unsold stock appears as an a ASSET	The business holds a valuable asset which can be sold in the future

Example 2

Fred set up a business on 1 March. The following are his first month's transactions.

1 Mar	Introduced £2,000 cash
2 Mar	Borrowed £500 from Tom
3 Mar	Purchased stock for £1,200
4 Mar	Purchased a van for £1,100
5 Mar	Paid rent of £150
10 Mar	Sold part of stock for £900
12 Mar	Purchased further stock for £400
17 Mar	Paid van expenses of £70
25 Mar	Sold part of stock for £750
28 Mar	Withdrew £60 cash for private use
30 Mar	Paid electricity bill of £40

At the end of the month there was stock unsold which had cost £320.

The accounts will appear thus:

Capital account

	£			£
		1 Mar	Cash a/c – introduced	2,000

Cash account

		£			£
1 Mar	Capital a/c	2,000	3 Mar	Purchases a/c	1,200
2 Mar	Loan a/c	500	4 Mar	Van a/c	1,100
10 Mar	Sales a/c	900	5 Mar	Rent a/c	150
25 Mar	Sales a/c	750	12 Mar	Purchases a/c	400
			17 Mar	Van expenses a/c	70
			28 Mar	Drawings a/c	60
			30 Mar	Electricity a/c	40
			31 Mar	Balance c/f	1,130
		£4,150			£4,150
1 Apr	Balance b/f	1,130			

Loan account

		£			£
			2 Mar	Cash a/c – Tom	500
31 Mar	Balance c/f	500			
		£500			£500
			1 Apr	Balance b/f	500

Purchases account

		£				£
3 Mar	Cash a/c	1,200				
12 Mar	Cash a/c	400	31 Mar	Balance transferred		1,600
		£1,600				£1,600

Van account

		£				£
4 Mar	Cash a/c	1,100	31 Mar	Balance c/f		1,100
		£1,100				£1,100
1 Apr	Balance b/f	1,100				

Rent account

		£				£
5 Mar	Cash a/c	150	31 Mar	Balance transferred		150
		£150				£150

Sales account

		£				£
			10 Mar	Cash a/c		900
			25 Mar	Cash a/c		750
31 Mar	Balance transferred	1,650				
		£1,650				£1,650

Van expenses account

		£				£
17 Mar	Cash a/c	70	31 Mar	Balance transferred		70
		£70				£70

Drawings account

		£				£
28 Mar	Cash a/c	60	31 Mar	Balance transferred		60
		£60				£60

Electricity account

	£		£
30 Mar Cash a/c	40		
		31 Mar Balance transferred	40
	£40		£40

The Trial balance at 31 March appears thus:

	Debits £	Credits £
Capital introduced	–	2,000
Cash a/c	1,130	–
Loan a/c	–	500
Purchases a/c	1,600	–
Van a/c	1,100	–
Rent a/c	150	–
Sales ac	–	1,650
Van expenses a/c	70	–
Drawings a/c	60	–
Electricity a/c	40	–
	£4,150	£4,150

Note that stock unsold does not yet appear in the Trial balance. It is now entered as a final adjustment.

	Debits £	Credits £
Total per above	4,150	4,150
Stock at 31 March		
Trading a/c	–	320
Balance sheet	320	–
	£4,470	£4,470

We can now prepare the final accounts:

TRADING, PROFIT AND LOSS ACCOUNT for March

	£	£
Sales		1,650
Purchases	(1,600)	
Closing stock	320	

Cost of sales		(1,280)
Gross profit		370
Expenses		
Rent	(150)	
Van expenses	(70)	
Electricity	(40)	
		(260)
Net profit (transferred to Capital account)		£110

BALANCE SHEET at 31 March

	£
Assets	
Van	1,100
Stock	320
Cash	1,130
	2,550
Liabilities	
Loan from Tom	(500)
Total assets *less* liabilities	£2,050
Representing	£
Capital introduced	2,000
Net profit for month	110
	2,110
Drawings	(60)
Capital at 31 March	£2,050

Example 3

In the next month Fred continues to trade. The summarised transactions were:

	£
Total sales	2,100
Total purchases	1,830
Cash withdrawn for private use	70
Goods withdrawn for private use	40

Total expenses	£
— rent	160
— van expense	75
— electricity	45

On 30 April the cost of stock unsold amounted to £360.

The accounts will appear thus:

Capital account

	£			£
		1 Apr	Balance b/f	2,050

Cash account

		£			£
1 Apr	Balance b/f	1,130	X Apr	Purchases a/c	1,830
X Apr	Sales a/c	2,100	X Apr	Drawings a/c	70
			X Apr	Rent a/c	160
			X Apr	Van expenses a/c	75
			X Apr	Electricity a/c	45
			30 Apr	Balance c/f	1,050
		£3,230			£3,230
1 May	Balance b/f	1,050			

Sales account

		£			£
			X Apr	Cash a/c	2,100
30 Apr	Balance transferred	2,100			
		£2,100			£2,100

Purchases account

		£			£
X Apr	Cash a/c	1,830	X Apr	Drawings a/c – stock for private use	40
			30 Apr	Balance transferred	1,790
		£1,830			£1,830

Drawings account

		£			£
X Apr	Cash a/c	70			
X Apr	Purchases a/c	40	30 Apr	Balance transferred	110
		£110			£110

Rent account

		£			£
X Apr	Cash a/c	160			
			30 Apr	Balance transferred	160
		£160			£160

Van expenses account

		£			£
X Apr	Cash a/c	75			
			30 Apr	Balance transferred	75
		£75			£75

Electricity account

		£			£
X Apr	Cash a/c	45			
			30 Apr	Balance transferred	45
		£45			£45

The Trial balance will appear thus:

	Debits £	Credits £
Capital at 1 April	–	2,050
Cash a/c	1,050	–
Loan a/c	–	500
Van a/c	1,100	–
Sales a/c	–	2,100
Purchases a/c	1,790	–
Drawings a/c	110	–
Rent a/c	160	–
Van expenses a/c	75	–
Electricity a/c	45	–
Stock at 1 April – transferred to Trading a/c	320	–
	£4,650	£4,650

Stock at 30 April		
Trading a/c	–	360
Balance sheet	360	–
	£5,010	£5,010

N.B. 1. Stock at 1 April appears in the Trial balance. It is transferred to the Trading account where it is added to purchases, since it has either been sold or is included in the closing stock.

   2. Van and Loan accounts have not been shown, since the balances have remained unchanged.

The final accounts now appear thus:

TRADING, PROFIT AND LOSS ACCOUNT for April

	£	£
Sales		2,100
Opening stock	(320)	
Purchases	(1,790	
	(2,110)	
Closing stock	360	
Cost of sales		(1,750)
Gross profit		350
Expenses		
Rent	(160)	
Van expenses	(75)	
Electricity	(45)	
		(280)
Net profit		£70

BALANCE SHEET at 30 April

Assets	£
Van	1,100
Stock	360
Cash	1,050
	2,510
Liabilities	
Loan from Tom	(500)
Total assets *less* liabilities	£2,010

Representing:	
Capital at 1 April	2,050
Net profit for month	70
	2,120
Drawings	(110)
Capital at 30 April	£2,010

2.8 FIXED, CURRENT AND NON-CURRENT

In the previous example Fred purchased a van. This was not for resale, but for use in the business. We call this a FIXED ASSET. In general a fixed asset is an asset that is purchased and used by the business in its activities; it is not purchased to make a profit on resale. Such an asset will be used over a number of years, and will eventually need to be replaced when it is worn out, or becomes obsolescent. Other examples of fixed assets are property, plant and machinery, fixtures and fittings, office machinery and furniture. In addition to fixed assets Fred had other types of assets. These were stock (goods for resale) and cash. Stock was purchased for resale, and would be sold and replaced regularly. Cash is used to pay for assets and expenses, and is the form in which liabilities and revenues are received. Cash can be held in notes and coins, or in a bank account. These types of assets are called CURRENT ASSETS. In general a current asset is an asset that is not intended for use on a continuing basis in the business.

Liabilities are also divided into two groups. The split is made on the basis of when the liability is to be paid.

When payable	Heading on balance sheet
Within one year of the Balance-sheet date	'Creditors: amounts falling due within one year' (also referred to as 'current liabilities')
In more than one year of the Balance-sheet date	'Creditors: amounts falling due after more than one year' (also referred to as 'non-current liabilities')

The Balance sheet is ordered thus:

	£	£
Fixed assets	–	x
Current assets	x	
Creditors: amounts falling due within one year	(x)	
Net current assets		x
Total assets *less* current liabilities		x
Creditors: amounts falling due after more than one year		(x)
		£x
Represented by:		
Capital		£x

2.9 ACCRUALS AND PREPAYMENTS

In the examples so far, expenditure such as rent, electricity and motor expenses which were paid in each period were related to that period. In reality, though, rent may be paid quarterly, half-yearly or even annually; electricity will be paid quarterly.

Our objective is to charge the Profit and loss account with expenditure items which relate to that period rather than items which are paid for in that period. We call this the MATCHING-UP CONCEPT, alias ACCRUALS CONCEPT.

At the end of each accounting period each item of expense is reviewed to see if payments in the period relate to future periods (PREPAYMENTS) or if any expense has been incurred for which payment has not been made (ACCRUAL).

2.9.1 Prepayments

The entries necessary are shown below:

Transaction	Entry in accounts
Cash payment for expenditure	Debit (*Dr*) Expense a/c Credit (*Cr*) Cash a/c This is the normal entry for a payment.
At end of period, compute the amount already paid for future periods	Carry forward on Expense a/c from credit side to debit side. This balance appears on the Trial balance as a debit item and in the Balance sheet as a current asset. It is called a PREPAYMENT.

Balance transferred to Profit and loss a/c	This is the balancing figure on the Expense a/c. It appears on the Trial balance as a debit item and is then included in the Profit and loss a/c.

N.B. It is possible to make a similar adjustment following the Trial balance.

Example 4

Harriet commenced her business on 1 July 19X1. Her first accounting period was the six months to 31 December 19X1. On 30 September 19X1 she paid £300 to the local authority for rates for the nine months to 31 March 19X2.
    Show the Rates account.

Rates account

19X1		£	19X2		£
30 Sep	Cash a/c	300	31 Dec	Balance transferred (to Profit and loss a/c)	200
			31 Dec	Balance c/f (*Prepayment*)	100
		£300			£300
19X2					
1 Jan	Balance b/f (*Prepayment*)	100			

Points arising:

1 The payment of £300 was for nine months.
2 The balance carried forward related to the three months to 31 March 19X2. It is computed 3/9 × £300 = £100. It will appear in current assets on the Balance sheet
3 The balance transferred to the Profit and loss account relates to the six months to 31 December 19X1.

Example 5

Harriet (as in Example 4) continued to trade in 19X2. On 10 April 19X2 she paid £500 to the local authority for rates for the year to 31 March 19X3.
    Show the Rates account for 19X2.

Rates account

19X2		£	19X3		£
1 Jan	Balance b/f	100	31 Dec	Balance transferred	475
10 Apr	Cash a/c	500		(to Profit and loss a/c)	
			31 Dec	Balance c/f	125
				(*Prepayment*)	
		£600			£600
19X3					
1 Jan	Balance b/f	125			
	(*Prepayment*)				

Point arising:

1 The payment of £500 related to the twelve months to 31 March 19X3.
2 The balance carried forward at 31 December 19X2 relates to the three months to 31 March 19X3. It is computed $3/12 \times £500 = £125$.
3 The balance transferred to the Profit and loss account is the balancing figure. It is made up of:

	£
Three months to 31.3.X2	100
Nine months to 31.12.X2 (*9/12 × £500*)	375
	£475

2.9.2 Accruals

The entries necessary are shown below:

Transaction	Entry in accounts
Cash payment for expenditure	Dr Expense a/c Cr Cash a/c This is the normal entry for a payment
At end of period compute the amount not yet paid for, but which relates to the current period.	Carry forward on Expense a/c from debit side to credit side. This balance appears on the Trial balance as a credit item, and in the Balance sheet as a creditor due within one year. It is called an ACCRUED EXPENSE.

Balance transferred to Profit and loss a/c	This is the balancing figure on the Expense a/c. It appears on the Trial balance as a debit item, and is then included in the Profit and loss a/c.

N.B. It is possible to make a similar adjustment following the Trial balance.

Example 6

Dick commenced trading on 1 March 19X1. His first accounting period was the four months to 30 June 19X1. The first payment of rent of £1,200 was made on 31 August 19X1, and was for the six months to that date.
    Show the Rent account.

Rent account

19X1		£	19X1		£
30 June	Balance c/f (*accrued expense*)	800	30 June	Balance transferred (*to Profit and loss a/c*)	800
		£800			£800
			1 Jul	Balance b/f	800

Points arising:

1 The eventual payment of £1,200 on 31 August 19X1 will be for the six months to that date.
2 The balance carried forward at 30 June 19X1 relates to the first four of those six months. It is computed $4/6 \times £1,200 = £800$.
3 This same amount becomes the balance transferred to the Profit and loss account.

Example 7

Dick (as in Example 6) continued to trade for a further year to 30 June 19X2. On 31 August 19X1 he duly paid the £1,200 rent. On 28 February 19X2 he paid a further £1,200 rent for the six months to that date. The next payment of rent was due on 31 August 19X2 for the six months to that date, and amounted to £1,500.
    Show the Rent account for the year to 30 June 19X2.

32

Rent account

19X1		£	19X1		£
31 Aug	Cash a/c	1,200	1 Jul	Balance b/f	800
19X2			19X2		
28 Feb	Cash a/c	1,200	30 Jun	Balance transferred	2,600
30 Jun	Balance c/f	1,000		(*to Profit and loss a/c*)	
		£3,400			£3,400
			1 Jul	Balance b/f	1,000

2.10 CREDIT TRANSACTIONS AND DISCOUNTS

2.10.1 Credit given to customers – trade debtors

So far we have considered only cash transactions. It is quite usual for a business to give credit to customers, i.e. the goods are sold, but payment is not required until some time in the future. An account is opened for each credit customer in order to keep a running total of the balance due from each customer. At the Balance-sheet date such balances due from customers are called TRADE DEBTORS and are included in the Balance sheet under CURRENT ASSETS. Entries are as follows:

Transaction	Debit entry	Credit entry
Goods sold to Smith	Smith's a/c	Sales a/c
Goods returned by Smith	Sales returns a/c	Smith's a/c
Cash received from Smith	Cash a/c	Smith's a/c

N.B. Sales returns are maintained on a separate account, and at the end of the period the balance is deducted from the sales for the period.

2.10.2 Credit taken from suppliers – trade creditors

Similarly it is quite usual for a business to receive credit from its suppliers of goods. An account is opened for each supplier in order to keep a running total of the balance due to each supplier. At the Balance-sheet date such balances due by the business are called TRADE CREDITORS and are included in the Balance sheet under CREDITORS: AMOUNTS FALLING DUE WITHIN ONE YEAR. Normally these balances would be paid in the month following supply. Entries are as follows:

Transaction	Debit entry	Credit entry
Goods purchased from Jones	Purchases a/c	Jones's a/c
Goods returned to Jones	Jones's a/c	Purchases returns a/c
Cash paid to Jones	Jones's a/c	Cash a/c

Since an account is maintained for each customer, and each supplier, a realistic business situation will require hundreds, perhaps thousands, of such accounts, and a system for maintaining them.

The individual accounts are therefore separated from the other accounts.

Individual accounts of	Collectively called
Customers	The Sales ledger
Suppliers	The Purchase ledger

In order to keep control over the individual accounts, and facilitate a more rapid preparation of the accounts, two total accounts are also maintained. One is for the total of customers' accounts and is called the DEBTORS' CONTROL ACCOUNT. The second, for the total of suppliers' accounts is called the CREDITORS' CONTROL ACCOUNT. Control accounts are dealt with fully in Section 3.5 in the next chapter. Example 8, which illustrates credit transactions, appears after the next sub-section.

2.10.3 Discounts

Two types of discount are possible:

(a) *Trade discounts*. These are given by businesses to other businesses in the same trade, e.g. the builders' merchants will offer a trade discount to a builder, a motor-parts dealer will offer a trade discount to a garage. Typically such discounts will amount to about 10 per cent or 20 per cent of basic price. They appear as deductions on the invoice and only the net amount is ever recorded in the accounts as a purchase or sale.

(b) *Cash discounts*. These are offered to all credit customers for paying balances due within a specified period of time. The purpose is to encourage customers to settle their accounts promptly. Percentages involved are much smaller than trade discounts, and 2 per cent or 3 per cent of invoice price would be typical. The discount only arises when the account is paid, and a separate account is opened to record discounts allowed (to all customers) which is an expense item, and another account to record discounts received (from all suppliers) which is a revenue item.

The entries may be summarised thus:

Transaction	Debit entry	Credit entry
Goods purchased from Smith. Basic price £100. 10% trade discount received. Net price £90.	Purchases a/c £90	Smith's a/c £90
Pays £88 to Smith in full settlement (£2 cash discount received).	Smith's a/c £88 Smith's a/c £2	Cash a/c £88 Discounts received a/c £2
Goods sold to Jones. Basic selling price £200 20% trade discount allowed. Net price £160.	Jones's a/c £160	Sales a/c £160
Receives £155 from Jones in full settlement (£5 cash discount allowed).	Cash a/c £155 Discounts allowed a/c £5	Jones's a/c £155 Jones's a/c £5

In each case the trade discount is never recorded, but is deducted before any entry is made. Subsequently when the cash is paid or received the Suppliers'/customers' account is not reduced merely by the cash paid/received, but by the cash together with the cash discount. This is logical, since there is now no balance outstanding.

At the end of each period the balance of discounts received (credit balance) and the balance of discounts allowed (debit balance) are included in the Trial balance, and thereafter transferred to the Profit and loss account.

Example 8

In Example 3 we left Fred at 30 April, with the following Balance sheet:

	£	£
Fixed assets		
Van		1,100
Current assets		
Stock	360	
Cash	1,050	
	1,410	

Creditors: amounts falling due
within one year
  Loan from Tom   (500)
                                        ────
                                                    910
                                                  ──────
                                                  £2,010
                                                  ──────
Representing:
Capital at 30 April   £2,010
                                                  ──────

Fred continued to trade in May. The following transactions took place:

2 May   Purchased goods from Robinson on credit for £400.
3 May   Sold goods to Brown on credit for £600.
5 May   Purchased goods from Davis on credit. List price was £700, but
        Davis gave a 10 per cent trade discount.
10 May Sold goods to Green on credit for £550.
13 May Withdrew £120 cash for private use.
16 May Paid rent of £320 for the months of May and June.
20 May Paid Robinson for goods supplied, less a 2 per cent cash discount.
21 May Green returned part of the goods sold to him. They had a selling
        price of £70.
22 May Received £582 in full settlement of goods sold to Brown.
24 May Sold goods for cash £1,500.
25 May Purchased goods for cash £1,200.
27 May Repaid £125 of the loan from Tom. The balance is repayable
        within one year.
28 May Sold further goods to Brown on credit for £420.
29 May Paid electricity bill of £55. In addition a further £15 worth of
        electricity had been used, but no payment had been made.
31 May Stock unsold amounted to £390.

The accounts will appear thus:

Cash account

		£			£
1 May	Balance b/f	1,050	13 May	Drawings a/c	120
22 May	Brown's a/c	582	16 May	Rent a/c	320
24 May	Sales a/c	1,500	20 May	Robinson's a/c	392
			25 May	Purchases a/c	1,200
			27 May	Loan a/c	125
			29 May	Electricity a/c	55
			31 May	Balance c/f	920
		£3,132			£3,132
1 June	Balance b/f	920			

Purchases account

		£			£
2 May	Robinson's a/c	400			
5 May	Davis's a/c	630			
25 May	Cash a/c	1,200	31 May	Balance transferred	2,230
		£2,230			£2,230

Sales account

		£			£
			3 May	Brown's a/c	600
			10 May	Green's a/c	550
			24 May	Cash a/c	1,500
31 May	Balance transferred	3,070	28 May	Brown's a/c	420
		£3,070			£3,070

Sales returns account

		£			£
21 May	Green's a/c	70			
			31 May	Balance transferred	70
		£70			£70

Robinson's account

		£			£
20 May	Cash a/c	392	2 May	Purchases a/c	400
20 May	Cash discount received a/c	8			
		£400			£400

Brown's account

		£			£
3 May	Sales a/c	600	22 May	Cash a/c	582
28 May	Sales a/c	420	22 May	Cash discount allowed a/c	18
			31 May	Balance c/f	420
		£1,020			£1,020
1 June	Balance b/f	420			

Davis's account

		£			£
			5 May	Purchases a/c	630
31 May	Balance c/f	630			
		£630			£630
			1 Jun	Balance b/f	630

Green's account

		£			£
10 May	Sales a/c	550	21 May	Sales returns a/c	70
			31 May	Balance c/f	480
		£550			£550
1 Jun	Balance b/f	480			

Cash discounts received account

		£			£
			20 May	Robinson's a/c	8
31 May	Balance transferred	8			
		£8			£8

Cash discounts allowed

		£			£
22 May	Brown's a/c	18			
			31 May	Balance transferred	18
		£18			£18

Loan account

		£			£
27 May	Cash a/c	125	1 May	Balance b/f	500
31 May	Balance c/f	375			
		£500			£500
			1 Jun	Balance b/f	375

Rent account

		£				£
16 May	Cash a/c	320	31 May	Balance transferred		
				(*to Profit and loss a/c*)		160
			31 May	Balance c/f		
				(*prepayment ½ × £320*)		160
		£320				£320
1 Jun	Balance b/f	160				

Electricity account

		£				£
29 May	Cash a/c	55				
31 May	Balance c/f		31 May	Balance transferred		
	(*accrued expense*)	15		(*to Profit and loss a/c*)		70
		£70				£70
			1 Jun	Balance b/f		15

Drawings account

		£				£
13 May	Cash a/c	120				
			31 May	Balance transferred		120
		£120				£120

TRIAL BALANCE at 31 May

	Debit	Credit
Capital at 1 May	–	2,010
Van a/c	1,100	–
Cash a/c	920	–
Purchases a/c	2,230	–
Sales a/c	–	3,070
Sales returns a/c	70	–
Brown's a/c	420	–
Davis's a/c	–	630
Green's a/c	480	–
Discounts received a/c	–	8
Discounts allowed a/c	18	–
Loan a/c	–	375
Rent a/c – Profit and loss a/c	160	–
– Prepayment	160	–

Electricity a/c – Profit and loss a/c	70	–
– Accrued expense	–	15
Drawings a/c	120	–
Opening stock	360	–
Closing stock		
Trading a/c	–	390
Balance sheet	390	–
	£6,498	£6,498

TRADING, PROFIT AND LOSS ACCOUNT for May

	£	£
Sales		3,070
Sales returns		(70)
		3,000
Opening stock	(360)	
Purchases	(2,230)	
	(2,590)	
Closing stock	390	
Cost of sales		(2,200)
Gross profit		800
Expenses		
Rent	(160)	
Electricity	(70)	
Discounts allowed	(18)	
Discounts received	8	
		(240)
Net profit		£560

(N.B. Discounts received appears positive, since it is revenue.)

BALANCE SHEET at 31 May

	£	£
Fixed assets		
Van		1,100
Current assets		
Stock	390	

Trade debtors		
Brown	420	
Green	480	
Prepayments – rent	160	
Cash	920	
	2,370	

Creditors' amounts falling due within one year		
Trade creditors		
Davis	(630)	
Accrued expenses – electricity	(15)	
Loan from Tom	(375)	
	(1,020)	
Net current assets		1,350
Total assets *less* current liabilities		£2,450
Representing		£
Capital at 1 May		2,010
Net profit for month		560
		2,570
Drawings		(120)
Capital at 31 May		£2,450

Exercises to Chapter 2

1. The following transactions occurred in March. You are required to write up the Cash account and compute the balance carried forward at the end of the month.

		£
1 Mar	Balance brought forward	2,520
2 Mar	Paid to Smith to clear account	360
3 Mar	Cash sales	1,490
4 Mar	Received from Red, a debtor	240
8 Mar	Office expenses paid	850
10 Mar	Cash purchases	1,100
12 Mar	Drawings by proprietor	500
15 Mar	Received from Blue, a debtor	1,390
17 Mar	Purchase of furniture for office	870
21 Mar	Cash sales	1,540

24 Mar	Rates paid	600
27 Mar	Paid to Jones for goods supplied	420
29 Mar	Repayment of loan	800

2. The following transactions relate to rent and rates for the year to 31 December 19X5. You are required to write up the Rent account and the Rates account.

   Rent is paid half-yearly in arrears on 31 March and 30 September. Payments made were 31 March 19X5 - £500, 30 September 19X5 - £500, 31 March 19X6 - £600.

   Rates are paid annually in advance on 1 April. Payments made were 1 April 19X4 - £800, 1 April 19X5 - £900.

3. The following transactions, which occurred in May, relate to the personal account of Brown, a customer.

		£
1 May	Balance brought forward	5,670
5 May	Payment from Brown	2,430
7 May	Sales at full invoice price (a 10 per cent trade discount was given on these goods)	3,000
10 May	Goods returned from Brown (full credit given)	500
20 May	Sales at full invoice price (a 15 per cent trade discount was given on these goods)	4,000
25 May	Payment from Brown	4,550
25 May	Cash discount given	130

You are required to record the transactions in the personal account of Brown and identify the balance at 31 May.

ACCOUNTING SYSTEMS

3.1 BOOKS OF PRIME ENTRY AND THE ACCOUNTING SYSTEM

In the previous chapter we considered a simple situation where each transaction was entered directly into an account which later appeared in a Trial balance. Collectively the accounts are referred to as the GENERAL LEDGER or NOMINAL LEDGER. (Other terms may be found, but these are the most common.) Frequently, the General ledger is in the form of a handwritten loose-leaf book, although it may be a set of machine-written cards, or a computer print-out of a magnetic file. Clearly, for a business which is handling hundreds, or perhaps thousands, of different transactions each day, it is not possible to enter each transaction in the General ledger as it happens.

The solution adopted is to use six additional 'books' to summarise similar transactions, and to enable subtotals to be entered in the General ledger at convenient intervals. Typically this would be once a month. These 'books' are called BOOKS OF PRIME ENTRY, since they show the initial recording of each transaction. Although referred to as 'books' the recording may appear on machine cards, or on a computer print-out. They are not part of the double-entry system. The double entry only arises when the books of prime entry are posted to the General ledger. The six books of prime entry are listed below, together with a brief description of the purpose and contents of each.

The accounting system from books of prime entry can be shown by the following flow diagram (Figure 3.1).

In the following sections we will examine each part of the system in more detail, and illustrate with examples. The books of prime entry are illustrated in Example 2 in Section 3.2.

fig 3.1   *accounting system from books of prime entry*

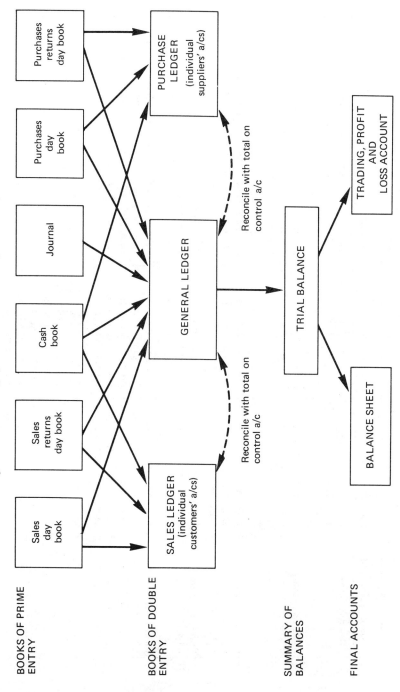

BOOKS OF PRIME
ENTRY

BOOKS OF DOUBLE
ENTRY

SUMMARY OF
BALANCES

FINAL ACCOUNTS

Book of prime entry	Purpose	Used to post	Details recorded
Sales day book	List sales invoices, and compute the total sales	Sales account; Customer's account	Date, invoice number, customer's name and reference number, amount
Sales returns day book	List credit notes issued and compute the total sales returns.	Sales returns account; Customer's account	Date, original invoice number, credit note number, customer's name and reference number, amount
Purchase day book	List purchase invoices, and compute the total purchases	Purchases account; Supplier's account	Date, goods-received note number, supplier's name and reference number, amount
Purchase returns day book	List credit notes received, and compute the total purchase	Purchase returns account; Supplier's account	Date, credit note number, customer's name and reference number, amount
Cash book	List receipts and payments, compute total cash received and paid, and any cash discounts received or allowed	Cash account, Customers' and Suppliers' accounts, Expense accounts, Fixed-asset accounts, Loan accounts, Cash discounts received and allowed accounts (any other General ledger account which may be affected by cash)	Date, name of payer/payee, cheque number, total amount, account to which posting is to be made, cash discount deducted before receipt or payment

Book of prime entry	Purpose	Used to post	Details recorded
Journal	Record and explain any miscellaneous entries, e.g. stock adjustment, correction of errors	Any General ledger accounts	Date, accounts to be posted, amount, reason for journal entry

3.2 VALUE ADDED TAX

3.2.1 Nature of the tax

Value added tax is an indirect tax on the supply of goods and services. When the sales of a business cross a fixed threshold, the business is required to 'register for value added tax' or VAT, as it is often called. This means that whenever the business sells goods, with a few exceptions, VAT must be added to the selling price. The tax is being collected by the business on behalf of the Customs and Excise. Both the registration threshold and the rate of VAT are changed from time to time, and are announced by the Chancellor of the Exchequer in the budget speech. Since the tax's inception in the early 1970s rates have varied between 8 per cent and 25 per cent, depending on the fiscal requirements of the day. The registration threshold was set originally at £7,500, and has moved roughly in line with inflation. The tax is paid to the Customs and Excise each quarter. This VAT is called 'output VAT' since it relates to sales or outputs from the business. Conversely, when a business buys goods, at a purchase price which includes VAT, the tax may be reclaimed by deduction from VAT due to the Customs and Excise authorities. Where purchases exceed sales, a repayment occurs. This VAT which is reclaimed is called 'input VAT' since it relates to purchases or inputs to the business. There are a few exceptions regarding reclaiming of input VAT. The major one is the purchase of fixed assets, since the business itself is the end user of the asset, and not merely a link in a purchase and resale chain.

3.2.2 Recording the tax

The effect of VAT on a business is widespread. Sales invoices, purchase invoices, bills for expenses, payments and receipts all involve VAT, and require separate recording in the Sales day book, Purchase day book, Sales returns day book, Purchase returns day book and Cash book.

An account is maintained in the General ledger in order to keep a record of VAT owed to the Customs and Excise authorities, less VAT reclaimable. The following examples serve to illustrate the calculation and recording of VAT.

Example 1

For each sale or purchase compute the VAT.

(i) Sell goods for £100 + VAT at 10 per cent. VAT = 10 per cent × £100 = £10. (Gross selling price = £110.)

(ii) Purchase goods for £220 + VAT at 15 per cent. VAT = 15 per cent × £220 = £33. (Gross purchase price = £253.)

(iii) Sell goods for £230 which includes VAT at 15 per cent. If the net selling price were 100, the VAT would be 15 and the gross selling price would be 115. In this case the gross selling price is £230. VAT = $\frac{15}{115}$ × £230 = £30. (Net selling price = £200.)

(iv) Purchase goods for £432, which includes VAT at 8 per cent. If the net purchase price were 100, the VAT would be 8 and the gross purchase price would be 108. In this case the gross purchase price is £432. VAT = $\frac{8}{108}$ × £432 = £32. (Net purchase price = £400.)

Example 2

Harry owns a retail business and is registered for VAT. The following details relate to the month of February.

Purchases:

3 Feb	Smith on credit	£230 (including VAT)
6 Feb	Jones on credit	£414 (including VAT)
12 Feb	Robinson on credit	£368 (including VAT)
18 Feb	Brown for cash	£598 (including VAT)

Sales:

10 Feb	Green on credit	£600 + VAT
12 Feb	Grey for cash	£460 + VAT
19 Feb	Black on credit	£280 + VAT
26 Feb	White on credit	£120 + VAT

Cash paid (in addition to cash purchases)

26 Feb	Smith	£230
28 Feb	Robinson	£368

Cash received (in addition to cash sales)

28 Feb	Black	£322

VAT is at 15 per cent in all cases.

Required:
Record these transactions in the Sales and Purchase day books and Cash book, and write up the VAT account in the General ledger.

fig 3.2 *example of books of prime entry*

Sales day book

Date	Customer	Invoice no.	Customers' reference no.	Net £	VAT £	Gross £	
10 Feb	Green	S/2B1	6923	600	90	690	
19 Feb	Black	S/232	6959	280	42	322	Posted to Customers' accounts
26 Feb	White	S/233	6842	120	18	138	
				£1,000	£150	£1,150	
				Posted to Sales account	Posted to VAT account		

Purchases day book

Date	Supplier	Suppliers' reference no.	Net £	Vat £	Gross £	
3 Feb	Smith	4296	200	30	230	
6 Feb	Jones	4268	360	54	414	Posted to Suppliers' accounts
12 Feb	Robinson	4250	320	48	368	
			£880	£132	£1,012	
			Posted to Purchases account	Posted to VAT account		

fig 3.3 *example of cash book (two sides)*

Cash book – receipts

Dat	Name	Gross £	Analysis		
			VAT £	Goods £	Customers £
12 Feb	Grey – cash sale	529	69	460	–
28 Feb	Black – settlement of account	322	–	–	322
		£851	£69	£460	£322
Posted to:		Cash a/c	VAT a/c	Sales a/c	Customers' a/c

Cash book – payments

Date	Name	Cheque no.	Gross £	Analysis		
				VAT £	Goods £	Suppliers £
18 Feb	Brown	268694	598	78	520	–
26 Feb	Smith	268695	230	–	–	230
28 Feb	Robinson	268696	368	–	–	368
			£1196	£78	£520	£598
Posted to:			Cash a/c	VAT a/c	Purchases a/c	Suppliers' a/c (individually posted)

50

VAT account

	£		£
Purchase day book – VAT credit purchases	132	Sales day book – VAT on credit sales	150
Cash book – VAT on cash purchases	78	Cash book – VAT on cash sales	69
Balance c/f – due to Customs and Excise	9		
	£219		£219
		Balance b/f	9

Points arising:

(i) Only the net sales and purchase price is recorded in the Sales and Purchases accounts.

(ii) The gross sales and purchase prices are recorded in the Customers' and Suppliers' accounts.

(iii) Double entry from the Sales day book is:
  Dr Customers' accounts – gross selling price
  Cr Sales account – net selling price
  Cr VAT account – VAT on sales

(iv) The double entry from the Purchase day book is:
  Dr Purchases account – net purchase price
  Dr VAT account – VAT on purchases
  Cr Suppliers' accounts – gross purchase price.

(v) In the Balance sheet, value added tax owing to the Customs and Excise, but not yet paid by the business is shown as a liability under 'Creditors: amounts falling due within one year'. Conversely, where the business is reclaiming value added tax which has not yet been received, the amount receivable is shown as an asset under 'Current assets'.

3.3 THE CASH BOOK AND BANK RECONCILIATIONS

3.3.1 Cash and bank working accounts

In Example 2, above, we saw an analysed cash book illustrated. Such a cash book is widely used by businesses to keep their own record of cash in the bank.

In a retail business we have an added dimension – the till. This gives us two locations where cash is held as an asset. Cash in the till is referred to as 'cash in hand'. Cash at the bank is referred to as 'cash at bank'.

Frequently, and particularly so in examination orientated situations, we require a summary working which deals with both cash in hand and cash at bank, but without any detailed analysis dealing with repeat transactions. Such a working is called a 'cash and bank account', and takes the form of a T account with two columns.

Cash and bank account

Date	Cash £	Bank £	Date	Cash £	Bank £

Essentially we have two separate T accounts, which are laid down side by side. This is called a COLUMNAR presentation. It will help if we set out a few ground rules before proceeding to an example.

1. There are two balances; cash in hand and cash at bank. Both appear on the Balance sheet as current assets.
2. Whenever a customer pays money to the business it is first placed in the till. This happens whether it was cash or a cheque received. Thus cash in hand may represent cash and cheques not yet banked.
3. When cheques in the till are banked the double entry is:
   Dr   Bank a/c
   Cr   Cash a/c
   Since both entries appear in the same account we call this a contra entry, and place the symbol '₵' beside both entries.
4. Cash payments can only be made from the cash column.
5. Cheque payments can only be made from the bank column.
6. If the business cashes one of their own cheques at the bank the entry is:
   Dr   Cash a/c
   Cr   Bank a/c
7. If a customer is given cash from the till for a cheque which is then placed in the till, no change has occurred. There is less cash in the till, but a cheque has replaced the cash. The total cash in hand is the same. Consequently there is no entry required.
8. When a cheque is dishonoured by the bank (that is, the drawer's bank refuse to accept their customer's cheque due to an inadequate bank

balance) the money is still owed by the customer. The entry is:

Dr   Debtors' a/c
    Dr   Bank a/c

Example 2

Stan owns a shop. On 1 April he had £240 cash in the till and £1520 cash in the bank. During April the following transactions occurred.

2 Apr   Sold goods for cash for £50.
3 Apr   Paid for goods purchased from *X* during March amounting to £75 by cheque.
4 Apr   Received a cheque from *A* for £130 for goods sold in March.
5 Apr   Paid wages in cash £40.
8 Apr   Paid £150 cash and cheques into the bank.
9 Apr   Sold goods on credit to *B* for £120.
10 Apr   Cashed a cheque at the bank for £20 to provide change for the till.
11 Apr   Paid rent of £50 by cheque.
12 Apr   Bank charged £10 to the bank account for service charges.
15 Apr   Sold goods for cash £180.
16 Apr   Sold goods to *C* for £200. *C* paid by cheque.
17 Apr   Cashed *D*'s personal cheque for £15.
18 Apr   Purchased goods on credit from *Y* for £90.
19 Apr   Received cheque from *B* for £120 in settlement of goods purchased.
22 Apr   Paid £22 cash for stationery.
23 Apr   Took his wife out to dinner and used a business cheque to pay the £40 bill.
24 Apr   Paid £470 cash and cheques into the bank.
25 Apr   Paid monthly salaries by cheque amounting to £260.
26 Apr   Took £25 cash from the till for personal use over the weekend.
29 Apr   Sold goods for cash £230.
30 Apr   Paid cleaning lady £30 in cash.

Cash and Bank account

Date		Cash £	Bank £	Date			Cash £	Bank £
1 Apr	Balances b/f	240	1,520	3 Apr	X's a/c		–	75
2 Apr	Sales a/c	50	–	5 Apr	Wages a/c		40	–
4 Apr	A's a/c	130	–	8 Apr	Bank a/c	¢	150	–
8 Apr	Cash a/c ¢	–	150	10 Apr	Cash a/c	¢	–	20
10 Apr	Bank a/c ¢	20	–	11 Apr	Rent a/c		–	50
15 Apr	Sales a/c	180	–	12 Apr	Bank charges			
16 Apr	Sales a/c	200	–		a/c		–	10
19 Apr	B's a/c	120	–	22 Apr	Stationery a/c		22	–
24 Apr	Cash a/c ¢	–	470	23 Apr	Drawings a/c		–	40
29 Apr	Sales a/c	230	–	24 Apr	Bank a/c	¢	470	–
				25 Apr	Salaries a/c		–	260
				26 Apr	Drawings a/c		25	–
				30 Apr	Cleaning a/c		30	–
				30 Apr	Balances c/f		433	1,685
		£1,170	£2,140				£1,170	£2,140
1 May	Balances b/f	433	1,685					

Points arising:

1 The sales on credit (3 April) and purchase on credit (18 April) do not appear until the accounts are settled.
2. The bank charges (12 April) represent a payment of cash at bank.
3. The cheque cashed for *D* (17 April) does not appear since the cheque would be put into the till.
4. The payments on 23 April (cheque) and 26 April (cash) both represent drawings.

3.3.2 Cash discounts and the cash book

In Sub-section 2.10.3 we discussed cash discounts and how they arise. In Section 3.1 we said that cash discounts appear in the Cash book. We can now demonstrate how our Cash and Bank account can be modified to accommodate a record of cash discounts received and allowed. We do this by adding an extra column to each side of the columnar account. The total at the bottom of each column is then used to post the Discounts received account and the Discounts allowed account.

Example 3

Dorothy runs a small retail business. On 1 June she had £100 cash in the till, and £400 cash in the bank. The following are the transactions for the week beginning 1 June.

1 June   Sold goods for cash - £80
2 June   Paid a cheque to *M* for £135. This was in settlement for goods with an invoice price of £140
3 June   Received a cheque from *P*. *P*'s account stood at £100, but Dorothy allowed a 2 per cent cash discount.
4 June   Sold goods for cash - £90. Paid electricity bill of £35 by cheque.
5 June   Purchased goods for cash - £70. Received a cheque from *Q* in settlement of *Q*'s account which stood at £250. Dorothy allowed a 2 per cent cash discount.
6 June   Paid a cheque to *R* for £180, to settle an account for £184. Took £25 cash for private expenses. Lodged £418 cash and cheques in the night safe at the bank.

Points arising (See account on next page):

1   *P*'s account will be credited with £100.
2   *Q*'s account will be credited with £250.
3   *M*'s account will be debited with £140.
4   *R*'s account will be debited with £184.
5   The total discounts allowed of £7 will be debited to the discounts allowed account.
6   The total discounts received of £9 will be credited to the discounts received account.

3.3.3 Bank reconciliation statements

The Cash book contains the business record of cash held at the bank. A favourable balance is a debit balance since it is an asset to the business.

However, the bank also keeps a record of its customers' accounts. In fact it periodically sends a copy of the account, called a BANK STATEMENT, to the customer. Three areas of difference between the bank and the business version of the same account will arise.

1   A debit balance in the cash book will appear as a credit balance on the bank statement. Such a favourable balance to the business is cash owed by the bank; hence it appears as a liability in their records. It follows that cash paid into the bank appears as credits on the bank statement;

Example 3
Cash and bank account

Date		Discounts allowed £	Cash £	Bank £	Date		Discounts received £	Cash £	Bank £
1 Jun	Balances b/f	–	100	400	2 Jun	*M*'s a/c	5	–	135
1 Jun	Sales a/c	–	80	–	4 Jun	Electricity a/c	–	–	35
3 Jun	*P*'s a/c	2	98	–	5 Jun	Purchases a/c	–	70	–
4 Jun	Sales a/c	–	90	–	6 Jun	*R*'s a/c	4	–	180
5 Jun	*Q*'s a/c	5	245	–	6 Jun	Drawings a/c	–	25	–
6 Jun	Cash a/c ¢	–	–	418	6 Jun	Bank a/c ¢	–	418	–
					6 Jun	Balances c/f	–	100	468
		£7	£613	£818			£9	£613	£818

and, conversely, cheques drawn and payments from the bank balance appear as debits on the bank statement:

Provided we take account of which set of records we are dealing with there is no problem.

2 Certain items will appear on the bank statement that do not yet appear in the cash book. Examples are bank charges, dishonoured cheques, standing orders, direct debits and bank giro credits. In each case the entry has been made directly by the bank. The only reason it did not appear in the Cash book is that the business did not know about it. Therefore, when the bank statement is received such items must be entered in the Cash book for the relevant period now ended.

3 Certain items will appear in the Cash book, but do not yet appear on the bank statement. Examples are lodgements into the bank and cheques drawn on dates close to the last date on the bank statement. The items will appear on the next bank statement. The reason is simply that the banking system will take a few days to process lodgements and cheques. Also cheques sent to suppliers must first pass through the suppliers' accounting procedures before they are sent to the bank. We call such items 'reconciling items', and prepare a BANK RECONCILIATION STATEMENT to show that the two versions of the same account will agree after these reconciling items are taken into account.

N.B. The period in which such items are included is determined by the date of entry to the cash book and not the date they appear on the bank statement.

	£
Format of a bank reconciliation statement:	
Balance per the bank statement (brackets denote an overdraft)	x
Add: Lodgements uncleared	x
	x
Less: Cheques unpresented	(x)
Balance per the Cash book	£x

If the bank has made an error, to be reversed in the next period, then this would also appear on the reconciliation statement.

Example 4

Glen runs a small business. On 31 December the Cash book showed a favourable cash balance of £845. When the bank statement was received it showed a favourable balance of £607 on the same day. The following differences are discovered:

(i) A lodgement of £769 paid in on 30 December did not appear on the bank statement until January.

(ii) Bank charges of £52 for the six months to 31 December had not been entered in the Cash book.

(iii) The business had entered a hire-purchase agreement in November. The first payment of £60 by standing order in December had not been entered in the Cash book.

(iv) Cheques drawn, entered in the Cash book and sent to suppliers, but not presented to the bank until January amounted to £534.

(v) One customer, H, had paid £152 directly to the Bank account in settlement of his account. The item had not been recorded in the Cash book.

(vi) A cheque for £25 received from P, a customer, had been paid into the bank and duly credited on the bank statement. However, the bank statement now shows a debit entry for this cheque of £25, described as 'cheque returned – no funds available'. Glen intends to ask this customer for cash in January.

(vii) The bank has, in error, debited Glen's business Bank account with a cheque for £18 drawn on his private account.

Required:

(a) Entries to the Cash book to show the adjusted balance; and

(b) A bank reconciliation statement at 31 December.

Bank account (entries in Cash book)

	£		£
Balance b/f per Cash book	845	Bank charges a/c	52
H's a/c	152	Hire-purchase a/c	60
		P's a/c	25
		Balance c/f	860
	£997		£997
Balance b/f (1 Jan)	860		

Bank reconciliation statement at 31 December:

		£
Balance per bank statement		607
Add: Lodgements uncleared		769
Add; Error by bank – cheque for private account		18
		1,394
Less: Cheques unpresented		(534)
Balance per Cash book		£860

Points arising:

1 The reconciliation should always show the cash book figure at the bottom since this is the figure that will appear in the Balance sheet as cash at bank.
2 The cheque from *P* for £25 has been dishonoured by the bank, and is worthless. The entry in Glen's accounts is to:

    Dr *P*'s a/c   £25
      Dr Bank a/c   £25

This has the effect of reversing the receipt of the cheque, and *P*'s account will again show a balance due to Glen of £25.

3.4 THE SALES LEDGER – BAD AND DOUBTFUL DEBTS

The sale of goods on credit is a normal part of business activity. Stock is converted into a debtor. The debtor is converted into cash. The cash is reinvested in more stock. We call this the 'working capital cycle'. But there is a hitch. Suppose that the debtor fails to pay the cash. Clearly the business takes care (or at least it ought to take care) to extend credit only to customers who are creditworthy. But frequently some unexpected problem arises and the debtor is unable to pay. Legal proceedings are expensive, and even if successful the customer may be in liquidation with a small chance of any cash at all being forthcoming. To cater for this eventuality it is usual for a business to maintain two special accounts. These are:

Name of account	Purpose
Bad debts a/c	To collect together debtor balances which are regarded as uncollectable. The total of such balances is written off as expense in the Profit and loss a/c.

Provision for doubtful debts	To create a provision for debtor balances which are not yet written off, but which are suspect.

We will now look in more detail at each account.

3.4.1 Bad debts account

The Bad debts account is debited with debtor balances which are recognised as uncollectable, and are thus removed from the sales ledger. The credit entry is to the customer's Debtors' account. At the end of each accounting period the total balance on the Bad debts account is charged to the Profit and loss account. There is no balance brought forward or carried forward. The charge to the Profit and loss account represents debtors written off in that period alone. The entries can be summarised:

Entry	Debit	Credit
Debtor regarded as uncollectable (repeated for each relevant customer)	Bad debts a/c	Debtors' a/c
Total balance on Bad debts a/c at end of accounting period	Profit and loss a/c	Bad debts a/c

3.4.2 Provision for doubtful debts account

The term 'provision' is used to indicate that a loss or liability exists, but the exact amount or date of occurrence is in doubt. In the case of debtors, two separate calculations are made to arrive at the amount of the provision. These are:

Specific provision	Particular customers identified as possible failures. Their balances outstanding will be provided for in full.
General provision	A percentage (typically 2–5%) is applied to the total remaining balances to cover small balances and unknown future failures. The percentage is based on past experience.

The Provision for Doubtful debts account will show a credit balance. Each period, the balance is reviewed and increased or reduced as necessary. It is only the increase (charge) or decrease (credit) which is posted to the Profit and loss account. The entries are as follows:

Entry	Debit	Credit
Balance brought forward from previous period	–	–
Compute balance to be carried forward based on closing debtors, and enter as balance carried forward	–	–
Increase from opening to closing balance	Profit and loss a/c	Provision for Doubtful debts a/c
Decrease from opening to closing balance	Provision for Doubtful debts a/c	Profit and loss a/c

In the Balance sheet the debtor balances (*debit*) and the Provision for Doubtful debts balance (*credit*) are shown together.

Current assets	£	£
Stock		x
Debtors	x	
Provision for doubtful debts	(x)	
		x
Prepaid expenses		x
Cash at bank		x
Cash in hand		x
		£x

Example 5

Mike sells goods on credit to small businessmen. Due to a recession many have gone out of business and Mike has consequently failed to collect certain balances due.

At the beginning of the year total debtor balances stood at £18,560, and a provision for doubtful debts of £928 had been made.

During the year Roy (£960), Jenny (£1,460) and Louisa (£770) went out of business and the balances due were written off by Mike.

At the end of the year total debtors (after writing off the balances above) stood at £22,740. Mike wishes to carry forward a provision of 5 per cent of these debtors.

Requires:

(a) Bad debts account; and
(b) Provision for Bad debts account.

Bad debts account

Debtors' a/c	£		£
Roy	960	Profit and loss a/c:	
Jenny	1,460	total written off	3,190
Louisa	770		
	£3,190		£3,190

Provision for doubtful debts account

	£		£
		Balance b/f	928
Balance c/f		Profit and loss a/c:	
(5% × £22,740)	1,137	increase in provision	209
	£1,137		£1,137
		Balance b/f	1,137

Points arising:

1 Both the bad debts written off (£3,190) and increase in the provision for doubtful debts (£209) appear in the Profit and loss account as financial expenses.
2 In the Balance sheet presentation is:

	£
Debtors	22,740
Provision for doubtful debts	(1,137)
	21,603

3.5 SALES AND PURCHASE LEDGER – CONTROL ACCOUNTS

Whenever we have dealt with customers' accounts (trade debtors) and suppliers' accounts (trade creditors) in the worked examples we have made entries for sales, purchases, cash received and paid, bad debts written off and discounts allowed and received into the individual customers' and suppliers' accounts. On this basis the Trial balance needs to show all

62

the individual trade debtor and trade creditor balances. Clearly, where the business has hundreds or thousands of customers and suppliers a quicker system is needed, otherwise the Trial balance will run to dozens of pages. The solution is to use a single account for the total of trade debtors and a single account for the total of trade creditors called a CONTROL ACCOUNT. The balance on each control account represents the total trade debtors and the total trade creditors. The control account forms part of the double-entry system, and as such is contained in the General ledger. The Sales ledger, which contains the individual customers' accounts, and the Purchase ledger, which contains the individual suppliers' accounts, become supporting records. They are not part of the double-entry system, but are still maintained to keep a record of individual customer and supplier balances. The individual balances must periodically be added together and checked against the control account total balance. This would normally be done monthly. Figure 3.1 in Section 3.1 (p.43) illustrates how these ledgers and accounts fit into the overall accounting system. We can identify three functions of control accounts. These are:

Expediency	The trade debtors' and trade creditors' total can be computed from the control accounts quickly. The General ledger can be written up and the Trial balance prepared more rapidly than if individual accounts were included.
Control	The General ledger (containing the control accounts) and supporting Sales and Purchase ledgers can be maintained by separate persons. This adds an internal check to the accounting system.
Tracing errors	Differences between the list of individual customers' and suppliers' balances from the Sales and Purchase ledgers and the control account balances can be identified at an early stage and traced. (This is dealt with in the next section.)

The normal entries to each control account appear below.

Debtors' control account (alias Sales ledger control account)

	£		£
b/f – opening total debtors' balance	x	Sales returns a/c – total credit returns (entered from Sales returns day book)	x
Sales a/c – total credit sales (entered from sales day book)	x	Cash a/c – total cash and cheques received from credit customers (entered from Cash book)	x
		Bad debts a/c – total bad debts written off (entered from journal)	x

		Discounts allowed a/c – total discounts allowed (entered from Cash book)	x
		c/f – closing total debtors' balance	x
£x			£x

Creditors' control account (alias Purchase ledger control account)

	£		£
Purchases returns a/c – total credit purchase returns (entered from purchase returns day book)	x	b/f – opening total creditors' balances	x
Cash a/c – total cash paid to suppliers (entered from Cash book)	x	Purchases a/c – total credit purchases (entered from Purchase day book)	x
Bank a/c – total cheques paid to suppliers (entered from Cash book)	x		
Discounts received a/c – total discounts received (entered from Cash book)	x		
c/f – closing total creditors' balances	x		
	£x		£x

Occasionally a credit balance may appear on an individual customer's account, or a debit balance on an individual supplier's account. This would arise where goods have been supplied, and paid for, but later returned. The adverse balance may be repaid or held against future supplies.

Example 6

Paula purchases and sells on credit. The following details have been extracted from her accounts for a particular calendar year:

	£
Total customers' balances at 1 January	6,923
Total suppliers' balances at 1 January	4,249
Credit sales	72,450
Credit purchases	47,475
Cheques received from customers	69,420
Cheques paid to suppliers	45,427
Cash paid to suppliers	245

64

	£
Allowance to customer for faulty goods	50
Sales returns	1,028
Purchase returns	904
Discounts allowed	1,464
Discounts received	1,273
Customers' balances written off as bad	1,550
Balance due from Smith as a customer cancelled against the balance due to Smith as a supplier	109
Total customers' balances at 31 December	?
Total suppliers' balances at 31 December	?

Required:

(a) Sales ledger control account; and
(b) Purchase ledger control account.

Sales ledger control account

	£		£
b/f – 1 January	6,923	Cash a/c – cheques received	69,420
Sales a/c – credit sales	72,450	Allowances a/c – faulty goods	50
		Sales returns a/c – returns	1,028
		Discounts allowed a/c – discounts	1,464
		Bad debts a/c – written off	1,550
		Purchase ledger control a/c – Smith	109
		c/f – 31 December	5,752
	£79,373		£79,373

Purchase ledger control account

	£		£
Bank a/c – cheques paid	45,427	b/f – 1 January	4,249
Cash a/c – cash paid	245	Purchases a/c – credit purchases	47,475
Purchase returns a/c – returns	904		
Discounts received a/c – discounts	1,273		
Sales ledger control a/c – Smith	109		
c/f – 31 December	3,766		
	£51,724		£51,724

Points arising:

1 The allowance of £50 to a customer reduces the balance of debtors (*hence a credit entry*). The Allowances account is written off in the Profit and loss account since it is an expense.
2 Smith is both a customer and a supplier. The debtor balance of £109 is cancelled against amounts owed to him. Thus both debtors (*credit entry*) and creditors (*debit entry*) are reduced by £109.
3 The missing balances of debtors and creditors at 31 December are found as balancing figures in the respective control accounts.

3.6 JOURNAL ENTRIES, SUSPENSE ACCOUNTS AND CORRECTION OF ERRORS

3.6.1 Journal entries

In Section 3.1 we saw that a journal was one of the books of prime entry. Its purpose is to keep a record of any unusual and one-off entries to the General ledger, and to enable a brief explanation to be recorded. In fact some businesses summarise all their General ledger entries in the journal. A typical entry in the journal to record the Cash book entries for a month may be as follows:

Date	Folio	Accounts	Debit	Credit
			£	£
31 May	A/7	Cash a/c	56,235	
	E/10	Discounts allowed a/c	1,350	
	A/9	Sales ledger central a/c		57,585
			£57,585	£57,585
		Being cash received from debtors and discounts allowed for the month of May.		

Points arising:

1 Each journal entry is dated.
2 There is a separate column for debit and credit entries.
3 The 'folio' column indicates the General ledger code number of the relevant account, so that it can be found easily.
4 A total is added to show that the debits equal the credits.
5 There is a brief explanation of the entry.

3.6.2 Suspense accounts and correction of errors

When an accounting system operates correctly the debit entries will always equal the credit entries, accounts are always correctly cast, all balances are listed correctly on the Trial balance, and the Trial balance balances!

However, in the real world, and particularly so in exam questions, the Trial balance regularly fails to balance.

Reasons why a Trial balance may fail to balance:
• Balances brought forward from previous period incorrectly.   • Debit entries in the General ledger do not equal credit entries.   • An account in General ledger has been miscast.   • An account balance has been omitted from the Trial balance.   • An account balance has been included in the Trial balance, but has been written down incorrectly, e.g. a balance of £523 written down as £532. This is called a 'transposition'.   • The Trial balance has been miscast.

The method of correction adopted is a two-stage method:

Stage 1 – Insert an artifical account balance in the Trial balance in order to make it balance. This is called a SUSPENSE ACCOUNT, e.g. Trial balance debits total £342,350, but credits total £329,640. A Suspense account is inserted with a credit balance of £12,710 such that debits and credits are now equal.

Stage 2 – The errors which led to the Trial balance difference are then located and cleared using double entry. One of the entries goes to the Suspense account such that, when all errors have been dealt with, the Suspense account is cleared.

Example 7 – use of Suspense account

Hugh has prepared a Trial balance at 31 December which, unfortunately, fails to balance. The debit balances total £56,790 whereas the credit balances total £63,267.

The following errors are located:

(a) The balance brought forward on Sales ledger control account of £5,900 had been completely omitted from the Sales ledger control account.

(b) In writing off a bad debt the amount of £210 has been correctly credited to the Sales ledger control account, but has also been credited to the Bad debts account.

(c) The Purchase ledger control account has been undercast on the credit side by £140.

(d) The balance on the Cash account of £855 has been recorded on the Trial balance as £558.

(e) A sales invoice to Jones of £300 has not been entered in the books at all.

Required:

Summarise the journal entries (omitting 'folio' column) necessary to correct the errors, and write up the Suspense account.

The Suspense account is opened with a debit balance of £6,477 (i.e. £63,267 *less* £56,790).

Journal entries

Date	Account	Debit £	Credit £
31 Dec	Sales ledger control account Suspense account Being balance brought forward omitted.	5,900 –	– 5,900
31 Dec	Bad debts account Suspense account Being reversal of a bad debt of £210 credited instead of debited.	420 –	– 420
31 Dec	Purchase ledger control account Suspense account Being undercast on Purchase ledger control account.	– 140	140 –
31 Dec	Cash account Suspense account Being correct cash balance entered incorrectly on Trial balance.	297 –	– 297
31 Dec	Sales ledger control account Sales account Being sales invoice not posted.	300 –	– 300

68

Suspense account

	£		£
Balance b/f	6,477	Sales ledger control a/c	5,900
Purchase ledger control a/c	140	Bad debts a/c	420
		Cash a/c	297
		Balance c/f	–
	£6,617		£6,617

Points arising:

1 The correction to the Bad debts account is twice the error. Once to reverse the incorrect credit, and once again to enter the correct debit.
2 The Cash account correction is not a genuine entry to the Cash account, since that balance was correct. The adjustment is to the figure for Cash account on the Trial balance only.
3 The sales invoice omitted does not affect the Suspense account since both debit and credit entries were omitted. (This item would also need to be entered in Jones's account in the Sales ledger, but this is not part of the General ledger and does not affect the Trial balance.)

Example 8 – correction of errors involving control accounts

Sadie has prepared draft accounts for her business. Unfortunately the Trial balance did not balance, the debits exceeding the credits by £171. From the draft information Sadie has computed her net profit to be £10,950. The Sales ledger control account showed a balance of £17,825 and the Purchase ledger control account a balance of £14,960. Unfortunately neither of these control accounts agreed to the list of Sales and Purchase ledger totals, these being £18,595 and £15,300 respectively. The following errors and omissions have been traced.

(a) A sales invoice to Smith of £320 has not been posted anywhere.
(b) The Purchase day book has been undercast by £60.
(c) The Sales day book total of £20,960 for one month had been correctly debited to Sales ledger control account, but credited to Sales account as £20,609.
(d) An electricity bill for £160 had been paid and Cash account credited correctly. However, the debit entry was posted in error to the Purchase ledger control account.
(e) The balance of £650 due from Vera Robinson, a customer, has been included in the list of Sales ledger balances twice.

(f) At the end of the previous period a debit balance of £90 being rates prepaid was carried forward. In the current year the balance was brought forward as a credit entry in the Rates account.

(g) John Hughes is both a supplier and a customer. A contra adjustment of £120 between his Sales and Purchase ledger accounts was correctly recorded in the control accounts, but no entry made in either the Sales or Purchase ledger accounts.

Required:

Journal entries (omitting date and folio) to deal with items (a) to (g); Suspense account; adjusted control accounts, and Sales and Purchase ledger totals; and a revised net profit figure.

Journal entries

Account	Debit £	Credit £
(a) Sales ledger control account	320	–
Sales account	–	320
Being sales invoice omitted. (In addition, Smith's Sales ledger account must be debited with £320.)		
(b) Purchase account	60	–
Purchase ledger control account	–	60
Being correction of undercast in Purchase day book. (Purchase ledger is not affected.)		
(c) Sales account	–	351
Suspense account	351	–
Being sales of £20,960 enterd as £20,609.		
(d) Purchase ledger control account	–	160
Electricity account	160	–
Being electricity bill posted incorrectly.		
(e) (No entry, but Sales ledger list of balances is reduced by £650.)	–	–
(f) Rates account	180	–
Suspense account	–	180
Being rates prepaid brought forward from previous period on wrong side.		
(g) (No entry, but both Sales and Purchase ledger list of balances are reduced by £120.)		

Suspense account

	£		£
Sales a/c (Item (c))	351	Balance b/f	171
		Rates a/c (item (f))	180
	£351		£351

Sales ledger control account

	£		£
Balance b/f – draft	17,825		
Sales a/c (item (a))	320	Balance c/f – adjusted	18,145
	£18,145		£18,145

Purchase ledger control account

	£		£
		Balance b/f – draft	14,960
Balance c/f – adjusted	15,180	Purchase a/c (item (b))	60
		Electricity a/c (item (d))	160
	£15,180		£15,180

List of balances

	Sales ledger Dr £	Cr £	Purchase ledger Dr £	Cr £
Per draft	18,595	–	–	15,300
Smith's a/c (item (a))	320	–	–	–
Robinson's a/c included twice (item (e))	–	–	–	–
Hughes a/c – contra (item (g))	–	650	–	–
	–	120	120	–
	18,915	770	120	15,300
	(770)			(120)
Agreed to control accounts	£18,145			£15,180

	Dr £	Cr £
Adjusted net profit		
Per draft	–	10,950
Sales a/c (item (a))	–	320
Purchases a/c (item (b))	60	–
Sales a/c (item (c))	–	351

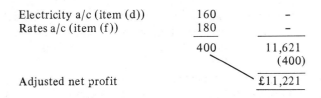

Electricity a/c (item (d))	160	–
Rates a/c (item (f))	180	–
	400	11,621
		(400)
Adjusted net profit		£11,221

(N.B. The items included in the adjustment of net profit are all those items which affect an account which is closed off and taken into the Trading, or profit and loss accounts.)

Note: Many students find this type of example very difficult to handle. The reason is that it requires both a firm grasp of double entry, and a clear understanding of how an accounting system fits together. It is thus an acid test of a student's ability at this stage of the subject. It is an area where the best preparation is application to past examination questions.

Exercises to Chapter 3

1. Compute the VAT for each of the following situations:
   (a) Purchase goods for £160 + VAT at 12 per cent.
   (b) Sell goods for £340 + VAT at 8 per cent.
   (c) Purchase goods for £250 including VAT at 15 per cent.
   (d) Sell goods for £350 including VAT at 10 per cent.

In each case calculations should be to the nearest £.

2. On 31 December the bank statement of a certain business showed a favourable balance of £1,340. This did not agree with the Cash book. The following points arose:
   (a) Bank charges of £55 had been charged by the bank for the period to 31 December.
   (b) Cheques drawn, but not presented to the bank until January, totalled £352.
   (c) The bank had debited the account in error with an amount of £15. This was corrected in January.
   (d) Lodgements totalling £420 had been paid into the bank, but had not yet appeared on the bank statement.
   (e) A standing order payment of £45 had been made by the bank, but not recorded by the business.

You are required to prepare a bank reconciliation statement and identify the corrected Cash-book balance.

3. On the first day of an accounting period trade debtors totalled £50,520, and a provision for bad debts stood at £2,526. During the year the following events occurred:

   (a) Sales totalled £510,000
   (b) Cash received from debtors totalled £492,500
   (c) Bad debts of £1,850 were written off.
   (d) Cash discounts of £12,350 were given.
   (e) Sales returns totalled £10,940.

   At the end of the period the Provision for bad debts account is to be adjusted to 5 per cent of trade debtors' balance.
   You are required to write up the Debtors' control account and the Provision for bad debts account, and identify the balances carried forward.

4. For each error identified below you are required to show the journal entry to correct the error. A Suspense account has been opened.

   (a) The debit side of the Debtors' control account has been overcast by £40.
   (b) Purchase returns of £90 have been entered to the wrong side of the Creditors' control account.
   (c) A purchase invoice for £110 has not been recorded at all.
   (d) The Sales day book has been undercast by £65.

A DOSE OF CONCEPTS

4.1 FUNDAMENTAL ACCOUNTING CONCEPTS

A frequent misapprehension of accountancy students is that there is always a unique answer to every accounts problem. In other words, accountancy is an exact science. In reality there may be many different answers to a given situation. This is due to the need to value certain items within the accounts (e.g. fixed assets, stock), estimate liabilities (e.g. taxation), estimate whether assets are valuable (e.g. bad debts). These examples affect both Balance sheet and Profit and loss account. In each case, and this is by no means an exhaustive list, the accountant must exercise JUDGEMENT. Different accountants may come to differing opinions. Hence we must say that accountancy is often more of an art than a science.

However, underlying such areas of judgement there exist certain principles or concepts upon which the practical treatment of all items are based. The purpose of this chapter is to consider the fundamental accounting concepts and to examine certain key areas where they are of importance.

We will start with four concepts which have been identified as the four fundamental accounting concepts. Their names are prudence, going concern, matching-up and consistency.

4.1.1 Prudence concept

Prudence is also known as conservatism. It means that accountants will never count their chickens before they're certain to be hatched. In practical terms it means that revenue (e.g. sales, discounts received) is not recognised (i.e. credited to the Trading, profit and loss account) until it is reasonably certain that the ultimate realisation (i.e. receipt of cash) will occur. In the case of sales this recognition is made at the invoice date.

In the case of discounts received the recognition does not occur until the cheque is drawn and entered into the books.

Conversely, provision for liabilities or claims upon the business and loss in value of assets are recognised within the accounts at the earliest possible date. Examples are the writing-off of bad debts, the provision for doubtful debts and the writing-down of stock in hand where its value has fallen below its cost due to deterioration.

Prudence is the overriding concept. Whenever there is a conflict between the fundamental concepts then it is prudence which is given priority.

4.1.2 Going concern

In preparing the accounts of a business it is assumed that the business will continue to trade into the future. We say that the business is a 'going concern'. The alternative assumption would be that the business is about to be terminated. The main effect would be on the amount at which assets are stated in the Balance sheet. Under the going-concern concept it is assumed that fixed assets will continue to be used in future periods (i.e. until the business is finished with that asset) and that stock will be sold to customers in the normal course of trade (i.e. at normal selling prices). If the business were to be terminated, fixed assets would have to be sold as second-hand assets and stock would be heavily discounted in order to sell as quickly as possible. In both cases the assets are certain to be worth less than under a going-concern situation, the one exception being land and buildings.

4.1.3 Matching-up

Matching-up is also known as the 'accruals concept'. It means that revenue and expenses are included in the Trading, profit and loss account in the accounting period to which they relate, rather than the period in which cash is received or paid. There are numerous examples. Sales is credited when the goods are sold (i.e. invoice date) rather than when cash is received from the customer. The Trading account is adjusted for opening and closing stock so that it is cost of sales and not purchases that are deducted from sales in arriving at gross profit. Prepaid expenses such as rates, and accrued expenses such as rent, are carried forward to the next period. One other important application is the depreciation of fixed assets. This is discussed fully in Section 4.3 of this chapter.

4.1.4 Consistency

It is desirable that accounts should be comparable from period to period.

The proprietor will wish to know if the business is going uphill or down-hill. To this end it is necessary that the accounting treatment of each item is consistent from period to period.

4.1.5 The doctrine of materiality

One important idea which is not included within the fundamental con-cepts is the doctrine of materiality, or size. This means quite simply that the larger an item is relative to other items within a particular set of accounts, then the more important it becomes. The more material an item is, then the greater the importance of the way in which it is pre-sented in the financial statements.

Conversely, items which are considered to be immaterial are given low priority in the financial statements. In individual businesses it is a matter of judgement as to which items are material and those which are not.

4.2 CAPITAL AND REVENUE EXPENDITURE

In Section 2.8 of Chapter 2 we first drew the distinction between fixed and current assets. We now reach the stage where we can formalise the division in the light of the fundamental accounting concepts.

4.2.1 Capital expenditure

Capital expenditure may be defined as the cost of *acquiring* or *improving* an asset which will be used by the business over a *number of accounting periods* in order to *generate revenue*.

The cost of such assets is included under *fixed assets*.

Examples fall into three groups:

(a) Intangible items such as goodwill, deferred development expenditure, patents and trade marks;
(b) Tangible items such as land and buildings, plant, machinery and equipment, fixtures and fittings, motor-vehicles, office equipment. Legal costs associated with the acquisition of property should be included in fixed assets;
(c) Investments such as shares or stock held in other companies.

4.2.2 Revenue expenditure

Revenue expenditure may be defined as the cost of materials and services which are *consumed* by a business in carrying out *normal trade operations* and *maintenance of assets*.

Such costs are charged in the *Trading, profit and loss account*. Examples are establishment costs (i.e. rent, rates, repairs to property, heat, light); administrative costs (i.e. wages, salaries, telephone, postage, stationery); selling costs (i.e. commission, advertising, distribution); and financial costs (i.e. cash discounts, interest). The four headings given here (establishment, administrative, selling and financial) are normally used as subheadings in a profit and loss account.

Frequently, problems arise in the differentiation of improvements to fixed assets (capital expense) from repairs to fixed assets (revenue expense).

4.3 DEPRECIATION

Having defined capital expenditure, and stated that such costs are treated as fixed assets, we must now recognise that fixed assets are themselves consumed over a number of years. Each asset has a finite useful life, at the end of which it will have a small or negligible residual value.

Two consequences arise:

(a) In the Balance sheet we need to show how the asset is being consumed. The proportion of the cost of the asset consumed is called ACCUMU-LATED DEPRECIATION. At any point the cost less accumulated depreciation to date is called NET BOOK VALUE.

(b) In the Profit and loss account we need to charge the appropriate portion of the fixed-asset cost which has been consumed in earning the profits of each period. This is called the CHARGE FOR DEPRECI-ATION.

The full definition is 'a measure of the wearing out or consumption of an asset due to use, obsolescence or effluxion of time'.

In order to compute depreciation for each period, four items must be established:

(a) *Cost* of the asset to be depreciated;
(b) Estimate of the asset's *useful life*;
(c) Estimated *residual value* at the end of the useful life; and
(d) a *method* of allocating the total depreciation to accounting periods within the total useful life.

Item (d), the method of allocation, requires some examination, since there are two methods in very common use, and perhaps a dozen further possible methods. The two common methods are called the STRAIGHT-LINE method and the REDUCING-BALANCE method. These are now considered.

4.3.1 The straight-line method

As the name suggests, the straight-line method spreads the depreciation out evenly over the assets life. The amount allocated to each period may be found by the following formula:

$$\text{Depreciation for each period} = \frac{\text{Cost} - \text{Estimated residual value}}{\text{Estimated useful life in years}}$$

Frequently the computation will be expressed as a PERCENTAGE OF COST.

Example 1

An asset is purchased on 1 January 19X1 for £10,000. It is estimated that at the end of four years it will have a residual value of £1,000.

$$\text{Depreciation for each year 19X1 to 19X4} = \frac{£10,000 - £1,000}{4 \text{ years}}$$
$$= £2,250 \text{ per annum.}$$

We can express this as a percentage of cost:

$$\frac{£2,250}{£10,000} \times 100 \text{ per cent} = 22.5 \text{ per cent per annum.}$$

The cost, accumulated depreciation, net book value and charge for depreciation can be shown in the following table.

	Cost £	Accumulated depreciation £	Net book value £
1.1.X1	10,000	–	10,000
19X1 charge for depreciation	–	(2,250)	(2,250)
31.12.X1	10,000	(2,250)	7,750
19X2 charge for depreciation	–	(2,250)	(2,250)
31.12.X2	10,000	(4,500)	5,500
19X3 charge for depreciation	–	(2,250)	(2,250)
31.12.X3	10,000	(6,750)	3,250
19X4 charge for depreciation	–	(2,250)	(2,250)
31.12.X4	£10,000	£(9,000)	£1,000

78

At the end of 19X4 the net book value is equal to the residual value. A total of £9,000 has been charged against the Profit and loss accounts, but spread evenly over the years 19X1, 19X2, 19X3 and 19X4.

The advantage of the straight-line method is that it is simple to use.

It is best suited to the type of asset that has even use over its life. Examples would be buildings, fixtures and fittings, and furniture. In each case the even spread of depreciation complements the even spread of use and fall in value of the asset.

4.3.2 The reducing-balance method

We stated that the straight-line method can be expressed as a percentage of cost. The reducing-balance method is expressed as a PERCENTAGE OF NET BOOK VALUE. Since the net book value is decreasing, so the annual charge for depreciation will decrease.

fig 4.1 *comparison of depreciation methods*

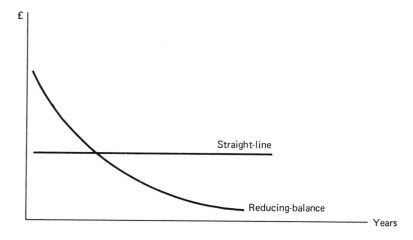

The percentage to be applied to the net book value can be found from the following formula:

$$\frac{i}{100} = 1 - \sqrt[n]{\frac{r}{c}}$$

where i = percentage depreciation;
r = estimated residual value;
c = cost;
n = number of years of useful life.

Mathematicians will spot that the formula does not work where the residual value is nil.

Example 2

Facts as in Example 1, but the reducing-balance method is used. The percentage is found as:

$$\frac{i}{100} = 1 - \sqrt[4]{\frac{1,000}{10,000}}$$ which solves to i = 43.77 per cent

(to two decimal places). We can construct the table as before.

	Cost £	Accumulated depreciation £	Net book value £
1.1.X1	10,000	–	10,000
19X1 charge for depreciation			
43.77% × £10,000	–	(4,377)	(4,377)
31.12.X1	10,000	(4,377)	5,623
19X2 charge for depreciation			
43.77% × £5,623	–	(2,461)	(2,461)
31.12.X2	10,000	(6,838)	3,162
19X3 charge for depreciation			
43.77% × £3,162	–	(1,384)	(1,384)
31.12.X3	10,000	(8,222)	1,778
19X4 charge for depreciation			
43.77% × £1,778	–	(778)	(778)
31.12.X4	£10,000	£(9,000)	£1,000

At the end of 19X4 the net book value is again equal to the residual value. The total depreciation of £9,000 has been spread £4,377 to 19X1, £2,461 to 19X2, £1,384 to 19X3 and £778 to 19X4.

The method is best suited to the type of asset that shows a heavier fall in value in earlier years, and repair costs that increase over the asset's life. The obvious example is a motor-vehicle. The reducing charge for depreciation is complemented by the increasing repair costs giving an even total cost in each period. The change in net book value gives a better indication of the asset's fall in value than it would using the straight-line method.

4.3.3 Year of purchase and sale

Where an asset is purchased during an accounting period a decision must be made whether to charge a fraction of a year's depreciation, or a full year's depreciation for that first period: either is possible and acceptable. Likewise, where an asset is sold during an accounting period, a decision must be made whether to charge a fraction of a year's depreciation, or no depreciation for that period – again either is possible and acceptable.

Two combinations are widely used:

(a) 'AT THE RATE OF . . . ' where this phrase appears it will mean that a fraction of a years charge in both the year of purchase and the year of sale.
(b) ' . . . IN USE AT THE YEAR END . . . ' where this phrase appears it will mean a full year's charge in the year of purchase, and no charge at all in the year of sale.

4.3.4 Double entry

In the Balance sheet two accounts are used. A Cost account, which does not normally change over the assets life, and an Accumulated depreciation account, which indicates the depreciation charged to date. Changes to the cost account will only arise if there is an addition or disposal.

Entries	Debit	Credit
Purchase of asset (entry on purchase date only)	Cost a/c	Cash a/c
Charge for depreciation for period (entry once in each period)	Profit and loss a/c	Accumulated depreciation

Example 3

For the facts in Example 2 prepare the Cost account and Accumulated depreciation account.

Cost account

	£		£
1 Jan Cash a/c – purchase of asset	10,000		

The balance on this account remains unchanged, and would be carried forward in each period.

Accumulated depreciation account

19X1		£	19X1		£
			31 Dec	Profit and loss a/c	4,377
31 Dec	Balance c/f	4,377			
		£4,377			£4,377
19X2			19X2		
			1 Jan	Balance b/f	4,377
			31 Dec	Profit and loss a/c	2,461
31 Dec	Balance c/f	6,838			
		£6,838			£6,838
19X3			19X3		
			1 Jan	Balance b/f	6,838
			31 Dec	Profit and loss a/c	1,384
31 Dec	Balance c/f	8,222			
		£8,222			£8,222
19X4			19X4		
			1 Jan	Balance b/f	8,222
			31 Dec	Profit and loss a/c	778
31 Dec	Balance c/f	9,000			
		£9,000			£9,000

In the Balance sheet at 31 December 19X1 both balances will appear:

Fixed assets

	£
Cost (*debit balance*)	10,000
Accumulated depreciation (*credit balance*)	(4,377)
Net book value	£5,623

4.3.5 Disposal of a fixed asset

In computing depreciation two estimates were made. These were the useful life and the residual value. If either of these two estimates proves to be anything other than completely accurate we will find that either two little or too much depreciation has been provided by the date of sale. Put another way it means that the assets net book value on the date of sale may not equal the proceeds from selling the asset. To identify this difference we use a DISPOSAL ACCOUNT. The difference arising is called an over or underprovision for depreciation' (alias a profit or loss on sale). The treatment is to take any profit or loss on sale to the Profit and loss account, thus decreasing or increasing any depreciation charged for the period.

Entry	Debit	Credit
Open Disposal account	–	–
Transfer cost of asset to be sold	Disposal a/c	Cost a/c
Transfer accumulated depreciation on asset to be sold	Accumulated depreciation a/c	Disposal a/c
Record sale proceeds	Cash a/c	Disposal a/c
Debit (*credit*) balance remaining on Disposal account represents loss (*profit*) on disposal (*reverse the entry if a profit on disposal*).	Profit and loss a/c	Disposal a/c

Example 4

Donna started to trade on 1 January 19X1. On that date Donna purchased plant which cost £15,000. She decides that all plant should be depreciated at 20 per cent of cost in sue at the year end.

On 1 April 19X2 a further item of plant was purchased which cost £20,000.

On 30 September 19X3 the plant acquired in 19X1 was sold for £8,500.

Required:

The Plant cost and Accumulated depreciation accounts for the three years ending 31 December 19X3, together with a Disposal account to record the sale.

Plant account

19X1		£	19X1		£
1 Jan	Cash a/c	15,000	31 Dec	Balance c/f	15,000
		£15,000			£15,000
19X2			19X2		
1 Jan	Balance b/f	15,000			
1 Apr	Cash a/c	20,000	31 Dec	Balance c/f	35,000
		£35,000			£35,000
19X3			19X3		
1 Jan	Balance b/f	35,000	30 Sep	Disposal a/c	15,000
			31 Dec	Balance c/f	20,000
		£35,000			£35,000

Accumulated depreciation account

19X1		£	19X1		£
			31 Dec	Profit and loss a/c	
31 Dec	Balance c/f	3,000		(*20% × £15,000*)	3,000
		£3,000			£3,000
19X2			19X2		
			1 Jan	Balance b/f	3,000
			31 Dec	Profit and loss a/c	
31 Dec	Balance c/f	10,000		(*20% × £35,000*)	7,000
		£10,000			£10,000
19X3			19X3		
30 Sep	Disposal a/c		1 Jan	Balance b/f	10,000
	(*2 years × 20% ×*		31 Dec	Profit and loss a/c	
	£15,000)	6,000		(*20% × £20,000*)	4,000
31 Dec	Balance c/f	8,000			
		£14,000			£14,000

Disposal account

19X3		£	19X3		£
30 Sep	Cost a/c	15,000	30 Sep	Accumulated depreciation a/c	6,000
			30 Sep	Cash a/c – proceeds	8,500
			31 Dec	Profit and loss a/c	
				– loss on sale	500
		£15,000			£15,000

Points arising:

1 The amounts charged to Profit and loss account were:

	£
19X1 – depreciation	3,000
19X2 – depreciation	7,000
19X3 – depreciation	4,000
– loss on sale of plant	500
	£4,500

2 Depreciation was '20 per cent of cost in use at the year end'. There was thus a full year's charges in 19X2 for plant purchased on 1 April and no charge in 19X3 for plant sold on the 30 September.

3 It was necessary to compute the accumulated depreciation on the plant sold in order to transfer that amount to the Disposal account.

4.3.6 **What about the fundamental concepts?**

We can see all four fundamental concepts within the charge for depreciation:

1 Going concern – use of cost in fixed assets rather than second-hand value.
– assumption that the asset will have a full useful life.
2 Matching up – cost less estimated residual value is allocated over the estimated useful life.
3 Prudence – in estimating the useful life and the residual value.
4 Consistency – use of the chosen method of allocation in every period.

4.4 **STOCK VALUATION**

It has been assumed in the examples considered so far that stock is valued at cost, and in each case this figure of cost has always been given. We must now ask two questions.

(a) How do we compute the cost of stock?   and
(b) Is there any value of stock other than cost which may be relevant?

The valuation placed upon stock is important since it affects three separate financial statements:

(a) Balance sheet, where it indicates the amount of stock held;
(b) Trading, profit and loss account of the current period, when the stock value represents closing stock; and
(c) Trading, profit and loss account of the next period, when the same stock value represents opening stock.

Thus any errors which may (and in practice frequently do) arise in counting, valuing, summarising and ensuring that the paperwork ties up with the physical movements (we call this 'stock cut-off') will affect the net profit of two accounting periods.

The area of cut-off is often particularly difficult. It requires that the purchase invoices relating to goods delivered by suppliers are included in Purchases and Creditors' accounts, but that invoices for goods not delivered at the Balance-sheet date are excluded. Conversely, the sales invoices relating to goods delivered to customers are included in Sales and Debtors' accounts, but that invoices for goods not yet delivered, and still in stock, are excluded. The general rule is that the paperwork should be brought into line with the physical situation at the Balance-sheet date.

4.4.1 How do we compute the cost of stock?

We are attempting to compute the cost of bringing the stock to its current location and condition. This would include:

(a) the purchase invoice cost of the materials which would be net of trade discounts;
(b) The cost of transport to its current location (delivery, handling and distribution to outlying warehouses); and
(c) The cost of insurance while in transit.

The cost of transport is often called CARRIAGE IN. This idea of cost will require some amplification when we consider manufacturing companies. However, it will suffice for the present.

A major problem arises in determining the appropriate purchase invoice cost when there have been two or more purchases of identical stock items. We call such identical items FUNGIBLE ASSETS.

Example 5

Henry buys and sells one type of radio. During 19X1, his first year of trading, he had the following purchases and sales.

	Purchases	Sales
1 Jan	100 radios @ £10.30 each	
15 Feb	80 radios @ £13.00 each	
		30 Mar 70 radios @ £15.00 each

Required:
Compute the cost of stock on three alternative bases.

The closing stock is 110 radios (100 + 80 − 70). The problem is in deciding which radios were sold on 30 March. There are three possible assumptions:

1 First-In-First-Out   (FIFO)
   This method assumes that the first items purchased are the first to be sold. In the example the 70 radios sold were purchased on 1 January. The closing stock would be computed:

		£
1 Jan	30 radios @ £10.30 =	309
15 Feb	80 radios @ £13.00 =	1,040
Total	110 radios	£1,349

2 Last-In-First-Out   (LIFO)
This method assumes that the latest items purchased are the first to be sold. In the example the 70 radios sold were purchased on 15 February. The closing stock would be computed:

		£
1 Jan	100 radios @ £10.30 =	1,030
15 Feb	10 radios @ £13.00 =	130
Total	110 radios	£1,160

3 Average cost
The purchases on 1 January and 15 February are added together to find the average cost.

		£
1 Jan	100 radios @ £10.30	1,030
15 Feb	80 radios @ £13.00	1,040
Total	180 radios	£2,070

Average purchase cost $= \dfrac{£2,070}{180} = £11.50$

Applied to 110 radios of closing stock gives £1,265.
Comparison of gross profit arising:

	FIFO		LIFO		Average	
	£	£	£	£	£	£
Sales (70 @ £15)		1,050		1,050		1,050
Purchases	(2,070)		(2,070)		(2,070)	
Closing stock	1,349		1,160		1,265	
Cost of sales		(721)		(910)		(805)
Gross profit		£329		£140		£245

N.B. The higher the figure of closing stock, then the higher the figure of gross profit, and hence net profit.

Of the three methods, FIFO and average cost are widely used and accepted. The reason is that the assumptions are realistic in relation to what is likely to have occurred physically. Therefore, the resulting stock value must give a reasonable approximation to actual cost. LIFO, on the other hand, has attracted much criticism and is not widely used in the United Kingdom, although it is popular in the United States. The main criticism is that it is an unrealistic assumption in relation to physical movements, since the stock held is deemed to be getting older and older, and eventually obsolete. In its favour its supporters point out that it gives the lowest profit figure of the three methods, and is therefore a more prudent method in an economy where stock purchase prices are increasing due to inflation or other factors.

4.4.2 Is there any value of stock other than cost which may be relevant?

The quick answer is 'yes'. The relevant figure is called NET REALISABLE VALUE. This is defined as the estimated selling price less any costs of completion or costs of selling and distribution. The net realisable value becomes relevant when it is LOWER than cost. This may occur when stock has been damaged, become obsolete or when the market selling price has fallen. In order to determine whether net realisable value is lower than cost, we must make the comparison on individual stock items (or groups of fungible items), and then add together the results for all stock items. It should never be done by comparing total cost and total net realisable value.

Example 6

Mavis buys and sells ladies' wristwatches. She deals in three models, gold, silver and steel. The market is volatile due to the rapid changes in fashion. Mavis values stock at the lower of cost and net realisable value, which are given below.

	Cost	Net realisable value
	£	£
Gold	10,500	11,200
Silver	6,900	6,300
Steel	2,100	2,500
	£19,500	£20,000

Required: Mavis's stock valuation.

	Cost	Net realisable value	Lower
	£	£	£
Gold	10,500	11,200	10,500
Silver	6,900	6,300	6,300
Steel	2,100	2,500	2,100
Stock valuation			£18,900

4.4.3 Further alternatives to cost

Two other alternatives to actual cost are possible. These are:

(a) *Selling price less gross profit.* This method works backwards by taking the estimated selling price and deducting a percentage representing gross profit. The method assumes that gross profit is uniform over different lines of stock, and is used by retailers.

(b) *Standard cost.* This is a predetermined budget or estimate of the cost, and is widely used in manufacturing companies as part of an overall costing and management control system.

The criterion for accepting either of these two methods as an alternative to actual cost is that they give a reasonable approximation to the actual cost. Once this is justified, these methods can avoid the need for maintaining detailed records of stock transactions.

4.4.4 What about the fundamental concepts?

Two concepts are particularly in evidence in the valuation of stock:

1 Matching-up – by computing the cost of stock purchased in one period and carrying forward to the future period when that stock is sold.

2 Prudence – by taking the net realisable value when lower than cost we are providing for any fall in value immediately.

4.5 PURCHASE OF ASSETS ON HIRE-PURCHASE

4.5.1 Substance over form concept

The terms of a hire-purchase contract will require the payment of a deposit at the date of the contract followed by a series of instalments.

89

Typically, such instalments would be paid monthly, and continue for 24 or 36 months.

Together, the deposit and instalments will amount to more than the outright cash purchase price. This extra amount is called a 'finance charge' or 'hire-purchase interest'. It is a form of interest charged by the seller (or vendor) to the purchaser on the outstanding instalments.

So far as the law is concerned the asset does not become the property of the purchaser until all the instalments have been paid. In the meantime the purchaser has had full use of the asset. This poses two questions when we consider the accounting treatment of a fixed asset purchased under a hire-purchase contract. They are:

(a) When should the purchaser record the asset purchased as a fixed asset?
(b) What figure should be recorded as the cost of the fixed asset?

Before dealing with the answers we will set out a fifth accounting concept. It is the SUBSTANCE OVER FORM CONCEPT. It means that where the substance or financial reality of a transaction differs from the form or legal position, then it is the substance which is reflected within the accounts. In the case of a hire-purchase contract the substance of the transaction is that the purchaser acquires an asset at the contract date and uses it over the asset's useful life. Such useful life commences immediately and is independent of the hire-purchase contract period. In addition the purchaser has contracted to pay instalments to the vendor, part of which is to cover interest charges.

In the light of this concept we can now answer the two questions:

(a) The purchaser records the fixed asset on the date of the contract, i.e. immediately the asset comes into use.
(b) The fixed asset is recorded at the price the purchaser would have paid if the asset had been acquired outright for cash. The difference between this figure and the total deposit plus instalments is the hire-purchase interest and is charged to the Profit and loss account as a financial expense evenly over the duration of the contract.

4.5.2 Double entry

Entry	Debit	Credit
Open a Hire-purchase a/c	–	–
Equivalent cash purchase price is recorded	Fixed-asset cost a/c	Hire-purchase a/c

Cash payments to vendor (deposit, instalments)	Hire-purchase a/c	Cash a/c
Proportion of hire-purchase interest related to instalments paid in current period	Profit and loss a/c	Hire-purchase a/c
Deprecation for period based on fixed-asset cost recorded, and normal factors affecting depreciation	Profit and loss a/c	Accumulated depreciation

The balance carried forward on the hire-purchase account represents the capital element only of the instalments not yet paid. It will appear in the Balance sheet under 'creditors: amounts falling due within one year'. Where the contract has more than one year left to run, then part of the balance will appear under 'creditors: amounts falling due after more than one year'.

Example 7

Jenny owns a shop and makes her accounts up to 30 June each year. On 1 January 19X2 Jenny entered a hire-purchase contract to purchase a display refrigerator. The terms of the contract required a deposit of £136 followed by 24 monthly instalments of £15 commencing on 1 February 19X2. The outright cash purchase price would have been £400. All instalments were paid on their due dates. Jenny's policy is to depreciate all refrigerators at the rate of 12 per cent per annum on cost.

Required:

Record these transactions in the books of Jenny for the accounting period ended 30 June 19X2.

It is first necessary to compute the hire-purchase interest and depreciation.

WORKINGS

		£
(1)	Hire-purchase interest	
	Deposit	136
	Instalments 24 × £15	360
	Total hire-purchase cost	496
	Cash price	400
	Hire-purchase interest	£96

Instalments paid before 30.6.X2   5
Total instalments   24
Hire-purchase interest related to period
    ended 30.6.X2 = 5/24 × £96 =   £20
(2) Depreciation for six months to 30.6.X2
    12% × 6/12 × £400 = £24

(N.B. Depreciation is ' . . . at the rate of . . . ', hence for six months only.)

Display refrigerator cost account

19X2		£	19X2		£
1 Jan	Hire-purchase a/c	400			
			30 Jun	Balance c/f	400
		£400			£400
1 Jul	Balance b/f	400			

Accumulated depreciation account

19X2		£	19X2		£
			30 Jun	Profit and loss a/c (*W2*)	24
30 Jun	Balance c/f	24			
		£24			£24
			11 Jul	Balance b/f	24

Hire-purchase account

19X2		£	19X2		£
1 Jan	Cash a/c – deposit	136	1 Jan	Display refrigerator Cost a/c	400
1 Feb	Cash a/c – instalment	15			
1 Mar	Cash a/c – instalment	15			
1 Apr	Cash a/c – instalment	15	30 Jun	Profit and loss a/c – hire-purchase interest (W1)	20
1 May	Cash a/c – instalment	15			
1 Jun	Cash a/c – instalment	15			
30 Jun	Balance c/f	209			
		£420			£420
			1 Jul	Balance b/f	209

N.B. Cross-reference to workings is made by indicating *W1*, *W2*, etc.

The balance of £209 on the hire-purchase account can be explained as:

	£
Instalments not yet due *19 × £15*	285
Hire purchase interest on those instalments	
19/24 × £96	(76)
Capital element of instalments	£209

For balance-sheet presentation the figure is split by reference to the twelve instalments due in the next year, and the further seven thereafter:

£

Creditors: amounts falling due within one year $\dfrac{12}{19} \times £209 =$ 132

Creditors: amounts falling due after more than one year $\dfrac{7}{19} \times £209 = 77$

£209

Exercises to Chapter 4

1. An asset was purchased on 1 June 19X2 for £10,000. The business makes up its accounts to 31 December each year. The asset was sold on 1 April 19X5 for £3,500. Compute the profit or loss on sale, assuming alternatively that:

   (a) depreciation is charged at 20 per cent on cost in use at each year end; and
   (b) depreciation is charged at the rate of 30 per cent on the reducing balance.

2. Stock purchased and used by a certain business during one period was as follows:

Opening stock	5,000 units @ £15
Purchased	2,000 Units @ £16
Used	4,000 Units
Purchased	3,000 units @ £17
Used	1,800 units
Purchased	3,500 Units @ £18
Used	3,100 units

You are required to value the closing stock on the alternative bases of:

(a) First-in-last-out: and

(b) Last-in-first-out.

3. An asset was purchased by a business on 1 January 19X3 on hire-purchase terms. Payments required were a deposit of £432, followed by 36 monthly payments of £20 each. The first payment of £20 was due on the 31 January 19X3. The outright cash purchase price of the asset would have been £840. Accounts are made up to 31 December each year. Assuming that the asset has no residual value you are required to:

(a) Calculate the hire-purchase finance charge for each of the three years; and

(b) Calculate the annual depreciation charge on straight-line basis.

PART II

PREPARATION OF

INTERNAL ACCOUNTS

ACCOUNTS FROM

INCOMPLETE RECORDS

5.1 GROSS PROFIT PERCENTAGES

Gross profit represents the excess of sales over the cost of sales. Gross profit can be expressed as a percentage of either sales or cost of sales.

Gross profit as a percentage of	Basis	Name
Sales	$\dfrac{\text{Gross profit}}{\text{Sales}} \times 100$	Margin
Cost of sales	$\dfrac{\text{Gross profit}}{\text{Cost of sales}} \times 100$	Mark-up

Frequently examination questions will supply a gross profit margin or mark-up in order to compute some missing information. If sales are known, then cost of sales, and hence purchases, opening stock or closing stock could be computed as a balancing figure. If cost of sales are known, then sales could be computed. The key is to work out the 'profit equation'. This is:

Cost of sales + Gross profit = Sales

The technique is:

1 If gross profit is given as a margin, then make sales 100. If gross profit is given as a mark-up, then make cost of sales 100.
2 Enter gross profit as a percentage of 100.
3 Complete the profit equation.
4 Compute sales or cost of sales as required:

$$\text{Sales} = \text{Cost of sales} \times \frac{\text{Sales factor}}{\text{Cost of sales factor}}$$

$$\text{Cost of sales} = \text{Sales} \times \frac{\text{Cost of sales factor}}{\text{Sales factor}}$$

Example 1

	£
Opening stock	5,000
Purchases	56,000
Closing stock	7,000

Gross profit is constant at 25 per cent on cost.

Required: Compute sales

Cost of sales = £5,000 + 56,000 − 7,000
          = £54,000

Profit equation

Cost of sales + Gross profit = Sales

$$\begin{array}{ccccc} 100 & + & 25 & = & 125 \\ & & & & (balance) \end{array}$$

$$\text{Sales} = £54,000 \times \frac{125}{100}$$

$$= £67,500$$

Example 2

Facts as in Example 1, but gross profit is constant at 25 per cent on sales.

Required: Compute sales.

Profit equation

Cost of sales + Gross profit = Sales

$$\begin{array}{ccccc} 75 & + & 25 & = & 100 \\ (balance) \end{array}$$

$$\text{Sales} = £54,000 \times \frac{100}{75}$$

$$= £72,000$$

Example 3

	£
Sales	90,000
Opening stock	8,000
Purchases	70,000

Gross profit is constant at 20 per cent on sales
Required: Closing stock.

Profit equation
Cost of sales + Gross profit = Sales
    80   +   20   = 100
  (balance)

$$\text{Cost of sales} = £90,000 \times \frac{80}{100}$$
$$= £72,000$$

	£
Opening stock	8,000
Purchases	70,000
	78,000
Cost of sales	72,000
Closing stock	£6,000

Example 4

Facts as in Example 3, but gross profit is constant at 20 per cent on cost.

Profit equation
Cost of sales + Gross profit = Sales
   100   +   20   = 120
                    (*balance*)

$$\text{Cost of sales} = £90,000 \times \frac{100}{120}$$
$$= £75,000$$

	£
Opening stock	8,000
Purchases	70,000
	78,000
Cost of sales	75,000
Closing stock	£3,000

5.2 TOTAL SALES AND PURCHASES ACCOUNTS

In Chapter 3 we examined the use of control accounts. The main function of these was to summarise transactions relating to credit sales and credit purchases. In certain types of incomplete records questions it is not possible to separate credit and cash transactions. In such a situation the control accounts are modified to incorporate cash and credit transactions, and are then called 'total accounts'. Total accounts are an examination technique working, never part of an actual double-entry system. A comparison is given in Figure 5.1 opposite.

5.3 PREPARATION OF ACCOUNTS FROM PARTIAL INCOMPLETE RECORDS

5.3.1 Situation

Two typical situations arise which require the preparation of accounts from partial incomplete records. These are:

1 A business which has maintained records of cash and bank transactions, debtors and creditors outstanding, but which has no double-entry records; and
2 A business where double-entry records have been maintained but destroyed due to a fire or some other catastrophe.

In each case the objective is to construct a Trading, profit and loss account and Balance sheet from available information.

5.3.2 Accounts required

There are a limited number of accounts which will deal effectively with most situations, and certain information can be deducted from these as balancing figures. Figure 5.2 on page 102 describes these accounts and their use.

5.3.3 Technique

1 Prepare opening Balance sheet to identify opening balances, and opening capital. (This will not be required where the business commences to trade at the beginning of the period.)
2 Open pro-forma Trading, profit and loss account and Balance sheet, so that figures may be entered as they are computed.

fig. 5.1 *Comparison of control account and total account*

Sales ledger control account (credit only)

	£		£
Balance b/f debtors	x	Cash a/c – received from debtors	x
Trading a/c – credit sales	x	Profit and loss a/c – bad debts	x
		– discounts allowed	x
		Balance c/f – debtors	x
	£x		£x

Total sales account (cash and credit)

	£		£
Balance b/f – debtors	x	Cash a/c – received from debtors + cash sales	x
Trading a/c – total sales (cash + credit)	x	Profit and loss a/c – bad debts	x
		– discounts allowed	x
		Balance c/f – debtors	x
	£x		£x

fig. 5.2 *accounts required for incomplete records workings*

Account	Potential missing information	Debit/Credit	Other side of entry	Comments
Cash account	(i) Cash from sales	Debit	Total sales a/c	Cash sales and credit from debtors. It is assumed that this first goes into the Cash account, and from there to the Bank account.
	(ii) Cash drawings	Credit	Drawings a/c	
Total sales account	(i) Total sales	Debit	Trading a/c	
	(ii) Cash from sales	Credit	Cash a/c	
Total purchases account	Total purchases	Credit	Trading a/c	Cash (Cash a/c) and cheques (Bank a/c) paid are generally known.
Trading account	(i) Total sales	Credit	Total sales a/c	The Trading a/c will be needed as a working whenever gross profit percentage is given.
	(ii) Closing stock	Credit	Balance sheet	
Sundry expense accounts (rent, rates, light and heat, etc.)	Charges to Profit and loss account	Credit	Profit and loss a/c	

3 Open working accounts. The exact combination will depend on the individual question. A typical selection would be: Cash and Bank account, Total sales account, Total purchases account, profit equation, Rent account, Rates account.
4 Work systematically through the information provided ensuring strict double entry is maintained in the workings.
5 Review workings for missing figures, and identify balances to complete Trading, Profit and loss account and Balance sheet.

Example 5

John was made redundant in May 19X4 and decided to set up his own business as a shopkeeper. He commenced to trade on 1 July 19X4. Most sales are for cash, but there are a few credit customers. John acquired an existing shop, which is rented, and paid the vendor for existing stock, shop fittings, prepaid rates less an amount for rent outstanding.

John maintains a separate business Bank account, a small notebook which records payments made from the till, and a file of suppliers and customers' invoices outstanding.

The following information is relevant for the year to 30 June 19X5:

(1) Summary Bank account

	£		£
Redundancy cheque paid in	15,000	Paid to Vendor	5,815
Loan from Mike		Rent – 6 m. to 30.9.X4	320
(*interest at 10% p.a.*)	3,000	– 6 m. to 31.3.X5	360
Cash and cheques banked	59,240	Rates – 12 m. to 31.3.X6	540
		Suppliers of food for resale	66,145
		Electricity	425
		Private expenses	75
		Interest on loan	300
		Purchase of ice-cream freezer	800
		Balance at 30.6.X5	2,460
	£77,240		£77,240

(2) The payment to the vendor consisted of:

	£
Stock	3,500
Shop fittings	2,100
Rates for nine months to 31.3.X5	375
c/f	5,975

Rent outstanding for three months to 30.6.X4	(160)
	£5,815

(3) The notebook of payments from the till showed:

	£
Wages for sales staff	4,680
Cash used for private expenses	5,720
Wrapping materials	470
Purchases of food for resale	2,385
Cash in the till on 30 June 19X5	235

(4) There was no stock count at the Balance-sheet date, but John sells all goods at a selling price which yields a 20 per cent profit on selling price.

(5) Credit customers owed a total of £1,260 at 30 June 19X5, and a total of £1,845 was owing to suppliers. In addition rent for the three months to 30 June 19X5 amounting to £200 was outstanding.

(6) Depreciation is to be provided at 10 per cent on the cost of shop fittings and 20 per cent on the cost of the ice-cream freezer.

Required:

A Trading, profit and loss account for the year ended 30 June 19X5 and a Balance sheet on that date.

WORKINGS (cross-referenced as *W1*, *W2*, etc.)

(1) *Cash account (the till)*

	£		£
Total sales a/c – cash		Profit and loss a/c –	
and cheques (balance)	72,730	wages	4,680
		Drawings a/c	5,720
		Profit and loss a/c –	
		wrapping materials	470
		Total purchases a/c –	
		goods for resale	2,385
		Bank a/c – paid to bank	59,240
		Balance c/f	235
	£72,730		£72,730

(2) *Total sales account*

	£		£
Trading a/c – total sales (*balance*)	73,990	Cash a/c – cash and cheques	72,730
		Balance c/f	1,260
	£73,990		£73,990

(3) *Total purchases account*

	£		£
Cash a/c – payments	2,385	Trading a/c – total purchases (*balance*)	70,375
Bank a/c – payments	66,145		
Balance c/f	1,845		
	£70,375		£70,375

(4) *Rent account*

	£		£
Bank a/c – payment	320	Balance b/f	160
Bank a/c – payment	360	Profit and loss a/c (*balance*)	720
Balance c/f	200		
	£880		£880

(5) *Rates account*

	£		£
Balance b/f	375	Profit and loss a/c (*balance*)	510
Bank a/c – payment	540	Balance c/f (*9/12 × £540*)	405
	£915		£915

(6) Cost of sales

Cost of sales + gross profit = Sales

$$80 \quad + \quad 20 \quad = 100$$

$$\text{Cost of sales} = £73,990 \ (W2) \times \frac{80}{100}$$

$$= £59,192$$

JOHN

Trading, profit and loss account for year to 30 June 19X5

	£	£
Sales (W2)		73,990
Opening stock	(3,500)	
Purchases (W3)	(70,375)	
	(73,875)	
Closing stock (*balance*)	14,683	
Cost of sales (W6)		(59,192)
Gross profit		14,798
Establishment costs		
Rent (W4)	(720)	
Rates (W5)	(510)	
Depreciation of shop fittings (*10% × £2100*)	(210)	
	£(1,440)	
Selling costs		
Wrapping materials	(470)	
Staff wages	(4,680)	
Depreciation of freezer (*20% × £800*)	(160)	
	£(5,310)	
Administration and general		
Electricity	(425)	
Financial		
Loan interest	(300)	
Total overheads		(7,475)
Net profit		£7,323

Balance sheet at 30 June 19X5

	£	£
Fixed assets – tangible		
Shop fittings at cost	2,100	
Accumulated depreciation	(210)	
		1,890
Freezer at cost	800	
Accumulated depreciation	(160)	
		640
		2,530

Current assets		
Stock	14,683	
Debtors	1,260	
Prepaid rates	405	
Cash at bank	2,460	
Cash in hand	235	
	£19,043	
Creditors: amounts falling due within one year		
Suppliers of goods	(1,845)	
Rent accrued	(200)	
	£(2,045)	
Net current assets		16,998
Total assets less current liabilities		19,528
Creditors: amounts falling due after more than one year – loan from Mike		(3,000)
		£16,528
Representing		£
Capital introduced		15,000
Net profit for year		7,323
		22,323
Drawings (£75 + 5,720)		(5,795)
		£16,528

5.4 CAPITAL STATEMENTS – TOTAL INCOMPLETE RECORDS

5.4.1 Situation

Capital statements are used where a business has no separate business accounts at all. This arises in two situations:

1 A new business where the proprietor has no knowledge of accounting matters, and has mixed business and private transactions in a single bank account; and
2 A business where accounting records deliberately fail to record all transactions, possibly giving rise to an Inland Revenue investigation.

5.4.2 Basis of capital statement

A capital statement is a computation of an individual's wealth, represented by net assets, at a particular date. Both private and business assets and liabilities are included. By preparing a capital statement on two dates, the beginning and the end of a period, we can compute the increase or decrease in wealth during the period. Part of the change in wealth will be due to private income and expenses. The balance of the change must then represent business net profit or loss.

5.4.3 The capital statement equation

Opening net assets	business +net profit	private + income	private − expenditure	Closing = net assets

It follows that:

Business net profit	Closing = net assets	Opening − net assets	private − income	private + expenditure

Example 6

Susan owned net assets worth £10,000 on 1 January. During the next twelve months she received private income of £6,000 and spent £5,500 on private expenses. By 31 December her net assets were £25,000.

Required: Compute Susan's business net profit.

	£
Closing net assets	25,000
Opening net assets	(10,000)
Increase in net assets	15,000
Private income	(6,000)
	9,000
Private expenditure	5,500
Business net profit	£14,500

5.4.4 Special points

(a) *Purchase and sale of private assets.* Purchase of a private asset (e.g. house, car) does not qualify as private expenditure. The cost of the asset is included as an asset in the next capital statement. Only the cost continues to appear in subsequent capital statements until the asset is sold. On sale it is the profit or loss only that is included in private income or expenditure. The proceeds do not qualify as private income.

(b) *Mortgages and loans.* In computing the net assets at any date it is the capital outstanding on a private mortgage or loan which is included as a liability. The interest element only of repayments are included as private expenditure.

(c) *Depreciation of business assets.* In listing business assets only the cost of each asset is included. Any amounts to be charged for depreciation are deducted from the final net profit figure.

Example 7

Dave started a business during 19X7, but failed to open a separate Bank account or keep any records. The following were his assets and liabilities:

	31.13.X6 £	31.12.X7 £
Private house at cost	25,000	25,000
Business fixed assets at cost	–	10,000
Building society a/c	12,300	2,200
Business stock	–	4,500
Business debtors	–	2,800
Business creditors	–	1,500
Mortgage on house	18,000	17,500
Business loan	–	3,000
Bank a/c	2,100	1,550
Motor-car – Mini at cost	4,200	–
– Jaguar at cost	–	9,800

The following information is relevant:

1 The building society credited Dave's account with £325 interest during the year.
2 Mortgage repayments totalled £2,400.
3 The Mini motor-car was sold in the year for £3,500.
4 Dave spent £4,200 on living expenses and £1,050 on holidays.

5 During the year, Dave received a £600 legacy from his Aunt's will.
6 Depreciation of £1,000 on the business fixed assets is to be provided.

Required: Compute Dave's net profit after depreciation for the year.

Capital statements	31.12.X6		31.12.X7	
	Liabilities	Assets	Liabilities	Assets
	£	£	£	£
House	–	25,000	–	25,000
Fixed assets	–	–	–	10,000
Building society a/c	–	12,300	–	2,200
Stock	–	–	–	4,500
Debtors	–	–	–	2,800
Creditors	–	–	1,500	–
Mortgage – capital	18,000	–	17,500	–
Loan	–	–	3,000	–
Bank a/c	–	2,100	–	1,550
Car	–	4,200	–	9,800
	18,000	43,600	22,000	55,850
		(18,000)		(22,000)
Net assets		25,600		33,850
				25,600
Increase in net assets	–	–	–	8,250
Private expenditure (W1)	–	–	–	7,850
				16,100
Private income (W2)	–	–	–	(925)
Net profit before depreciation	–	–	–	15,175
Depreciation	–	–	–	(1,000)
Net profit after depreciation	–	–	–	£14,175

WORKINGS

(1) Private expenditure	£	£
Mortgage interest		
Repayments	2,400	
Reduction in capital (£18,000 – 17,500)	500	
		1,900
Loss on sale of Mini motor-car		
Proceeds	3,500	
Cost	4,200	
		700

Living expenses	4,200
Holiday expenses	1,050
	£7,850

(2) Private income	£
Legacy	600
Building society interest	325
	£925

Exercises to Chapter 5

1. For each of the following sets of data compute the missing item by using the gross profit percentage.

   (a) Opening stock £1,500, purchases £8,500, closing stock £2,000, gross profit 30 per cent on cost, compute sales.
   (b) Opening stock £3,200, purchases £6,300, closing stock £1,300, gross profit 20 per cent on sales, compute sales.
   (c) Opening stock £1,100, closing stock £1,500, sales £12,000, gross profit $33\frac{1}{3}$ per cent on cost, compute purchases.

2. From the limited data given below you are required to compute gross profit.

	£
Opening Stock	2,500
Closing Stock	3,500
Opening trade debtors	800
Closing trade debtors	1,300
Opening trade creditors	500
Closing trade creditors	900
Opening cash in hand	150
Closing cash in hand	250
Total cash payments (including drawings)	10,500
Total payments to suppliers (all by cheque)	7,200
Bad debts written off	350

There were no cash receipts other than for sales or receipt of debtor accounts.

3. A private individual who has confused private and buisness affairs in a single Bank account has requested a calculation of net profit.

Business assets, excluding cash, grew from £10,500 to £13,200 in the period, while business liabilities decreased from £2,200 to £1,800. Private assets were £50,000 at the outset of the period. The only change was the sale of a house which had cost £40,000 for proceeds of £82,000. A new house was purchased for £90,000. A building society mortgage of £15,000 was raised. Apart from the above, other private income totalled £1,200 and private expenditure totalled £3,600. The single Bank account balance decreased in the period from £5,650 to £4,840.

INCOME AND EXPENDITURE ACCOUNTS

6.1 NON-PROFIT-MAKING ORGANISATIONS

All the examples considered so far have assumed a profit motive. Certain organisations, however, require financial statements to record the activities over a period and the position at the closing date, but do not set out to earn a profit. The motive may be social, sporting, educational or charitable, and the organisation concerned a club, society, school or trust.

The differences apparent in the financial statements are due mainly to different terminology.

6.2 TERMINOLOGY

Profit-making organisation	Non-profit-making organisation
Trading a/c	No equivalent
Profit and loss a/c	Income and expenditure a/c
Net profit for period	Excess of income over expenditure for period
Balance sheet	Balance sheet
Capital a/c	General fund or accumulated fund

6.3 SUBSCRIPTIONS

Subscriptions will normally form the main source of income of a club or society. It is therefore the first item of income to be shown on the Income and expenditure account. When preparing a Subscriptions account, there may be two balances brought forward and two balances carried forward. Subscriptions in arrears for an earlier period would be a debit balance, whereas subscriptions paid in advance for the next period would be a credit balance.

Example 1

On 1 January subscriptions in arrears for the Jolly Social Club amounted to £320, while subscriptions in advance amounted to £155.

Receipts of subscriptions during the next year totalled £17,750.

On 31 December subscriptions in arrears and in advance amounted to £430 and £170 respectively.

Required:

Prepare a Subscriptions account indicating the total subscriptions for the period credited to Income and expenditure account.

Subscriptions account

	£		£
Balance b/f – in arrears	320	Balance b/f – in advance	155
Income and expenditure a/c		Cash a/c – receipts	17,750
– subscriptions for period		Balance c/f – in arrears	430
(*balance*)	17,845		
Balance c/f – in advance	170		
	£18,335		£18,335

6.4 PRESENTATION OF INCOME AND EXPENDITURE

In order that the Income and expenditure account gives as much information as possible certain items of income and of expenditure are grouped together, while other items may be excluded.

6.4.1 Bar trading account

Social and sporting clubs and societies often have a bar. In order to show whether the bar earned a profit or loss we prepare a Bar trading account. This shows bar sales, opening stock of bar supplies, purchases and closing stock. Together these show gross profit from which any barman's wages and other costs are deducted to show net profit or loss. In the context of the bar, the terms 'profit' and 'loss' are used.

6.4.2 Dances, fetes and special events

Income from sale of tickets and side shows are shown, together with related expenditure (prizes, hire of premises, music, etc.) to show whether the event was a financial success or failure.

6.4.3 One-off receipts

Receipts which are substantial and unusual, such as legacies received, are not shown as part of income in the Income and expenditure account, but are credited directly to the general fund. The reason is that inclusion in the Income and expenditure account would give a misleading picture of income for the period when compared with the previous or next accounting periods. The treatment is comparable with capital introduced in a business.

6.5 SPECIAL FUNDS

Occasionally a special fund may be set up to meet the cost of a particular project such as a building extension, or to provide scholarship payments. Such a special fund is separate within the Balance sheet. There will be a credit balance representing the capital of the fund, and an equal amount of assets. The two are always equal. It follows that income earned from special-fund assets is added to the Special-fund account and the special-fund assets.

Example 2

On 1 January 19X3 the Balance sheet of the Orange Squash Club showed the following position:

	£	£
Fixed assets		
Freehold property at cost		15,000
Accumulated depreciation		(5,100)
		9,900
Current assets		
Bar supplies at cost	4,300	
Subscriptions in arrears	420	
Prepaid rates	320	
Cash at bank	1,100	
	£6,140	

Creditors: amounts falling due within one year
  Due to brewery for bar supplies   (1,250)
  Subscriptions in advance   (270)
                                         ‾‾‾‾‾‾‾‾‾
                                         £(1,520)
                                         ‾‾‾‾‾‾‾‾‾

Net current assets   4,620
                                                       ‾‾‾‾‾‾‾‾
Net assets representing general fund   £14,520
                                                       ‾‾‾‾‾‾‾‾

The following information is relevant:

(1) Summary of receipts and payments (all through the Bank account):

Receipts	£	Payments	£
Balance b/f	1,100	Bar supplies	13,590
Subscriptions	21,560	Barman's wages	2,340
Legacy from Smith's		Maintenance of courts	2,950
estate	5,000	Electricity	1,875
Bar sales	20,400	Rates for twelve months	
Ticket sales of Valentine's		to 31.3.X4	1,500
Day banquet	1,100	Cleaning	550
Interest on Treasury		Cost of food and dance	
Stock	400	band for Valentine's	
		Day banquet	970
		Insurance	420
		Heating	1,975
		Purchase of furniture	5,800
		Investment in Treasury	
		Stock	5,000
		Secretary's salary	7,200
		Balance c/f	5,390
	£49,560		£49,560

(2) It was decided to set up a special fund to build new changing-rooms. To this end the legacy received was used to purchase Treasury Stock.
(3) At 31 December 19X3 bar stocks amounted to £3,800, subscriptions in arrears £550, subscriptions in advance £310 and owing for bar supplies £1,400.
(4) Freehold property is depreciated at 2 per cent on cost, and furniture at 10 per cent on cost.

Required:

Income and expenditure account for the year and a balance sheet at 31 December.

WORKINGS

(1) *Subscriptions account*

	£		£
Balance b/f – in arrears	420	Balance b/f – in advance	270
Income and expenditure a/c	21,650	Bank a/c	21,560
Balance c/f – in advance	310	Balance c/f – in arrears	550
	£22,380		£22,380

(2) *Creditors for bar supplies*

	£		£
Bank a/c	13,590	Balance b/f	1,250
Balance c/f	1,400	Income and expenditure a/c – purchases	13,740
	£14,990		£14,990

(3) *Rates account*

	£		£
Balance b/f	320	Income and expenditure a/c	1,445
Bank a/c	1,500	Balance c/f (3/12 × £1,500)	375
	£1,820		£1,820

ORANGE SQUASH CLUB

Income and expenditure account for year to 31 December 19X3

	£	£	£
Subscriptions (*W1*)			21,650
Bar Trading a/c			
Sales		20,400	
Opening stock	(4,300)		

Purchases (*W2*)	(13,740)	
	(18,040)	
Closing stock	3,800	(14,240)
Gross profit		6,160
Barman's wages		(2,340)
Net profit		3,820
Valentine's Day banquet		
Ticket sales		1,100
Costs		(970) 130
		25,600
Other costs:		
Maintenance of courts	(2,950)	
Electricity	(1,875)	
Rates (*W3*)	(1,445)	
Cleaning	(550)	
Insurance	(420)	
Heating	(1,975)	
Depreciation of freehold		
(*2% × £15,000*)	(300)	
Depreciation of furniture		
(*10% × £5,800*)	(580)	
Secretary's salary	(7,200)	(17,295)
Excess of income over expenditure		£8,305

Balance sheet at 31 December 19X3

	£	£
Fixed assets		
Freehold property at cost	15,000	
Accumulated depreciation	(5,400)	9,600
Furniture at cost	5,800	
Accumulated depreciation	(580)	5,220
		14,820
Current assets		
Bar supplies at cost	3,800	
Subscriptions in arrears	550	
Rates in advance (*W3*)	375	
Cash at bank (*see point arising below*)	4,990	
	£9,715	

Creditors: amounts falling due within one year		
Due to brewery for bar supplies	(1,400)	
Subscriptions in advance	(310)	
	£(1,710)	
Net current assets		8,005
Net assets in general fund		22,825
Special building fund assets		
Treasury stock at cost	5,000	
Cash at bank	400	5,400
		£28,225
General fund at 1 January		14,520
Excess of income over expenditure in period		8,305
		22,825
Special building fund		
Legacy	5,000	
Interest on Treasury stock	400	5,400
		£28,225

Point arising:

£400 of the balance of cash at bank relates to the special building fund, and has been shown as part of the special fund assets.

Exercises to Chapter 6

1. A club received a total of £15,545 for subscriptions during a particular year. At the beginning of the year a total of £185 had been owing in arrears and £75 had been received in advance. At the end of the year, arrears totalled £270 and receipts in advance totalled £110.

   You are required to prepare a Subscriptions account in order to identify the total subscriptions to be included in the Income and expenditure account.

2. A certain club runs a bar for members. During a particular year sales totalled £20,145. Payments to the brewery totalled £12,490. At the beginning of the year £460 was owed to the brewery and stocks at cost were £870. At the end of the year £630 was owed to the brewery and stocks at cost were £910.

   You are required to compute a Bar trading account to identify the bar profit for the period.

CHAPTER 7

PARTNERSHIP ACCOUNTS

7.1 DEFINITION AND PARTNERSHIP AGREEMENT

7.1.1 Definition of a partnership

The relationship which subsists between persons carrying on a business in common with a view to profit (*Section 1, Partnership Act 1890*).

7.1.2 Partnership agreements

A partnership agreement is the arrangement under which the business is conducted. Such an agreement may be:

(a) in writing; or
(b) verbal; or
(c) implied by a course of dealing.

It is desirable that the agreement should be in writing.
The points covered would include:

- name of business
- object of business
- capital contribution of each partner
- profit-sharing arrangements including partners' salaries and interest on capital
- drawings
- accounts preparation and audit
- conduct of meetings
- provisions for decision-making on day-to-day basis, admission of new partners and settlement of disputes

- arrangements covering the death and retirement of partners
- banking arrangements.

7.1.3 **Partnership Act 1890**

This Act contains provisions which will be applied by the Courts in the absence of any agreement to the contrary.

The provisions regarding accounting and administration are contained in Section 24

Capital contribution	Equal
Salaries	None
Interest on capital	None
Interest on advances beyond capital	5% per annum
Accounts	All partners entitled to view
Management	All partners partake
Admission of new partners	By unanimous agreement
Decisions – ordinary – nature of business	Simple majority Unanimous

7.1.4 **Capital and current accounts**

When we considered a sole trader only one Capital account was maintained. Capital introduced and net profit were added to the balance brought forward, and drawings and any net loss were deducted. There was a single balance carried forward.

In the case of a partnership we increase the number of separate balances for two reasons.

First, we keep separate the capital of each partner. This is done by using columnar T accounts.

Second, we draw a distinction between the permanent or fixed capital for which we use a CAPITAL ACCOUNT, and the undistributed shares of profit for which we use a CURRENT ACCOUNT. Both the Capital account and the Current account will have columns for each partner.

Account	Purpose	Entries
Capital a/c	Indicates each partner's contribution to the permanent capital of the business.	Only when there is some permanent adjustment, e.g. new partner, existing partner retires, alteration to asset book values including goodwill.

Current a/c	Indicates each partner's undrawn share of profits.	Credited with share of net profit. Debited with drawings. Normally there are no other entries to the Current account.

7.2 APPROPRIATION STATEMENTS

7.2.1 Computation of net profit

The Trading, profit and loss account of a partnership is very similar to any other Trading, profit and loss account. Items charged in arriving at net profit include establishment, administration, selling and financial expenses. The latter class would include interest charges on any loans, including loans from partners.

However, any amounts paid or allocated to partners such as salaries, interest on capital or share of residual profit do not appear in the Profit and loss account, but in the APPROPRIATION STATEMENT. Drawings represent a payment to partners on account of their total profit share, and are debited to the Current accounts.

7.2.2 Appropriation statements

The appropriation statement appears beneath the Profit and loss account. Its purpose is to show the division of net profit between the partners. The division is in three stages:

Item	Purpose
Interest on capital – expressed as a rate per annum on the Capital account balance.	Preferential share of profit intended as a reward for investment of fixed capital.
Salary – expressed as an annual sum.	Preferential share of profit intended as a reward for involvement in day-to-day activities.
Balance in profit-sharing ratio.	The surplus (or deficiency) remaining after the preferential shares is divided in an agreed ratio.

Example 1

A, *B* and *C* are in partnership. Their Capital account balances at 1 January 19X4 stand at £10,000, £8,000 and £6,000 respectively. The agreement specifies that partners are to receive interest on capital at the rate of 8 per cent per annum, *B* and *C* to receive salaries of £5,000 per annum, and the balance of profits to be shared in the ratio 5:3:2. Net profit for the year 19X4 was £50,000, and drawings by *A*, *B* and *C* were £15,000, £14,000 and £13,000 respectively. Balances brought forward on Current accounts at 1 January 19X4 were *A*: £2,500, *B*: £3,000 and *C*: £1,000.

Required: Appropriation statement, and Current accounts for the year to 31 December 19X4.

Appropriation statement for year to 31.12.X4

	Total	*A*	*B*	*C*
	£	£	£	£
Net profit available	50,000			
Interest on capital				
(*8% × capital balance*)	1,920	800	640	480
Salaries	10,000	–	5,000	5,000
Balance in profit-sharing				
ratio (*5:3:2*)	38,080	19,040	11,424	7,616
Total profit share	£50,000	£19,840	£17,064	£13,096

Current account

	A	*B*	*C*		*A*	*B*	*C*
	£	£	£		£	£	£
Cash a/c –				Balance b/f			
drawings	15,000	14,000	13,000	1.1.X4	2,500	3,000	1,000
Balance				Appropriation			
31.12.X4	7,340	6,064	1,096	a/c – net			
				profit share	19,840	17,064	13,096
	£22,340	£20,064	£14,096		£22,340	£20,064	£14,096

N.B. The only payments to partners are their drawings. Interest on capital and salaries are simply preferential shares of the profit, and are not automatically paid to the partners.

Example 2

Facts as in Example 1 except that the net profit for the year 19X4 was £8,000 only.

Required: Appropriation statement and current accounts.
Appropriation statement for the year to 31.12.X4

	Total	A	B	C
	£	£	£	£
Net profit available	8,000			
Interest on capital				
(*8% × capital balance*)	1,920	800	640	480
Salaries	10,000	–	5,000	5,000
Deficit in profit-sharing				
ratio *5:3:2*	(3,920)	(1,960)	(1,176)	(784)
Total profit (loss) share	£8,000	£(1,160)	£4,464	£4,696

Current accounts

	A	B	C		A	B	C
	£	£	£		£	£	£
Appropriation a/c – net loss share	1,160	–	–	Balance b/f 1.1.X4	2,500	3,000	1,
Cash a/c – drawings	15,000	14,000	13,000	Appropriation a/c – net share	–	4,464	4,
				Balance c/f 31.12.X4	13,660	6,536	7,
	£16,160	£14,000	£13,000		£16,160	£14,000	£13,

N.B. Each partner now has a debit (*adverse*) balance on Current account.

7.2.3 Interest charged on debit balances or drawings

A debit balance on a Current account indicates that a partner has withdrawn more than his or her entitlement. It can easily arise when profits are low, or if a loss is made. The partnership agreement may contain a penalty for such a situation by charging interest on the debit balance. An alternative may be to charge interest on all drawings. The treatment in both cases is to include a negative item in the appropriation statement. The effect will be to increase the balance shared in profit-sharing ratio.

Example 3

Facts as in Example 2. In the year ended 31 December 19X5 the business earned a net profit of £60,000. The partnership agreement requires that interest at the rate of 10 per cent per annum be charged on Current account adverse balances. Drawings for the year were A: £12,000, B: £10,500 and C: £9,000.

Required: Appropriation statement and Current accounts for the year to 31 December 19X5. All workings should be to the nearest £1.

Appropriation statement for the year to 31.12.X5

	Total	A	B	C
	£	£	£	£
Net profit available	60 000			
Interest on capital				
(*8% × £10,000/8,000/*				
6,000)	1,920	800	640	480
Salaries	10,000	–	5,000	5,000
Interest charged on Current				
accounts (*10% × £13,660/*				
6,536/7,304)	(2,750)	(1,366)	(654)	(730)
Balance in profit-sharing ratio				
(*5:3:2*)	50,830	25,415	15,249	10,166
Total profit share	£60,000	£24,849	£20,235	£14,916

Current account

	A	B	C		A	B	C
	£	£	£		£	£	£
Balance b/f				Appropriation			
1.1.X5	13,660	6,536	7,304	a/c – net			
Cash a/c –				profit share	24,849	20,235	14,"
drawings	12,000	10,500	9,000	Balances c/f			
Balance c/f				31.12.X5	811	–	1,
31.12.X5	–	3,199	–				
	£25,660	£20,235	£16,304		£25,660	£20,235	£16,:

N.B. *A* and *C* have adverse balances, *B* has a favourable balance carried forward.

7.2.4 Guaranteed minimum share of profit

When a new partner is admitted, he or she may be concerned that their total share of profits may fall below expectations. One remedy is for the incoming partner to seek a guarantee from some or all of the existing partners to make good any deficit for the first few years. The adjustment is between the partners and is effected as a transfer of profit at the foot of the appropriation statement.

Example 4

A and *B* are partners sharing profits in the ratio 3:2. No salaries or interest on capital are allowed. On 1 January 19X8 *C* is admitted as a partner. Previously *C* was a salaried manager earning a salary of £15,000. The new profit-sharing ratio is to be 3:2:1. No salary or interest on capital are allowed to *C*. *A* and *B* agree that if *C*'s share of profit falls below £15,000 they will make up the difference. The total net profit for 19X8 is £72,000.

Required: Appropriation statement for the year to 31 December 19X8.

Appropriation statement for year to 31.12.X8

	Total	A	B	C
	£	£	£	£
Net profit available	72,000			
Total shares in profit-sharing ratio *3:2:1*	72,000	36,000	24,000	12,000
Guaranteed minimum adjustment: £3,000 borne by *A* and *B* in ratio *3:2*	–	(1,800)	(1,200)	3,000
Credit to Current a/c	£72,000	£34,200	£22,800	£15,000

N.B. (i) *A* and *B* bear the £3,000 in their respective profit-sharing ratio.
(ii) The guarantee adjustment does not affect the total net profit.

7.2.5 Guaranteed maximum share of profit

We have seen the effect on an incoming partner of a guaranteed minimum share of profits. However, where it is envisaged that the incoming partner may receive more than expectations, the existing partners may be concerned that their share of profits will be affected. Therefore, one existing partner may guarantee another existing partner to make good the amount by which that partner has suffered. The adjustment is between the two existing partners, and is effected as a transfer of profits at the foot of the appropriation statement.

Example 5

A and *B* are partners sharing profits in the ratio 3:2. *C* is their manager earning a salary of £20,000. On 1 January 19X6 *C* is admitted as a partner. The new profit-sharing ratio is 3:2:1. *A* guarantees that he will indemnify *B* against the amount by which *B* suffers if *C*'s share of profit exceeds his previous salary as a manager. Net profit for 19X6 is £132,000.

Required: Appropriation statements for the year to 31 December 19X6.

Appropriation statement for year to 31.12.X6

	Total	A	B	C
	£	£	£	£
Net profit available	132,000			
Total shared in profit-sharing ratio 3:2:1	132,000	66,000	44,000	22,000
Guaranteed maximum adjustment:				
C's share of profit exceeds £20,000 by £2,000. This would be shared by A and B in the ratio 3:2.				
B's share is 2/5th	–	(800)	800	–
Credit to current account	£132,000	£65,200	£44,800	£22,000

N.B. (i) C is unaffected, since the guarantee is between A and B.

(ii) The adjustment is for B's share of the excess only, i.e. the amount B would have received had C received a £20,000 salary.

(iii) The total net profit is unaffected.

7.3 ADMISSION OF A PARTNER

7.3.1 Profit allocation

When a new partner is admitted the partnership agreement will be revised in relation to capital to be introduced, profit shares, salaries and interest on capital.

When the new partner is admitted at the beginning of a new accounting period no special points arise. The old agreement is used to appropriate the previous period's profit and the new agreement is used to appropriate the new period's profit.

However, when the new partner is admitted DURING an accounting period it is necessary to compute the net profit for the separate parts of the accounting period before and after the change. This is called a PROFIT ALLOCATION. It involves dividing gross profit and the various Profit and loss account expenses into the two part-periods. The resulting net profit figures are then appropriated to the partners, using two separate appropriation statements.

The technique of a profit allocation is as follows:

1 Compute total gross profit for the full period and allocate between the parts of the period by reference to SALES.

2 Compute total sales based expenses (e.g. commissions to salesmen, delivery costs) and allocate by reference to SALES.

3 Compute total time-based expenses (e.g. establishment, administration, interest charges on loans) and allocate by reference to TIME.

4 Identify any specific costs which occurred in one particular part of the accounting period (e.g. manager's salary prior to admission as a partner, bad debts) and allocate to relevant period.

Example 6

X and Y are partners together making up their accounts to 31 December each year. X and Y receive salaries of £10,000 each per annum and thereafter share profits and losses in the ratio 2:1. Z is their office manager earning a salary of £12,000 per annum.

On 1 September 19X7 Z is admitted as a partner. From that date, X, Y and Z are to receive salaries of £8,000 each per annum, and share profits and losses in the ratio 5:3:2. No interest on capital is allowed before or after Z's admission.

Details of Trading, profit and loss account items for the year ended 31 December 19X7 are as follows:

	£
Sales – for 9 m. to 30.9.X7	400,000
– for 3 m. to 31.12.X7	300,000
Stock at 1.1.X7	55,000
Purchases	520,000
Stock at 31.12.X7	15,000
Rent, rates, heat and light	13,500
Salaries (including Z's salary to 30.9.X7)	36,700
Delivery expenses	10,500
Other selling expenses	21,000
Loan interest	2,800
Bad debt written off in April	500
Bad debt written off in November	1,500

Required: Prepare a Trading, profit and loss account and appropriation statements for the year to 31 December 19X7.

Trading, profit and loss account for year to 31.12.X7

	£	£
Sales		700,000
Opening stock	(55,000)	
Purchases	(520,000)	
	(575,000)	
Closing stock	15,000	
Cost of sales		(560,000)
Gross profit		£140,000

	Total	9 months to 30.9.X7		3 months to 31.12.X7	
	£	£	£	£	£
Gross profit on sales ratio *400:300*	140,000		80,000		60,000
Sales-based costs:					
Delivery	10,500				
Other selling costs	21,000				
Sales ratio *400:300*	31,500	(18,000)		(13,500)	
Time-based costs:					
Salaries	36,700				
less: Z					
($9/12 \times £12,000$)	(9,000)				
	27,700				
Rent, rates, heat and light	13,500				
Loan interest	2,800				
Time ratio *9:3*	£44,000	(33,000)		(11,000)	
Specific costs:					
Z salary (*9 months*)		(9,000)			
Bad debts		(500)		(1,500)	
			(60,500)		(26,000)
Net profit			£19,500		£34,000

Appropriation statements

	Total	X	Y	Z
(i) For 9 months to 30.9.X7	£	£	£	£
Net profit available	19,500			
Salaries *for 9 months*	15,000	7,500	7,500	–
Balance in profit-sharing				
ratio *2:1*	4,500	3,000	1,500	–
	£19,500	£10,500	£9,000	–
(ii) For 3 months to 31.12.X7				
Net profit available	34,000			
Salaries *for 3 months*	6,000	2,000	2,000	2,000
Balance in profit-sharing				
ratio *5:3:2*	28,000	14,000	8,400	5,600
	£34,000	£16,000	£10,400	£7,600
Total for year – credited to				
current accounts	£53,500	£26,500	£19,400	£7,600

7.3.2 Cash introduced and cash paid privately

Whenever an incoming (or existing) partner pays cash into the business the capital account of that partner is credited, signifying an increase in the interest of that partner in the fixed capital of the business.

Frequently, however, an incoming partner will purchase an interest in the business from an existing partner. Cash is paid by the incoming partner to the existing partner privately. It does not pass through the business Cash account. In such cases the incoming partner's capital account is credited and the existing partner's Capital account is debited signifying that the paying partner has increased his or her interest in the fixed capital and that the receiving partner has reduced his or her interest.

Transaction	Debit	Credit
Cash introduced to business	Cash a/c	Capital a/c of partner who paid cash.
Cash paid privately for an interest in the business	Capital a/c of partner who received cash.	Capital a/c of partner who paid cash.

This double entry is demonstrated in Example 9 below.

Where other assets are introduced by an incoming partner the entry will be similar to cash introduced to the business, except that the relevant Asset account will be debited.

7.3.3 Goodwill - nature

Goodwill is an intangible asset. There is nothing physically to show, but there is value. Reputation, good location, expertise are all examples. The only precise way to value goodwill is to sell the business as a going concern. The amount by which the purchase price of the entire business exceeds the value of the separate net assets is attributable to goodwill.

In most businesses goodwill exists. However it is not normally shown as an asset in the Balance sheet. There are two reasons for this:

(i) goodwill cannot be separately sold. This follows from its nature and existence in a going-concern business. To show it as an asset in the Balance sheet would indicate it is a separate asset;
(ii) any method of valuation other than actually selling the business will be highly subjective, verging on arbitrary.

In a partnership the partners will wish to take account of goodwill when there is a change in the partners or in the profit-sharing ratio. This will ensure that an incoming partner pays a fair contribution towards the unrecorded asset, and that an outgoing partner receives a fair share of that same asset's value, to which he or she has contributed in the past.

7.3.4 Goodwill - methods of valuation

The partnership agreement will specify a method of valuation to be used in the event of a change in the partners or profit-sharing ratio. There are two methods:

(a) Purchase of a number of years' average profits. The technique is as follows:

    1 Identify profits of recent years. These may require adjustment for unusual items.
    2 Apply weighting, if required, to give greater emphasis to recent years.
    3 Compute average.
    4 Multiply by number of years required.

Example 7

The partnership agreement of A, B and C contains the following provision:

'Goodwill shall be valued at one and a half times the weighted average of net profits of the last three completed accounting periods. Weighting shall be one for the earliest year, two for the second year and three for the most recent year.'

Profits for the latest three completed accounting periods are 19X4 £11,000; 19X5 £14,000; 19X6 £16,500.

Required: Valuation of goodwill at 1 January 19X7

Year	Net profit	Weighting		
	£			£
19X4	11,000	× 1	=	11,000
19X5	14,000	× 2	=	28,000
19X6	16,500	× 3	=	49,500
Total		6		£88,500

Weighted average net profit $= \dfrac{£88,500}{6} = £14,750$

One and a half times thereof $= 1½ \times £14,750 = £22,125$

(b) Capitalised superprofits

A superprofit is a profit earned in excess of that which is expected from the separate net assets. In order to compute the goodwill we must decide upon the profit that we expect the separate net assets to generate. We called this the RETURN ON CAPITAL EMPLOYED. The technique for computing goodwill is as follows:

1 Identify the actual net profit of the partnership. (This could be an average or weighted average.)
2 Identify the return on capital employed expected from the business.
3 Divide the net profit by the return on capital employed to find the value of the capital (i.e. net assets) employed by the business.
4 Deduct the fair value of the separate net assets from the capital employed. The result represents goodwill (i.e. the value of capital employed which is not explained by separate net assets in the Balance sheet).

Example 8

The Balance sheet of *P*, *Q* and *R* shows net separate assets of £70,000. The partnership agreement provides that goodwill be valued on the basis of capitalised superprofits using the most recently completed accounting periods net profit and a return on capital employed of 20 per cent. Net profit for the year ended 31 December 19X7 was £19,000.

Required: Valuation of goodwill at 1 January 19X8.

Net profit to be used	£19,000
Expected return on capital employed	20 per cent
Value of capital employed:	

$$£19,000 \times \frac{100}{20} \quad = \qquad \begin{array}{c} £ \\ 95,000 \end{array}$$

Separate net assets per Balance sheet	(70,000)
Value of goodwill	£25,000

N.B. Alternative layout:

	£
Actual net profit	19,000
Net profit expected from separate net assets	
20 per cent × £70,000	(14,000)
Superprofit	£5,000
Capitalised at the rate of 20 per cent	

$$£5,000 \times \frac{100}{20} \qquad = \quad £25,000$$

7.3.5 Goodwill – double entry

Having valued the goodwill the double entry will be:

Event, and timing	Debit	Credit
Immediately BEFORE a new partner is admitted or the profit-sharing ratio is changed.	Goodwill a/c	Capital a/c – of OLD partners in OLD profit-sharing ratio

If goodwill is to be eliminated again, then immediately AFTER the change.	Capital a/c – of NEW partners in NEW profit-sharing ratio.	Goodwill a/c

Points arising:

1 The Goodwill account begins and ends with a zero balance.
2 Whenever an examination question states 'no goodwill account is to be raised' then the adjustment is still made, but the question is confirming that goodwill is to be eliminated after the change.
3 The adjustments for goodwill are normally recorded in the Capital accounts, and not the Current accounts. Individual exam questions may give a specific instruction to deviate from this norm.
This double entry is demonstrated in Example 9 below.

7.3.6 Revaluation of assets

Where the value of tangible assets recorded in the Balance sheet increase or decrease, then it is the existing partners who should benefit from the surplus or suffer the deficit.

Whenever a new partner is admitted we therefore need to review the value of tangible assets and take account of those values where they differ from book values.

The double entry is as follows:

Event, and timing	Debit	Credit
Asset valued higher than book value. Identify revaluation SURPLUS and enter BEFORE the change in partners.	Asset a/c – thus incresing the stated value of the asset.	Capital a/c – of OLD partners in OLD profit sharing ratio.
Asset valued lower than book value. Identify revaluation DEFICIT and enter BEFORE the change in partners.	Capital a/c – of OLD partners in OLD profit sharing ratio.	Asset a/c – thus reducing the stated value of the asset.

This double entry is demonstrated in Example 9 below.

Exceptionally, some exam questions require that the assets be returned to their original book values. In this case the above entries are made and then reversed AFTER the change in partners. The entry in the Capital account will then be to the NEW partners in the NEW profit-sharing ratio.

Example 9

R and *S* have been in partnership for some years, sharing profits in the ratio 3:2. Their Balance sheet at 31 December 19X3 included the following items;

	£
Capital accounts *R*	30,000
S	25,000
Land and buildings	12,000
Motor-vehicles	7,000

No goodwill account appears in the Balance sheet, and no goodwill account is to be maintained in the future.

On 1 January 19X9 *T* was admitted to the partnership. The terms of *T*'s admission were:
(a) Profit-sharing ratio be *R*, *S* and *T*   5:3:2.
(b) *T* pay £5,000 cash privately to *R* and £4,000 privately to *S*. In addition, *T* is to pay £8,000 cash into the business.
(c) Goodwill is to be valued at £12,000.
(d) Land and buildings are valued at £15,000 and motor-vehicles at £6,000. These values are to be recorded.
(e) *T* is to introduce his own car, valued at £4,500, into the partnership.

Required: Record the admission of *T* in the Capital account of the partnership and identify the balances carried forward. (Answer appears on page 137.)

7.3.7 Arrangement of capital balances to predetermined levels

The partners may agree that after the entries to admit a partner are complete, the capital balances should be adjusted to some predetermined balances. The excess or deficit arising in each partner's Capital account can be either:

(a) settled by withdrawing and paying in cash; or
(b) transferred to and from their Current accounts.

One special case arises when the Capital account balances are to be adjusted so that they are in the profit-sharing ratio. The technique is:

Capital account

	R £	S £	T £
Capital a/c – cash received privately from T	5,000	4,000	–
Goodwill a/c – £12,000 R, S and T 5:3:2	6,000	3,600	2,400
Motor-vehicles a/c – £1,000 deficit R and S 3:2	600	400	–
Balances c/f	27,400	23,000	19,100
	£39,000	£31,000	£21,500

	R £	S £	T £
1.1.X9 Balances b/f	30,000	25,000	–
Capital a/c – cash paid privately to R and S			9,000
Cash a/c – cash introduced			8,000
Goodwill a/c – £12,000 R and S 3:2	7,200	4,800	–
Land and buildings a/c – £3,000 surplus R and S 3:2	1,800	1,200	–
Motor-vehicles a/c – car introduced			4,500
	£39,000	£31,000	£21,500

1 Add together the capital balances of all partners.
2 Divide this total in profit-sharing ratio and carry forward as capital balances.
3 Identify the excess capital or capital deficiency for each partner and settle according to the instructions given.

Example 10

Facts as in Example 9. After completion of the entries in Example 9 the capital balances are to be adjusted to profit-sharing ratio by transfers to and from the Current account. The Current account balances on 31 December 19X8 were *R* £7,500 and *S* £4,700.

Required:
Show the necessary adjustment in the Capital and Current accounts.

Capital accounts

	R £	S £	R £		R £	S £	
Current a/c	–	2,150	5,200	Balances b/f from			
Balances c/f				Example 9	27,400	23,000	19,▮
(£69,500 in ratio				(total			
5:3:2)	34,750	20,850	13,900	£69,500)			
				Current a/c	7,350	–	–
	£34,750	£23,000	£19,100		£34,750	£23,000	£19,▮

Current accounts

	R £	S £	T £		R £	S £	T £
Capital a/c	7,350	–	–	Balances b/f	7,500	4,700	–
Balances c/f	150	6,850	5,200	Capital a/c	–	2,150	5,▮
	£7,500	£6,850	£5,200		£7,500	£6,850	£5,▮

7.4 RETIREMENT OR DEATH OF A PARTNER

7.4.1 Computing the balance due

On the retirement or death of a partner it is first necessary to compute the total amount to which he or she is entitled. There are three elements to the total:

Element of total	Adjustment required
Capital a/c balance	As for the admission of a partner: – goodwill (Section 7.3.5) – asset revaluations (Section 7.3.6)
Current a/c balance	Includes share of profit and drawings to date of retirement or death
Loan a/c	Includes accrued interest to date of retirement or death

7.4.2 Settlement of the total amount due

The balance due to a retired partner or to the executors of a deceased partner can be settled in three ways (or in any combination of the three ways). They are:

(a) Withdrawal of cash and assets;
(b) Transfer to a Loan account carrying an agreed rate of interest; and
(c) Acceptance of an annuity in lieu of the balance due.

Each of the three methods is considered in turn.

7.4.3 Withdrawal of cash and assets

A retired partner is entitled to payment of sums due in full. To this end the partnership may have set aside cash over some period to meet the often substantial payment of cash. In addition the retiring partner may wish to take certain assets such as a motor-car or office desk. In the context of a partnership of accountants or solicitors the retiring partner may wish to continue to act privately for certain clients, and would therefore collect any debtor and work-in-progress balances due from that client and pay any sums due to that client. The relevant entries are as follows:

Entry	Debit	Credit
Cash withdrawn	Capital a/c of partner to whom payment is made	Cash a/c
Assets taken AT VALUATION	Capital a/c of partner taking asset	Asset a/c
Liabilities assumed	Liability a/c	Capital a/c of partner assuming liability

7.4.4 **Transfer to a Loan account**

Although a retiring partner is entitled to be paid all sums due in full, it is unlikely that a going concern business would have sufficient cash available. One solution suggested above was to set aside funds over a period of years prior to the retirement; but this assumes that the retirement is planned some years ahead.

Another more common solution is for the retiring partner to leave some or all of the balance due as a loan to the partnership. Such a loan would carry an agreed rate of interest from the date of retirement. Where a rate of interest has not been agreed then the Partnership Act 1980 provides that the rate of 5 per cent per annum be used.

The loan could then be cleared by a series of payments, thus spreading the drain on the partnership assets over several periods.

The same arrangement may apply on the death of a partner, except that the loan would be from the executors of the deceased partner.

The relevant double entry would be:

Entry	Debit	Credit
Transfer Capital a/c balance to Loan a/c	Capital a/c	Loan a/c
Transfer Current a/c balance to Loan a/c	Current a/c	Loan a/c
Interest charged on Loan a/c	Profit and loss a/c (of the period AFTER the retirement or death	Loan a/c (where interest is not paid immediately) or Cash a/c (where interest is paid immediately)
Cash payments to retired partner/executors of deceased partner	Loan a/c	Cash a/c

7.4.5 **Acceptance of an annuity**

A further alternative to immediate payment in full of a retired partner's balances due is for the retired partner to accept an annuity from some or all of the continuing partners. This means that the continuing partners agree to pay an agreed sum to the retired partner each year for as long as he or she may live. It is similar to a pension and contains an element of risk on the part of the continuing partners, since they do not know how many payments they will have to make before the death of the retired partner. The following points are relevant:

1 The arrangement is a PRIVATE contract between the retired and continuing partners. Where any of the continuing partners use business cash•to pay their share of the annuity the payment will be treated as drawings.
2 The continuing partners will agree the ratio in which they will bear the annuity payments. This ratio need not be the profit-sharing ratio.
3 The balances due to the retired partner are transferred to the Capital accounts of the partners bearing the annuity payments in the ratio that they pay the annuity (this was the decision in the case Elliott *v.* Elliott). Thus no record is then maintained in the partnership books of any balances due to the retired partner, or any annuity payments made.

The relevant double entry would be:

Entry	Debit	Credit
Transfer Capital and Current a/c balances due to retired partner to continuing partners	Capital a/c and Current a/c of retired partner	Capital a/c of partners who agree to pay annuity in ratio that annuity is paid.
Annuity payments from partnership cash	Current a/c of partner for whom payment made (equivalent to drawings)	Cash a/c

7.4.6 Insurance policies

In order to provide the necessary funds to repay capital on the death or retirement of a partner the partnership may enter insurance policies on some or all of the partners' lives.
The particular points arising are:

1 Premiums paid are not charged in the Profit and loss account, but are debited to an Insurance policy account. This account appears in the Balance sheet as an investment.
2 On maturity the proceeds received will exceed the total premiums paid. The surplus is shared between all the partners in profit-sharing ratio.
3 The proceeds received may then be paid to the retiring partner or to the executors of the deceased partner.

142

The relevant double entry is:

Entry	Debit	Credit
Premiums paid	Insurance policy a/c	Cash a/c
Proceeds received	Cash a/c	Insurance policy a/c
Surplus arising on Insurance policy a/c	Insurance policy a/c	Capital a/cs in profit-sharing ratio.
Proceeds paid to one partner.	Capital a/c of receiving partner.	Cash a/c

Example 11

D, E and F have been in partnership for some years sharing profits and losses in the ratio 5:3:2. There were no salaries, and no interest on capital allowed. The trial balance of the partnership at 31 December 19X9 was as follows:

	Dr £	Cr £
Capital a/cs at 1 January 19X9		
D		10,000
E		8,000
F		6,000
Current a/cs at 1 January 19X9		
D		1,875
E		1,225
F	500	
Net profit for year to 31 December 19X9		15,000
Fixed assets – net book value	16,300	
Stock at 31 December 19X9	14,200	
Debtors	3,500	
Cash at bank	6,300	
Life-insurance policies at cost	4,000	
Creditors		2,700
	£44,800	£44,800

The following points are relevant:

1 On 1 October 19X9 D had retired. Goodwill was valued at £8,000 on that date. No adjustment has been made and no Goodwill account is to appear in the books. Other assets were agreed to be worth their book value.

Capital accounts

	D (£)	E (£)	F (£)		D (£)	E (£)	F (£)
Goodwill a/c £8000 7:3	–	5,600	2,400	b/f 1 January 19X9	10,000	8,000	6,000
Cash a/c	5,000			Goodwill a/c £8,000 5:3:2	4,000	2,400	1,600
Loan a/c balance transferred	9,500			Surplus on life-insurance			
				policies a/c £1,000 5:3:2	500	300	200
	£14,500				£14,500		
c/f 31 December 19X9		5,100	5,400				
		£10,700	£7,800			£10,700	£7,800

Current accounts

	D (£)	E (£)	F (£)		D (£)	E (£)	F (£)
b/f	–	–	500	b/f	1,875	1,225	–
Loan a/c balance transferred	7,500			Net profit			
				(i) 9 m. to 30.9.X9	5,625	3,375	2,250
				(ii) 3 m. to 31.12.X9	–	2,387	1,023
	£7,500				£7,500		
c/f 31 December 19X9		6,987	2,773				
		£6,987	£3,273			£6,987	£3,273

2 *E* and *F* are to continue in business, sharing profits in the ratio 7:3.
3 On 1 October 19X9 £5,000 was received in full settlement of the life-insurance policies which were surrendered. The proceeds have been paid to *D*.
4 Net profit has accrued evenly over the year.
5 Drawings have been debited to Current accounts.
6 Any balance due to *D* is to remain as a loan to the partnership carrying interest at the rate of 8 per cent per annum.

Required. Appropriation statements. Capital, Current and Loan accounts, and a Balance sheet at 31 December 19X9.

Appropriation statement for year to 31 December.

	Total £	D £	E £	F £
Net profit for year	15,000			
(i) 9 months to 30.9.X9				
9/12 × £15,000	11,250			
Shared in profit-sharing ratio 5:3:2		5,625	3,375	2,250
(ii) 3 months to 31.12.X9				
3/12 × £15,000	3,750			
Interest on loan from D				
3/12 × 8% × £17,000	340			
Shared in profit-sharing ratio 7:3	3,410		2,387	1,023

Loan account - D

	£		£
c/d 1.10.X9	17,000	Capital a/c	9,500
		Current a/c	7,500
	£17,000		£17,000
c/f 31.12.X9	17,340	b/f 1.10.X9	17,000
		Interest for three months	340
	£17,340		£17,340

E and *F*
Balance sheet at 31 December 19X9

	£	£
Fixed assets – net book value		16,300
Current assets		
Stock	14,200	
Debtors	3,500	
Cash at bank	6,300	
	24,000	
Creditors: amounts falling due within one year		
Trade creditors	(2,700)	
Net current assets		21,300
Total assets *less* current liabilities		37,600
Loan account – *D*		(17,340)
		£20,260

Representing:	Capital	Current	Total
	£	£	£
E	5,100	6,987	12,087
F	5,400	2,773	8,173
	£10,500	£9,760	£20,260

Example 12

Facts as in Example 11.
On 1 January 19Y0 *D* accepts an annuity from *E* and *F* of £4,500 per annum to be paid by *E* and *F* in the ratio 2:1.

Required: Show the transfer from the Loan account to the Capital accounts on 1 January 19Y0.

Capital accounts

	E £	F £		E £	F £
			b/f 1 January 19X0	5,100	5,400
			Loan a/c – balance transferred in		
c/d 1 January 19X0	16,660	11,180	lieu of annuity	11,560	5,780
	£16,660	£11,180		£16,660	£11,180

Loan account – D

	£		£
Capital a/cs – in ratio *2:1*		b/f 1 January 19X0	17,340
E	11,560		
F	5,780		
	£17,340		£17,340

7.5 DISSOLUTION OF A PARTNERSHIP

7.5.1 Accounts required

On a dissolution of a partnership two special accounts are used in addition to the normal partnership accounts. These are Realisation account and Purchasers' account. A typical dissolution situation will require a total of six accounts. These are briefly described below.

1 Realisation account
   This is essentially a disposal account which deals with the disposal of all the partnership assets (except cash which is kept separate). The purpose is thus to find the profit or loss arising on disposal of these assets which will be shared by the partners in profit-sharing ratio. The profit or loss is found by comparing the book value of assets and costs of dissolution with the proceeds of the assets.
2 Purchasers' account
   This account is only used where some or all of the partnership assets are being purchased by another business (which may be a company). The purpose of the account is to add together the various elements of the purchase consideration (cash received, shares and debentures in the company, liabilities taken over, costs borne) so that the total consideration can be transferred to the realisation account as a single figure.

3 Capital accounts
The final balances on Capital accounts will determine how much each partner will receive from the partnership (or in extreme cases, the amount a partner must contribute to a deficit). Current account balances will normally be transferred to the Capital accounts to determine this final settlement.
4 Creditors' account
It is necessary to pay all creditors before any payments are made to partners. To ensure this is done the creditors are kept separate from the assets (which are dealt with in the Realisation account).
5 Loan account
Loans from partners will be settled before partners' capital is repaid.
6 Cash account
This is kept separate from the other assets, since there will be both receipts and payments before the final settlement is made to partners.

7.5.2 Double entry of a dissolution

Entry	Debit	Credit
Assets, at book value, are transferred to the Realisation account (N.B. Unrecorded goodwill and revaluations may be ignored.)	Realisation a/c	Asset a/cs
Cash received for assets sold	Cash a/c	Realisation a/c
Assets taken by partners *at valuation*	Capital a/c of receiving partner	Realisation a/c
Costs paid by partnership	Realisation a/c	Cash a/c
Costs paid by acquiring company	Realisation a/c	Purchasers' a/c
Cash received from acquiring company	Cash a/c	Purchasers' a/c
Shares received from acquiring company and distributed to partners	Capital a/c of each partner with *value* of shares received	Purchasers' a/c
Creditors paid in cash	Creditors' a/c	Cash a/c
Creditors taken over by acquiring company	Creditors' a/c	Purchasers' a/c
Discount on settlement of creditors	Creditors' a/c	Realisation a/c
Loan from partner settled in cash	Loan a/c	Cash a/c

Loan from partner settled by issue of debenture stock in acquiring company	Loan a/c	Purchasers' a/c
Balance on Purchasers' a/c represents total purchase consideration	Purchasers' a/c	Realisation a/c
Balance on Realisation a/c represents profit on realisation (reverse entries for a loss	Realisation a/c	Capital a/c *in profit-sharing ratio*
Current a/cs transferred	Current a/cs	Capital a/cs
Final balances on Capital a/cs settled in cash	Capital a/cs	Cash a/c

7.5.3 Debit balances on Capital account

At the final cash-settlement stage a partner with a debit (*adverse*) balance on Capital account is obliged to pay cash into the partnership to settle the balance.

Where a partner in this position is unable to meet such a payment, then the rule in the leading case of GARNER *v* MURRAY requires that the debit balance is borne by the other partners in the ratio of their last agreed capital balances. This would be the balances at the last Balance-sheet date.

Example 13

X, Y and Z have been partners for some years, sharing profits in the ratio 3:1:1. On 31 December 19X9 the summarised Balance sheet appeared as follows:

	£	£
Fixed assets at net book value		55,000
Current assets		
Stock and debtors	32,600	
Cash	9,200	
	£41,800	
Creditors: amounts falling due within one year		
Trade creditors	(15,100)	
Hire-purchase liability	(1,100)	
	£(16,200)	

Net current assets		25,600
Total assets *less* current liabilities		80,600
Creditors: amounts falling due after		
more than one year		
Loan account – Y		(5,000)
		£75,600

Representing:

	Capital accounts £	Current accounts £	Total £
X	20,000	8,300	28,300
Y	20,000	5,400	25,400
Z	20,000	1,900	21,900
	£60,000	£15,600	£75,600

On 1 January 19X0 they accepted an offer from Big Plc to acquire their business as a going concern. The dissolution was effect as follows:

(1) Big Plc paid a total of £121,000 being:
   (a) 50,000 shares in Big Plc valued at £1.60 each to be distributed among the partners in profit-sharing ratio;
   (b) £20,000 in cash;
   (c) £5,000 debenture stock in Big Plc at par to settle Y's Loan account;
   (d) The trade creditors assumed; and
   (e) Solicitors' costs of £900 paid;
(2) X took a car valued at £9,000 and assumed the hire-purchase liability which related to that car;
(3) The remaining fixed assets, stock and debtors were transferred to Big Plc;
(4) The partnership paid further costs of £500;
(5) Final amounts due to and from partners were settled in cash.

Required: Record the dissolution in the books of the partnership.

Realisation account

	£		£
Fixed assets	55,000	Capital a/c – X –	
Stock and debtors	32,600	motor-car	9,000
Purchasers' a/c – costs	900	Purchasers' a/c – total	
Cash a/c – costs	500	consideration	121,000
Capital a/c – profit on			
realisation	41,000		
	£130,000		£130,000

Purchasers' account

	£		£
Realisation a/c – total		Capital a/c – shares	
consideration transferred	121,000	(50,000 × £1.60)	80,000
		Cash a/c	20,000
		Loan a/c – debenture	
		stock	5,000
		Trade creditors' a/c	15,100
		Realisation a/c – costs	
		paid	900
	£121,000		£121,000

Cash account

	£		£
b/f	9,200	Realisation a/c – costs	500
Purchasers' a/c	20,000	Capital a/c – withdrawn	
Capital a/c – paid in by		to settlement	
X to settle deficit on		balances due:	
Capital a/c	3,000	Y	17,600
		Z	14,100
	£32,200		£32,200

Trade creditors' account

	£		£
Purchasers' a/c	15,100	b/f	15,100

Hire-purchase liability account

	£		£
Capital a/c – X	1,100	b/f	1,100

Capital and current accounts

	£	£	£		£	£	£
Purchasers' a/c – shares £80,000 3:1:1	48,000	16,000	16,000	Capital a/c	20,000	20,000	20,000
Realisation a/c – motor-car	9,000	–	–	Current a/c	8,300	5,400	1,900
Cash a/c – balance to settle	–	17,600	14,100	Hire-purchase liability a/c	1,100	–	–
				Realisation a/c – profit on realisation £41,000 3:1:1	24,600	8,200	8,200
				Cash a/c – balance to settle	3,000	–	–
	£57,000	£33,600	£30,100		£57,000	£33,600	£30,100

Loan account - X

	£			£
Purchasers' a/c – debenture stock	5,000	b/f		5,000

N.B. The profit arising on realisation represents goodwill and asset values in excess of book value. These items are not recognised separately.

7.5.4 Piecemeal dissolutions

When a partnership is dissolved, and the individual assets are sold for cash, then it is likely that it will be some months before all cash is received and the final settlement made. However, once the liabilities and costs have been settled the partners may make a series of distributions to themselves as the cash is received, but in such a way that no partner will be required to repay any sums at a future date.

The key is to assume that each distribution is the last, and consider the position which would arise as a result. This is achieved by carrying forward a balance on the Realisation account at each distribution date which represents the loss (or profit) on realisation if that distribution were the last. The cash distribution can then be determined from Capital account workings (NOT the actual Capital account).

The technique is as follows:

1 Enter receipts and payments as before.
2 At first distribution date carry forward the balance on the Realisation account – the maximum possible loss.
3 Open a vertical Capital account working and write off the maximum possible loss in profit-sharing ratio.
4 Apply the Garner *v*. Murray rule to any deficits arising.
5 Identify cash to be paid to each partner.
6 Identify revised balances on Capital account and return to step 2 for next distribution date.

N.B. The Garner *v*. Murray ratio will not change between successive distributions, since it is the last AGREED capital balances which determine the ratio.

Example 14

S, *T* and *U* have traded as partners for several years, sharing profits and losses in the ratio 5:3:2. Their summarised Balance sheet at 30 June 19X1 was as follows:

	£
Assets (excluding cash)	70,000
Cash	10,000
	80,000
Creditors	(12,000)
	£68,000
Capital accounts	
S	26,000
T	28,000
U	14,000
	£68,000

On 1 July 19X1 the partnership was dissolved. Transactions were as follows:

1 Jul   Received £4,000
5 Jul   Paid creditors in full
12 Jul   Received £5,000, and paid costs of £3,000
31 Jul   Received £6,000 and made first distribution to partners
31 Aug   Received £20,000 and made second distribution to partners
30 Sep   Received £30,000 and made final distribution to partners.

Required:
Realisation account and workings to show the distributions to the partners.

Realisation account

	£		£
Assets at book value	70,000	Cash a/c (1 July)	4,000
Cash a/c	3,000	Cash a/c (12 July)	5,000
		Cash a/c (31 July)	6,000
		Balance c/d – maximum possible loss on 31 July	58,000
	£73,000		£73,000
Balance b/d	58,000	Cash a/c (31 August)	20,000
		Balance c/d – Maximum possible loss on 31 Aug	38,000
	£58,000		£58,000
Balance b/d	38,000	Cash a/c (30 Sep)	30,000
		Capital a/c – actual loss on realisation	8,000
	£38,000		£38,000

First distribution – 31 July

	Total £	S £	T £	U £
Capital account balance	68,000	26,000	28,000	14,000
Maximum possible loss in profit-sharing ratio 5:3:2	(58,000)	(29,000)	(17,400)	(11,600)
	£10,000	(3,000)	10,600	2,400
Deficit written off in ratio of capital balances *28,000:14,000*		3,000	(2,000)	(1,000)
Distribution		£Nil	£8,600	£1,400

Second distribution – 31 August

	Total £	S £	T £	U £
Capital account balance	68,000	26,000	28,000	14,000
First distribution	(10,000)	–	(8,600)	(1,400)
	58,000	26,000	19,400	12,600
Maximum possible loss in profit-sharing ratio 5:3:2	(38,000)	(19,000)	(11,400)	(7,600)
Distribution	£20,000	£7,000	£8,000	£5,000

Final distribution – 30 September

	Total £	S £	T £	U £
Balance above	58,000	26,000	19,400	12,600
Second distribution	(20,000)	(7,000)	(8,000)	(5,000)
	38,000	19,000	11,400	7,600
Final loss on realisation in profit-sharing ratio 5:3:2	(8,000)	(4,000)	(2,400)	(1,600)
Final distribution	£30,000	£15,000	£9,000	£6,000

Exercises to Chapter 7

1. *A*, *B* and *C* are in partnership. *B* and *C* are entitled to salaries of £10,000 each. Interest on capital is allowed at the rate of 10 per cent per annum. The balance of profit or loss is shared in the ratio 5:3:2. Opening capital balances were £20,000:£12,000:£8,000, and Current account balances £5,000:£2,000:£2,500. You are required to prepare an appropriation statement to share a net profit of £32,000.
2. Facts as in exercise 1. Drawings were *A* £5,000: *B* £7,000: *C* £4,000. You are required to prepare Current accounts and identify the closing balances carried forward.
3. Facts as in exercise 1, but the profit amounted to £9,000 only. You are required to prepare an appropriation statement.
4. Facts as in exercise 1, but *B* and *C* have guaranteed *A* a share of profits, which is not less than £9,000. You are required to revise the appropriation statement.
5. Facts as in exercise 1, but *B* has guaranteed *C* that *A*'s share of profits will not exceed £5,000. You are required to revise the appropriation statement.
6. *X*, *Y* and *Z* are partners sharing profits and losses in the ratio 2:2:1. Their Capital account balances are £15,000:£12,000:£10,000 respectively. *Q* is admitted as a partner and pays £5,000 cash into the business. In addition he pays £2,500 privately to *X* for a one-fifth share of goodwill. The new profit-sharing ratio is *X*:*Y*:*Z*:*Q*; 1:2:1:1. No Goodwill account is carried in the books. Tangible assets are to be valued at £4,000 above their book value; this value is to remain in the books. You are required to record the above entries in the Capital accounts of the partners, and identify the balances carried down.
7. Facts as in exercise 6. Following the admission of *Q*, *X* retires. Goodwill is to be valued at £9,000. A life-insurance policy which appears in the books at cost of £13,000 was cashed for a sum of £15,000 and this was paid to *X* in part satisfaction of amounts due to him. The remaining balance is to be transferred to a Loan account. *Y*, *Z* and *Q* continue in business, sharing profits and losses equally. You are required to write up the Capital accounts of the partners and the Loan account of *X* and identify all relevant balances carried forward.

CHAPTER 8

INTRODUCTION TO LIMITED COMPANY ACCOUNTS

8.1 LEGAL STRUCTURE, BIRTH AND DEATH

8.1.1 The separate entity concept

In Chapter 1 we examined companies briefly in relation to the need for accounts. In particular we stated that:

1 A company is a legal person separate from its owners, managers and employees. This was decided in the leading case of Saloman *v*. Saloman. It is known as the SEPARATE ENTITY CONCEPT and implies that the company's life may be unlimited. Companies may be incorporated in one of three ways:

   (a) by Royal Charter (e.g. Hudson's Bay Company)
   (b) by Special Act of Parliament (e.g. Bank of England)
   (c) by registration under the Companies Acts.

2 Companies Acts contain a substantial amount of detail regulating companies accounting and administration. In 1985 a new Companies Act consolidated the provisions of several earlier Acts. In addition each company is further regulated by two documents which are unique for each company. These are:

   (a) *Memorandum of association*, which covers dealings with the outside world. In particular:

      – Name
      – Registered office
      – Objects
      – Declaration of limited liability
      – Capital of the company

(b) *Articles of association*, which covers the internal management of the company. The Companies Act 1985 contains a model set of Articles known as Table A.

3 The owners of a company are its shareholders (also called members). The total capital is divided into many, possibly thousands or millions, of shares. The shares may be held by many different shareholders, who may be individuals, or other companies. The shares carry votes which are used in the company's general meetings and represent the ultimate power behind a company. If one person or company owns a majority of the shares then they will control the company in which the shares are held. Shares may be purchased and sold independent of the company.

4 The management of a company is delegated to directors, who may or may not also own shares. The directors are appointed by shareholders in general meeting. The directors act in a stewardship capacity and are required to lay financial statements before the shareholders at each annual general meeting.

The life of a company is terminated by liquidation or by dissolution by a Court order.

8.1.2 Limited liability and nominal value

Each share has an assigned nominal value. Typical nominal (alias par) values are 25 p, 50 p and £1. Once a shareholder has fully paid the nominal value on shares held there can be no further obligation on the shareholder towards the liabilities of the company. We say that the shareholders have limited liability. The name of the company will include the word 'Limited'.

In addition to denoting the shareholder's liability the nominal value is the figure at which shares are stated in the Balance sheet. The total nominal value of all shares is called the 'company's share capital'.

8.2 PUBLIC AND PRIVATE COMPANIES

Companies are subdivided into two classes:

8.2.1 Public company

Conditions:

(a) Limited by shares or guarantee and has a share capital; and
(b) Has a memorandum which states that it is a public company; and

(c) Registered as a public company; and
(d) At least two shareholders; and
(e) Name ends with 'public limited company' or 'Plc'; and
(f) Minimum paid up share capital of £50,000.

Benefits:

May offer shares and debentures to the public.

8.2.2 Private company

This is any company which fails to meet any of the conditions above. The name will then end with 'Limited' or 'Ltd'. The company may not offer shares and debentures to the public.

8.3 SHARE CAPITAL

8.3.1 Classes of shares

Share capital is divided into various classes:

1 *Ordinary shares.* All companies must have ordinary shares since they carry the votes. Ordinary shareholders may receive a dividend for each accounting period which varies according to the amount which the directors recommend. This will depend on how well the company has traded. In addition the increase in a company's value will be reflected in an increase in the value of each ordinary share.
2 *Preference shares.* A few companies additionally issue preference shares. Preference shares do not normally carry votes and are entitled only to a fixed rate of dividend. Consequently the value of a preference share will not increase as an ordinary share will increase.
Preference shares may be CUMULATIVE. This means that if the dividend in any period is not paid, then it is not lost, but carried forward. The full backlog must be paid before any ordinary dividends are paid.

Both ordinary and preference shares may be REDEEMABLE. This means that the company may purchase back the shares at some future date, at an agreed price.

8.3.2 Authorised, issued and paid-up share capital

AUTHORISED share capital is the maximum nominal amount of share capital which the company is entitled to issue. The Memorandum of association will stipulate the authorised share capital.

ISSUED share capital is the full nominal value of that part of the authorised share capital which has been allotted to shareholders.

PAID-UP or CALLED-UP share capital is that part of the issued share capital for which the shareholders have paid the company. Where this is less than the full issued nominal value, then we say that shares are 'partly paid'.

Dividends may be expressed as either:

(a) pence per issued share; or
(b) a percentage of the called-up share capital.

Example 1

ABC Plc has an authorised share capital of 1,000,000 25p ordinary shares of which 800,000 have been allotted. Of this 15 p per share has been called-up and paid-up.

Required:
(a) Compute a 10 p per share dividend; and
(b) Compute a 10 per cent dividend.

(a) Number of shares issued = 800,000
Dividend = 800,000 × £0.10 = £80,000.
(b) Called-up share capital = 800,000 × £0.15 = £120,000
Dividend = £120,000 × 10 per cent = £12,000.

8.4 RESERVES

In addition to share capital the company's capital includes reserves. A reserve can be distinguished from a provision. A provision is an amount set aside to meet a probable liability, but the exact amount is uncertain. A reserve is any amount set aside in excess of probable liabilities. Below are the more common reserves:

8.4.1 Profit and loss account

The Profit and loss account or retained profits represents the accumulated balances of net profit which have not been used to pay dividends. The reserve remains available to charge dividends paid in the future. We there-fore say that it is a DISTRIBUTABLE RESERVE. The remaining reserves are UNDISTRIBUTABLE, since they are not available for the charging of dividends paid.

8.4.2 Share premium account

This reserve arises when shares are issued at a price above nominal value. The issue price is an estimate of what potential shareholders are willing to pay.

Example 2

DEF Plc issues 50,000 25 p ordinary shares at 125 p each fully paid in cash.

Required:
Prepare the journal entry to record the share issue.

		£	£
Dr	Cash account *(50,000 × £1.25)*	62,500	–
Cr	Ordinary share capital account *(50,000 × £0.25)*	–	12,500
Cr	Share premium account *(50,000 × £1.00)*	–	50,000
		£62,500	£62,500

The issue of shares is dealt with in more detail in Chapter 12.
The uses of a Share premium account are:

1 Writing-off preliminary expenses. These are expenses incurred in forming a company prior to trading;
2 Writing-off share issue expenses. These would constitute commissions, underwriting costs and professional fees;
3 Writing-off the premium payable on redemption or purchase of shares and debentures subject to limits (see Chapter 10);
4 Writing-off the discount on issue of debentures; and
5 Issue of bonus shares (described in Section 8.6 below).

8.4.3 Capital redemption reserve

This reserve arises when a company redeems or purchases its own shares. It is created by a transfer from the Profit and loss account to replace the lost share capital. (This is dealt with in more detail in Chapter 10.)

The uses of a Capital redemption reserve account are the issuing of bonus shares only (described in Section 8.6 below).

8.4.4 Fixed-asset replacement reserve

This account represents transfers from the Profit and loss account in order to retain funds within the company toward the increases in replacement costs of fixed assets.

8.4.5 Debenture redemption reserve

This reserve, known as a 'sinking fund', represents transfers from the Profit and loss account in order to retain funds within the company towards the cost of redeeming debentures.

8.4.6 Revaluation reserve

This reserve arises when the recorded value of fixed assets is increased to reflect some current measure of the assets value.

Example 3

GHI Plc owns a piece of land which is recorded in the accounts at a cost of £10,000. The directors wish to show the value of the land in the accounts. The value is agreed at £23,000.

Required:
Prepare the necessary journal entry to record the revaluation.

		£	£
Dr	Land account	£13,000	
Cr	Revaluation reserve		£13,000

8.5 LOAN CAPITAL

In addition to capital provided by shareholders a company may raise capital in the form of loan stock or debenture stock. Both will carry a fixed rate of interest and preferential rights to repayment of capital before share-holders.

8.5.1 Loan stock

Loan stock may carry a fixed repayment date or it may be irredeemable. The rate of interest will be set at or above the market rate depending on the risk involved. Generally loan stock is unsecured. This means that the loan stock ranks with creditors in a liquidation.

8.5.2 Debenture stock

Debenture stock carries additional rights to loan stock. It is covered by a debenture trust deed. This appoints a representative to safeguard the interests of the debenture holders. The debenture stock is normally secured on the assets of the company, and if interest or capital is not paid on the due date, then a receiver is appointed to seize specified assets and sell them to satisfy any amounts due to the debenture holders.

Both loan stock and debenture stock have a nominal value on which interest is calculated. They can both be issued and redeemed at a premium or discount.

Debenture stock may carry rights to convert into ordinary shares at some future date. It would then be called CONVERTIBLE DEBENTURE STOCK.

8.6 FORMS OF SHARE ISSUE

There are three basic types of share issue:

8.6.1 Market issue

A market issue involves the issue of new shares for cash at a price equal to the current market price, or an estimate thereof where no shares are previously in issue. Shares may never be issued at a price below nominal value.

The share issue is normally arranged by a separate expert body such as a merchant bank, or firm of stockbrokers.

Example 4

JKL Plc makes a market issue of 20,000 50 p ordinary shares at the current market price of 375 p.

Required:
Journal entry to record the issue.

		£	£
Dr	Cash account *(20,000 × £3.75)*	75,000	
Cr	Ordinary share capital account *(20,000 × £0.50)*		10,000
Cr	Share premium account *(20,000 × £3.25)*		65,000
		£75,000	£75,000

8.6.2 Rights issue

A rights issue is an issue of new shares for cash to existing shareholders in proportion to the number of shares already held, e.g. a 1-for-10 rights issue gives the right to acquire one new share for every ten held. The issue price will be below the current market price to make the issue attractive to shareholders.

Shareholders are not bound to take up their rights issue, but may sell the right to some other person. This is called a 'sale of rights nil paid' since the purchaser has still to pay the company the issue price.

Example 5

MNO Plc has 500,000 25 p ordinary shares in issue. A 1-for-5 rights issue was made at 160 p.

Required:
Journal entry to record the share issue.

Number of shares issued 500,000 × 1/5 = 100,000

		£	£
Dr	Cash account *(100,000 × £1.60)*	160,000	
Cr	Ordinary share capital account *(100,000 × £0.25)*		25,000
Cr	Share premium account *(100,000 × £1.35)*		135,000
		£160,000	£160,000

8.6.3 Bonus issue

A bonus issue alias scrip issue or capitalisation issue does not involve any cash at all. It is an issue of shares to existing shareholders in proportion to shares already held, which is charged to available reserves. The effect of a bonus issue is to divide the total share capital into a larger number of smaller units of nominal value. The reason for such an issue may be to make the shares more easily marketable.

The reserves available for making a bonus issue are:

1 Capital redemption reserve
2 Share premium account
3 Profit and loss account
4 Revaluation reserve.

Example 6

PQR Plc has 400,000 25 p ordinary shares in issue. A 1-for-5 bonus issue was made from the Share premium account.

Required:
Journal entry to record the share issue.

Number of shares issued 400,000 × 1/5 = 80,000

Dr	Share premium account (*80,000* × *25p*)	£20,000	
Cr	Ordinary share capital account		£20,000

In addition to these forms of share issue there are two further methods by which shares may be issued.

8.6.4 Options

Options are often given to directors and employees. They give the holder an option to purchase shares in the future at an agreed price. If the market price is above the agreed issue price then it is likely the options will be exercised, and shares issued.

8.6.5 Convertible debentures

Debentures may carry an option to convert into shares. There will normally be a cash redemption alternative and the decision to convert or have shares redeemed will depend on the market price of the shares at the time of choice.

Example 7

Specimen Plc is a trading company. The accountant has prepared the following Trial balance at 31 December 19X8

	£	£
Ordinary shares of 25p		230,000
Share premium account		40,000
Profit and loss account at 1 January 19X8		7,400
8% Debentures repayable 19Y8		70,000
Leasehold property at cost	270,000	
Accumulated depreciation		61,200
Office equipment and machinery at cost	145,000	
Accumulated depreciation		48,000
Proceeds of equipment sold		5,000
Stock at cost 1 January 19X8	47,000	
Trade debtors	54,570	
Balance at bank	18,400	
Trade creditors		29,930
Sales		455,200
Purchases	325,950	
Rent and rates	23,210	
Wages and salaries	39,300	
Distribution costs	16,900	
Debenture interest	5,600	
Telephone, postage and sundry costs	800	
	£946,730	£946,730

The following information is relevant:
1 Stock at cost on 31 December 19X8 was £62,570
2 A bonus issue of one new share for ten held was made during the year from Share premium account. This has not been recorded in the accounts. The new shares rank for dividend in the current period.
3 The proceeds of equipment sold relates to equipment which had cost £20,000, and accumulated depreciation £14,000, and was sold on 2 January 19X8. The equipment is still included in the Trial balance. Depreciation of £25,000 is to be provided, being 20 per cent on cost.
4 Leasehold property was revalued on 1 January 19X8 to £300,000. This is to be depreciated over 40 years.

5 Corporation tax of £8,000 is to be provided.
6 A dividend of 1 p per share is proposed.

Required:
A Trading, profit and loss account for the year and a Balance sheet at the 31 December 19X8 for management. (Ignore advance corporation tax.) (N.B. Published accounts are not required.)

SPECIMEN PLC

Trading, profit and loss account for the year to 31 December 19X8

	£	£
Sales		455,200
Opening stock	(47,000)	
Purchases	(325,950)	
	(372,950)	
Closing stock	62,570	
Cost of sales		(310,380)
Gross profit		144,820
Establishment costs		
Rent and rates	(23,210)	
Depreciation of leasehold (W1)	(7,500)	
	(30,710)	
Administration and general costs		
Wages and salaries	(39,300)	
Telephone, postage and sundry	(800)	
Depreciation of equipment	(25,000)	
Underprovision for depreciation on		
equipment sold (W2)	(1,000)	
	(66,100)	
Selling and distribution costs		
Distribution costs	(16,900)	
Financial costs		
Debenture interest	(5,600)	
Total overheads		(119,310)
Net profit before taxation		25,510
Corporation tax		(8,000)

	£	£
Net profit after taxation		17,510
Proposed dividend (*W3*)		(10,120)
Retained profit for year		£7,390

Balance sheet at 31 December 19X8

	£	£
Fixed assets – tangible		
Leasehold property at valuation (*W4*)	300,000	
Accumulated depreciation (*W4*)	(7,500)	
		292,500
Office equipment and machinery at cost (*W5*)	125,000	
Accumulated depreciation (*W5*)	(59,000)	
		66,000
		358,500
Current assets		
Stock at cost	62,570	
Trade debtors	54,570	
Cash at bank	18,400	
	£135,540	
Creditors: amounts falling due within one year		
Trade creditors	(29,930)	
Corporation tax	(8,000)	
Proposed dividend	(10,120)	
	£(48,050)	
		87,490
Total assets *less* current liabilities		445,990
Creditors: amounts falling due after more than one year		
8% Debenture stock 19Y8		(70,000)
		£375,990

	£	£
Capital and reserves		
Called-up share capital (*W3*)		253,000
Share premium account (*£40,000 – 23,000*)	17,000	
Revaluation reserve (*W4*)	91,200	
Profit and loss account (*£7,400 + 7,390*)	14,790	
		122,990
		£375,990

WORKINGS

1 Depreciation of leasehold

$£300,000 \times 1/40 =$ £7,500

2 Underprovision for depreciation on equipment sold

	£
Cost	20,000
Accumulated depreciation	(14,000)
Net book value	6,000
Proceeds	(5,000)
Loss	£1,000

3 Share capital and proposed dividend

	No.	£
Ordinary shares at 1 January 19X8	920,000	230,000
Bonus issue	92,000	23,000
	1,012,000	£253,000

Proposed dividend $1,012,000 \times £0.01 = £10,120$

4 Leasehold property

	Gross £	Depreciation £	Net £
At 1 January 19X8	270,000	(61,200)	208,800
Revaluation surplus	30,000	61,200	91,200
	300,000	-	300,000
Depreciation for 19X8	-	(7,500)	(7,500)
	£300,000	£(7,500)	£292,500

5 Office equipment and machinery

	Gross	Depreciation	Net
	£	£	£
At 1 January 19X8	145,000	(48,000)	97,000
Disposal	(20,000)	14,000	(6,000)
Depreciation for 19X8	–	(25,000)	(25,000)
	£125,000	£59,000	£66,000

Exercises to Chapter 8

1. A company has an authorised share capital of 400,000 25 p shares, of which 300,000 are in issue, but only 20 p per share has been called up. You are required to compute:

   (a) a 30 p per share dividend; and
   (b) a 30 per cent dividend.

2. A company has 100,000 ordinary shares of £1 each in issue, fully paid. You are required to make journal entries for the following transactions:

   (a) an issue of 30,000 shares for £2.50 each to the open market;
   (b) a bonus issue of 1-for-5 from share premium;
   (c) a rights issue of 1-for-13 at £1.80 each, and
   (d) a revaluation of land from its cost of £70,000 to market value of £120,000.

PART III

PREPARATION OF

STATUTORY ACCOUNTS

ACCOUNTING STANDARDS

9.1 WHAT IS AN ACCOUNTING STANDARD?

9.1.1 Background

In Chapter 1 we identified various reasons why accounts are prepared for a company. Those reasons fall into two major groups. These are:

(a) Preparation of *detailed* accounts for *management* and financial advisors to determine how the company has performed, and to *make decisions* regarding the future. Such accounts are not available to shareholders or the general public. They are referred to as 'internal or management accounts'.

(b) Preparation of accounts for distribution to *shareholders* and for placing on file at Companies House for inspection by the general public. Such accounts must comply with the requirements of the various Companies Acts in respect of format and *minimum disclosure*. They are referred to as 'STATUTORY accounts.'

The Companies Acts deal primarily with disclosure. They do not attempt to deal with the many problems of an accounting treatment nature. It is generally considered sensible to leave this area for accountants to sort out themselves.

To this end a committee now called the Accounting Standards Committee was formed in 1969. It draws representatives from the various professional bodies, in particular:

Institute of Chartered Accountants in England and Wales
Institute of Chartered Accountants of Scotland
Institute of Chartered Accountants in Ireland
Chartered Association of Certified Accountants

Institute of Cost and Management Accountants
Chartered Institute of Public Finance and Accountancy.

9.1.2 Objectives of the Accounting Standards Committee

The Accounting Standards Committee does not attempt to standardise accounting practice, nor to lay down rigid rules. Rather, its aim is to narrow the areas of difference and variety in accounting practice by publishing authoritative statements on best accounting practice. Two types of statement are issued:

(a) Statement of Standard Accounting Practice (SSAP)
These statements deal with areas of fundamental and major importance, and which affect companies generally. An example would be stock valuation. Members of the various bodies represented on the Accounting Standards Committee acting as preparers, directors, company officers or auditors are expected to observe the Standards. Where there is a departure, for justified reasons, from a Standard, then that departure should be clearly explained. Failure to comply with a Standard would be a disciplinary matter between the member body and the accountant involved. SSAPs are not limited in their application to companies. They are intended to apply to all accounts intended to give a true and fair view.
(b) Statement of Recommended Practice (SORP)
These statements are intended to deal with areas which are not of fundamental or major importance or which do not affect the generality of companies. An example would be the accounts of pension funds. Compliance with such statements is encouraged, but is not mandatory.
In preparing statements, both SSAP and SORP, the Accounting Standards Committee will first issue an exposure draft. This sets out the intended statement, and invites public comment which may then be taken into account in the final Statement.

It can thus be seen that there are three levels of accounting requirement.

Source	Status
Companies Acts	Enforced by the Courts (through the Department of Trade and Industry)
Statements of Standard Accounting Practice (SSAP)	Enforced by the various Institutes represented on the Accounting Standards Committee
Statements of Recommended Practice (SORP)	Voluntary compliance

9.2 CONCEPTS, BASES AND POLICIES (SSAP 2)

9.2.1 Purpose of the Standard

Due to an accident of history this Standard, which lays down the foundation for all other Standards, became SSAP 2! (SSAP 1, which deals with associated companies, is considered in Chapter 20.)

The Standard recognises four fundamental concepts, but accepts that for any given transaction there may be more than one acceptable method of putting these concepts into practical effect. It therefore requires that accounts disclose which of the acceptable alternatives have been applied in those accounts.

9.2.2 Definitions

There are three definitions:

(a) Fundamental accounting concepts
These are broad basic assumptions which underlie the periodic financial statements of business enterprises. Four such fundamental concepts are regarded as having general acceptability:

 (i) the 'going-concern' concept – Balance sheet and Profit and loss account are drawn up, assuming there is no intention to liquidate or reduce significantly the scale of operations;
 (ii) the 'accruals' concept (or matching-up) – revenues and costs related to a particular transaction are both included in the period when the transaction occurs rather than the period when cash flow occurs;
(iii) the 'consistency' concept – similar transactions are dealt with in a consistent manner both within any one period, and from one period to the next;
(iv) the 'prudence' concept – profits are not recognised until eventual cash receipt is reasonably certain, whereas losses are recognised in full as soon as they are foreseen.

(b) Accounting bases
These are the methods developed for applying fundamental accounting concepts to financial transactions and items for the purpose of preparing financial accounts, and in particular (i) for deciding the accounting periods in which particular revenues and costs should be dealt with in the Profit and loss account; and (ii) for deciding the amounts at which assets and liabilities are stated in the Balance sheet.

(c) Accounting policies

These are the specific accounting bases selected and consistently followed by a business enterprise as being, in the opinion of the management, appropriate to its circumstances and best suited to present fairly its results and financial position.

9.2.3 Accounting points and disclosure

The Standard requires that all company accounts include a list of accounting policies. The table below gives an indication of the major areas upon which an accounting policy will be disclosed, together with an indication of the matters covered by the policy.

Area	Nature of policy
Turnover (alias sales)	How computed
Stocks	Basis of valuation
Depreciation	Methods and rates
Government grants	Treatment of capital grants
Research and Development	Circumstances when expenditure deferred
Foreign currencies	Rates of translation
Consolidation and equity accounting	Treatment of acquisitions and disposals, unrealised profit, indirect holdings
Deferred tax	Basis of provision
Accounting conventions	Use of historic cost, revaluations and current cost
Goodwill	Whether fully eliminated or depreciated

9.3 STOCK VALUATION (SSAP 9)

9.3.1 Purpose of the Standard

The Standard deals with two distinct areas of stock valuation:

(a) Long-term contracts. This is fully dealt with in Chapter 27.
(b) Valuation of trading stocks, work-in-progress and finished production, including short-term contracts. This is dealt with in this chapter.

The purpose is to identify methods of achieving acceptable measures of the cost of stocks held, and to indicate situations where the prudence concept requires the use of a different measure of stock value called 'net realisable value'.

9.3.2 **Definitions**

(a) Cost

Cost is defined in relation to the different categories of stocks and work-in-progress as being that expenditure which has been incurred in the normal course of business in bringing the product or service to its present location and condition. This expenditure should include, in addition to cost of purchase, such costs of conversion as are appropriate to that location and condition.

(b) Cost of purchase

Cost of purchase comprises purchase price including import duties, transport and handling costs and any other directly attributable costs, less trade discounts, rebates and subsidies.

(c) Cost of conversion

Cost of conversion comprises:

   (1) costs which are specifically attributable to units of production, i.e. direct labour, direct expenses and subcontracted work;
   (2) production overheads (as defined);
   (3) other overheads, if any, attributable in the particular circumstances of the business to bringing the product or service to its present location and condition.

(d) Production overheads

Production overheads are overheads incurred in respect of materials, labour or services for production, based on the normal level of activity, taking one year with another. For this purpose each overhead should be classified according to function (e.g. production, selling or administration) so as to ensure the inclusion in cost of conversion of those overheads (including depreciation) which relate to production, notwithstanding that these may accrue wholly or partly on a time basis.

(e) Net realisable value

Net realisable value is the actual or estimated selling price (net of trade, but before settlement discounts) *less*:

   (1) all further costs to completion; and
   (2) all costs to be incurred in marketing, selling and distributing.

9.3.3 **Accounting points**

(a) Stocks and work-in-progress should be valued at the lower of cost and net realisable value. The comparison of cost and net realisable value should be applied to separate items or groups of similar items and then aggregated. It should never be a comparison of total cost and total net realisable value.

The use of cost is a direct application of the matching-up concept. The cost of items purchased or manufactured in the current period, but sold in a future period, is carried forward for matching with the sales revenue when the sale occurs.

The use of the lower net realisable value is an application of the prudence concept, which takes priority over all other concepts when there is a conflict. Where stock value has fallen due to physical deterioration, obsolescence or market changes, or where stock cannot be sold at current selling prices due to errors in production or purchasing, then any loss arising is recognised immediately.

(b) Acceptable alternatives to actual cost

Two methods other than actual costs are considered acceptable. These are:

(i) Selling price less an estimated profit margin. This is used in retail situations where stock records may be maintained at selling prices.

(ii) Standard cost. Where a manufacturing business operates a standard costing system, then the stock valuation will be an automatic by-product of that system.

In both cases it is necessary that the result gives a close approximation to actual cost, and it would be necessary for the management to justify their assumptions periodically.

The use of the latest purchase price per unit applied to all units is not considered an acceptable approximation to actual cost.

(c) Identification of units to be valued

Items (stock or fixed assets) which are indistinguishable one from another are referred to as fungible assets! Where a business buys and sells or uses identical units of stock, then they will need to make an assumption concerning which of the items purchased have been used, and which remain in stock. The commonly used methods are explained below, and an example of the various calculations is given.

Certain methods are not accepted in SSAP 9 since they are considered not to give a close approximation to actual cost or they are not realistic assumptions as to physical movements. However, these methods are found in use by a few businesses, who will be required to quantify the effect of not using an acceptable method.

Method	Accepted by SSAP 9	Not accepted by SSAP 9, but used in practice
Unit cost – Stock units are identifiable (e.g. by a reference number) and each unit is separately valued at actual cost.	YES	–
First-in-first-out (FIFO) – It is assumed that the oldest stock is used first, and that stock in hand represents the latest purchases. This is a sensible assumption of what may have occurred physically.	YES	–
Average cost – The total cost over a period is divided by the number of units purchased in that period. The calculation may be made each time a purchase occurs. This is called a 'moving average'. It assumes that new purchases are mixed with older stock and usage is random.	YES	–
Last-in-first-out (LIFO) – It is assumed that the most recent purchases are the first to be used and that stock in hand represents earlier purchases. In physical terms it assumes that the new stock is added to the top of a pile, and that sales are made from the top of the same pile. Unless there is heavy usage without replacement, the items at the bottom of the pile would never be used. This does seem an unrealistic assumption. However, it is claimed to be a prudent method, since the cost of the most recent purchases are charged in the Trading account, reducing profits available for distribution. The profit retained is then available to meet the higher cost of replacing stock.	NO	YES (particularly in the United States of America)
Base stock – A predetermined volume of stock is treated as the base stock, and valued at a historic cost which may remain constant, or be revalued from time to time. Any		

additional stock would be valued on some other basis. The method is used in continuous processing industries where there is always a volume of stock tied up inside the process. The process cannot function without that volume, although physically it changes as the process continues. The business will always require that volume of stock within the process, and are valuing it as if it were part of the plant itself (although it is disclosed under 'Stocks').	NO	YES (particularly sugar-refining businesses)
Replacement cost – Stock in hand is valued at the notional cost of replacement. It is sometimes called 'next-in-first-out'.	NO	Basis of current cost accounting

Example 1

The following purchases and sales of identical stock units occurred in the month of January. There was no opening stock.

		Units	Per unit £
1 Jan	Purchases	100	10
10 Jan	Sales	(65)	
15 Jan	Purchases	70	12
23 Jan	Sales	(45)	
31 Jan	Stock in hand	60	

Required:
The cost of the 60 units of closing stock on the alternative bases of:

(i) First-in-first out (FIFO)
(ii) Last-in-first-out (LIFO)
(iii) Moving average cost.

(i) and (ii)

		FIFO			LIFO		
		Units	Per unit £	£	Units	Per unit £	£
1 Jan	Purchase	100	10	1,000	100	10	1,000
10 Jan	Cost of sales	(65)	10	(650)	(65)	10	(650)
	Stock	35		350	35		350
15 Jan	Purchase	70	12	840	70	12	840
23 Jan	Cost of sales	(35)	10	(470)	(45)	12	(540)
		(10)	12				
31 Jan	Stock in hand	60		£720	60		£650

Under the FIFO basis the 60 units of stock represent units at £12 each.
Under the LIFO basis the 60 units of stock represent 35 units at £10, and
25 units at £12.

(iii) Moving average cost

		Units	Per unit £	£
1 Jan	Purchase	100	10	1,000
10 Jan	Cost of sales	(65)	10	(650)
		35	–	350
15 Jan	Purchase	70	12	840
	Total	105	11.33*	1,190
23 Jan	Cost of sales	(45)	11.33*	(510)
31 Jan	Stock	£60		£680

* The average calculation takes place each time there is a purchase. The average
cost per unit of £11.33 marked * was found by dividing the total units 105 into the
aggregate cost £1,190.

9.3.4 Disclosure

(a) Accounting policies regarding cost and net realisable value.
(b) The Balance sheet should show stock subdivided into main categories.
These are not defined. It is worth noting that the Companies Acts
require a specific classification into:

(i) raw materials and consumables
(ii) work-in-progress
(iii) finished goods
(iv) payments made to suppliers on account.

9.4 FIXED ASSETS - DEPRECIATION (SSAP 12)

9.4.1 Purpose of the standard

Prior to the issue of this standard in 1977 the charging of depreciation within accounts was normal practice, but there had never been a formal definition of depreciation written down. Views expressed include 'the setting aside of funds towards replacement' to 'the simple allocation of cost to accounting periods'. The Standard includes a definition of depreciation. It also deals with various areas of change which arise in a period affecting depreciation, and the thorny problem of depreciating freehold buildings. It was common practice at that time to view such depreciation as unnecessary, since freehold property prices were increasing. This latter problem was not fully resolved until the issue of SSAP 19 dealing with investment properties. This is dealt with in Section 9.5 below.

9.4.2 Definition

Depreciation is the measure of the wearing out, or consumption of a fixed asset whether arising from use, effluxion of time or obsolescence through technology and market changes.

9.4.3 Accounting points

(a) Depreciation is necessary for all assets with a finite useful life (with the exception of investment properties). In particular, this includes freehold buildings.
(b) Depreciation should be provided by allocating the cost (or revalued amount) less the estimated residual value of fixed assets as fairly as possible to the periods expected to benefit from their use. No indication is given of which method of depreciation should be used in a particular situation. However, the 'as fairly as possible' requirement would be met in the following instances:

Method	Typical example
Straight-line	Leasehold property and freehold buildings, since usage is spread evenly over useful life
Reducing-balance	Motor-vehicles since the value of the asset will fall steeply in the earliest years, and less in the later years when repair costs will be higher
Usage (hourly, mileage)	Assets which are hired out since the charge will match the revenue earned
Extraction	Quarry or mine, since the asset is consumed and revenue earned as material is extracted

(c) Revaluation of an asset during a period. Depreciation should continue to be allocated, and based on the revalued amount, since the asset's life has not changed.

(d) Change in the method of depreciation in order to allocate more fairly the cost or revalued amount. No alteration to past-period provisions should be made. The net book value brought forward from the previous period will be depreciated on the new method beginning in the current period.

(e) Revision in the estimate of useful life. No alteration to past-period provisions should be made, since it is accepted that accounting estimates may require periodic revision. The rate of depreciation is simply increased or decreased in the future, beginning in the current period.

(f) Where the recoverable amount of an asset falls below its net book value, then there should be an immediate write down to recoverable amount. This amount is then depreciated over the remaining life.

9.4.4 Disclosure

(a) Accounting policies regarding methods and rates or useful lives for each major class of depreciable asset;

(b) Total depreciation allocated, gross depreciable amount (cost or revaluation) and accumulated depreciation for each major class of depreciable asset;

(c) Effect of a revaluation in the period on that period's result;

(d) Effect of a change in method of depreciation in the period on that period's results.

9.5 FIXED ASSETS – INVESTMENT PROPERTIES (SSAP 19)

9.5.1 Purpose of the Standard

As indicated in subsection 9.4.1 above, it was common practice prior to 1977 not to depreciate freehold property. While SSAP 12 required depreciation of assets with a finite life, which includes the buildings element of freehold property occupied by a business, this later standard attempted to identify situations where property could justifiably avoid depreciation, and to indicate alternative procedures.

9.5.2 Definition

Investment property is an interest in land and/or buildings:

(a) in respect of which construction work and development have been completed; and
(b) which is held for its investment potential, any rental income being negotiated at arm's length.

The following are exceptions from the definition:

(a) A property which is owned and occupied by a company for its own purposes is not an investment property.
(b) A property let to and occupied by another group company is not an investment property for the purposes of its own accounts or the group accounts.

9.5.3 Accounting points

(a) No depreciation should be allocated.
(b) Investment properties should be stated in the Balance sheet at open market value.
(c) Surpluses and deficits on revaluation should be taken directly to an investment property revaluation reserve without passing through the Profit and loss account.

9.5.4 Disclosure

(a) Investment properties should be separated from other assets.
(b) Investment revaluation reserve should be disclosed, together with movements.
(c) Names or qualifications of the persons making the valuation.

(d) Basis of valuation.
(e) Indicate if the valuer is an employee or officer of the company.

9.6 FIXED ASSETS – GOVERNMENT GRANTS (SSAP 4)

9.6.1 Purpose of the standard

The Standard distinguishes between grants related to assets which are used over a number of periods (capital) and those relating to a single period (revenue). In relation to capital grants it excludes two treatments on the grounds of failure to match-up. These two treatments are immediate credit to Profit and loss account and credit to a non-distributable reserve.

9.6.2 Definitions

(a) Capital-based grants
      Grants which relate to fixed assets.
(b) Revenue-based grants
      Any other grants.

9.6.3 Accounting points

(a) Capital-based grants should be credited to revenue over the expected useful life of the asset. Two techniques are possible:

 (i) Deduct the grant from the assets cost, or
(ii) Credit the grant to a separate deferred Credit account, which is released to the Profit and loss account over the assets life.

Example 2

	Deduct from cost	Deferred credit
	£	£
Asset at gross cost	1,000	1,000
Grant	(150)	(150)
Net cost included in fixed assets	£850	

Depreciation (*say 10%*)	85	100
Grant released to Profit and loss		
account (*also 10%*)	–	(15)
Net effect on profit	£85	£85

The depreciation charge will be disclosed at differing amounts. The grant credited in the Profit and loss account need not be disclosed.

(b) Revenue-based grants should be included in the Profit and loss account in the period when the related expenditure is charged.

9.6.4 Disclosure

(a) The treatment adopted for capital-based grants.
(b) The amount of deferred credit (where that option was selected), which should be separate and never be included in capital or reserves.

9.7 EXTRAORDINARY ITEMS, EXCEPTIONAL ITEMS AND PRIOR-YEAR ADJUSTMENTS (SSAP 6)

9.7.1 Purpose of the Standard

Prior to the issue of this Standard in 1974, companies would frequently write-off large items directly to reserves without disclosure in the Profit and loss account. This treatment could be used to mask embarrassing items of loss. The Standard requires that all items of profit or loss be disclosed in the Profit and loss account, but draws a distinction between those arising from ordinary events and those from extraordinary events.

9.7.2 Definitions

(a) Extraordinary items are those items which derive from activities of the business and which are both material and expected not to recur frequently or regularly. They do not include items which, though exceptional on account of size and incidence (and which may therefore require separate disclosure), derive from the ordinary activities of the business. Neither do they include prior-year items merely because they relate to a prior year.
(b) Prior-year adjustments are those material adjustments applicable to prior years arising from changes in accounting policies and from the correction of fundamental errors. They do not include the normal

recurring corrections and adjustments of accounting estimates made in prior years.

9.7.3 Examples of extraordinary and exceptional items

Extraordinary	Exceptional
(a) Discontinuance of a significant part of a business	(a) Rationalisation costs relating to a continuing part of a business
(b) Sale or permanent diminution in value of an investment, including subsidiaries and associates	(b) Stock provisions
	(c) Long-term contract profits and losses
(c) Expropriation of assets (sequestration, nationalisation)	(d) Bad debts
	(e) Research and development costs
	(f) Adjustments to prior-year tax provisions

In addition there are a large number of 'grey area' items which will need to be tested against the definitions.

9.7.4 Accounting points

A Profit and loss account falls into two separate areas. These are the results from ordinary activities, and from extraordinary activities. In addition, changes to prior-year retained profits are disclosed at the foot of the Profit and loss account.

Structure of a Profit and loss account	
Ordinary activities	Turnover Operating costs (includes exceptional items) Investment income Interest payable Taxation on above items (includes tax on exceptional items)
	= Net profit from ordinary activities
Extraordinary activities	Extraordinary items
	= Net profit after extraordinary items or profit for the financial year
Statement of retained profits	Brought forward as previous reported Prior-year adjustment = Brought forward as restated Retained profit for year = Carried forward

9.7.5 **Disclosure**

(a) Extraordinary items
 (i) Nature of each item
 (ii) Aggregate tax effect.
(b) Exceptional items
 Nature of each item.
(c) Prior-year adjustments
 (i) Nature of each item
 (ii) Tax effect
 (iii) Effect of a change in policy on the results of the period.

9.8 **RESEARCH AND DEVELOPMENT** (SSAP 13)

9.8.1 **Purpose of the Standard**

The Standard sets out definitions of research and development, and identifies conditions when it is acceptable to carry expenditure forward to future periods.

9.8.2 **Definitions**

Research and development expenditure means expenditure falling into one or more of the following broad categories (except to the extent that it relates to locating or exploiting mineral deposits or is reimbursable by third parties either directly or under the terms of a firm contract to develop and manufacture at an agreed price which has been calculated to reimburse both elements of expenditure):

(a) *Pure (or basic) research*: original investigation undertaken in order to gain new scientific or technical knowledge and understanding. Basic research is not primarily directed towards any specific practical aim or application.
(b) *Applied research*: original investigation undertaken in order to gain new scientific or technical knowledge and directed towards a specific practical aim or objective.
(c) *Development*: the use of scientific or technical knowledge in order to produce new or substantially improved materials, devices, products, processes, systems or services prior to the commencement of commercial production.

9.8.3 **Accounting**

(a) The cost of fixed assets, such as laboratories, which are used for research and development activities should be disclosed under fixed assets in the normal way and depreciated over their useful life. The depreciation allocated should be considered a part of the research or development cost.

(b) All research expenditure, whether pure or applied, should be written-off as incurred. This is an application of the prudence concept. It follows from the definition of research that no future revenue is yet certain, and no basis for matching-up therefore exists.

(c) Development expenditure

  (i) Development expenditure should be written-off unless specific conditions (see (d) below) are shown to exist in which case the expenditure may be carried forward as deferred development expenditure.

  (ii) The deferred development expenditure should be amortised on a systematic basis, commencing with the commercial production of the product or process.

  (iii) Once written-off expenditure should never be recapitalised.

  (iv) There should be an annual review of the circumstances under which expenditure was carried forward.

(d) Conditions required for capitalisation of development expenditure

  (i) There is a separate project.

  (ii) Expenditure is separately identifiable.

  (iii) The projects technical feasibility and commercial viability are reasonably certain.

  (iv) It can be shown that estimated future revenues will cover costs to date plus further development, production, selling and administration costs.

  (v) There exist adequate resources to complete the project.

It can be seen that these conditions ensure adequate, certain future revenue in order that the matching-up concept is justified.

9.8.4 **Disclosure**

(a) Accounting policy in respect of expenditure written-off and deferred.

(b) Deferred development expenditure should be disclosed:

(i) Separately (as an intangible fixed asset);

(ii) Balance brought forward, movements in the period and balance carried forward.

9.9 POST-BALANCE-SHEET EVENTS (SSAP 17) AND CONTINGENCIES (SSAP 18)

9.9.1 Purpose of the Standards

These two closely related Standards seek to ensure that accounts give a full picture of the business position by disclosing events and conditions which occurred after the Balance-sheet date or which by their nature would not normally be included within a Balance sheet or Profit and loss account.

9.9.2 Definitions

(a) Post-Balance-sheet events are those events, both favourable and unfavourable, which occur between the Balance-sheet date and the date on which the financial statements are approved by the board of directors.

(b) Adjusting events are post-Balance-sheet events which provide additional evidence of conditions existing at the Balance-sheet date. They include events which because of statutory or conventional requirements are reflected in financial statements.

(c) Non-adjusting events are post-Balance-sheet events which concern conditions which did not exist at the Balance-sheet date.

(d) Contingency is a condition which exists at the Balance-sheet date, where the outcome will be confirmed only on the occurrence or non-occurrence of one or more uncertain future events. A contingent gain or loss is a gain or loss dependent on a contingency.

9.9.3 Accounting points

(a) A post-Balance-sheet event should be adjusted within financial statements if:

(i) it is an adjusting event; or

(ii) it indicates that the going-concern concept does not apply.

An example would be the discovery of errors.

(b) A post-Balance-sheet event should not be adjusted within financial

statements where it is a non-adjusting event. An example would be
a share issue occurring after the Balance-sheet date.
(c) *Contingency*. Figure 9.1 identifies the treatment of various gains and
losses.

fig 9.1 *evaluation of contingencies*

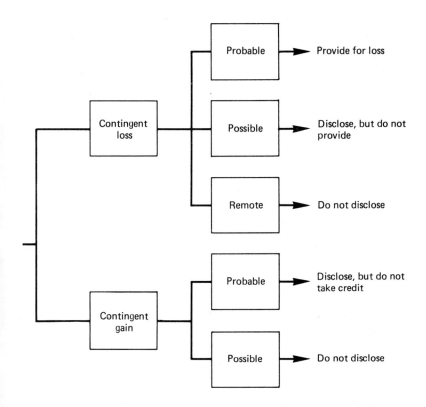

9.9.4 Disclosure

(a) Post-Balance-sheet events
   (i) Nature of the event; and
   (ii) Estimate of the financial effect.
(b) Contingency
   (i) Nature of the contingency;
   (ii) Uncertainties which affect ultimate outcome; and
   (iii) Prudent estimate of the financial effect.

192

9.10 **VALUE ADDED TAX** (SSAP 5)

9.10.1 **Purpose of the standard**

The standard deals with two areas of accounting treatment. It contains
no definitions. It remains the briefest standard issued to date.

9.10.2 **Accounting points**

(a) Turnover should be included in a Profit and loss account net of
VAT.
(b) Where VAT is not recoverable (for example on certain types of fixed
asset) it should be included in the cost of the asset.

TREATMENT OF TAXATION
IN COMPANY ACCOUNTS

10.1 WHAT ARE TAXABLE PROFITS?

10.1.1 The burden of taxation

A private individual resident in the United Kingdom suffers various types of taxation. Among them are income tax, capital gains tax, inheritance tax, value added tax and development land tax. (We could go on!)

A company will normally pay only one type of tax called CORPOR-ATION TAX. This tax may be charged at various rates. Historically, such rates have varied from 30 per cent to 52 per cent. (A company may also suffer development land tax, value added tax and petroleum revenue tax, but these would be under specialised circumstances.)

In addition to the corporation tax which a company suffers it is also engaged in the collection of various other taxes on the Inland Revenue's behalf, e.g. income tax on employees' wages and salaries (Pay-as-you-earn), income tax on interest payments to stockholders, value added tax on sales. In each case the company does not bear the burden of these taxes, but merely collects the tax from the employees or stockholders or customers and pays it to the Inland Revenue, or Customs and Excise.

10.1.2 Taxable profits

The profit which a company shows in its Profit and loss account is not the profit used for assessing the corporation tax liability. We would call this disclosed profit the ACCOUNTS PROFIT. It has been determined by applying the various fundamental concepts. In particular the prudence and matching-up concepts have given rise to charges for depreciation, provisions for bad debts and other items which are deemed to have arisen in the Current account period, although the related cash flow may have occurred in an earlier period (e.g. the purchase of a fixed asset which is now being depreciated) or in a later period (e.g. the payment of interest which has been accrued as interest payable).

In order to find the amount of profit upon which the company will pay corporation tax, called the 'TAXABLE PROFIT', a series of adjustments are made to the accounts profit. The major adjustments involve the replacement of depreciation with a standardised charge called a 'capital allowance' (roughly 25 per cent on the reducing tax balance), and the replacement of items accrued with the equivalent sums received and paid in the period. The subject of computing taxation, and dealing with the practical aspects of collection is a separate and complex area. A financial accounting examination will only expect a knowledge of how to account for corporation tax, and not how to compute that tax.

The following sections deal with those areas of accounting for taxation which are central to the preparation of company accounts, and lay the foundation for the study of published company accounts in Chapter 11.

10.2 CHARGES ON INCOME

Charges on income are those annual payments made by a company which may be deducted from revenue in arriving at taxable profits. Interest payments on debenture and loan stock and royalty payments are both examples of charges on income.

Section 53 of the Income and Corporation Taxes Act 1970 requires that whenever a company makes such a payment, then it deducts basic rate income tax from the payment. The income tax is paid to the Inland Revenue on behalf of the recipient of the payment. We say that the recipient's own income tax has been collected by 'deduction at source'.

The income tax which each company deducts from its charges on income is paid to the Inland Revenue at the end of each quarter. The system is called the *'quarterly accounting system'* and involves Inland Revenue form CT61.

Example 1

A company has in issue £100,000 of 10 per cent loan stock. Basic-rate income tax is 30 per cent.

Required:
Show the journal entry for the payment of a full year's interest on the loan stock.

		£	£
Dr	Profit and loss account (shown as interest payable) (10% × £100,000)	10,000	
Cr	Interest payable account (paid in cash to loan stockholder) (70% × £10,000)		7,000
Cr	Income tax due to Revenue account (paid in cash at end of quarter) (30% × £10,000)		3,000
		£10,000	£10,000

The charge to the Profit and loss account is the gross amount of interest. The full gross amount is allowable for corporation-tax purposes.

10.3 UNFRANKED INVESTMENT INCOME

In Section 10.2 above we saw that every company will deduct basic-rate income tax from charges on income. Where the recipient is a private individual no particular problems arise. However, when the recipient is another company the receipt is called 'unfranked investment income'. It is unfranked because it did not suffer corporation tax in the paying company's hands. Contrast this with a dividend which is shown in the Profit and loss account of the paying company after its corporation-tax charge, and is a franked payment.

Payment	Type
Interest, royalties	Unfranked
Dividends	Franked

A problem now arises. It is that the paying company will have deducted basic-rate INCOME TAX from the payment regardless of whether the recipient is a private individual or a company. A company, however, does not suffer income tax, but only CORPORATION TAX.

The solution is that a receiving company will reclaim the income tax deducted at source from the Inland Revenue. Then, the gross amount of the receipt will be added to taxable profit, and charged to corporation tax.

The recovery of the income tax is also dealt with under the quarterly accounting system. Only the net amount of income tax due to or from the Inland Revenue will eventually be paid or received.

Example 2

A company holds an investment of £120,000 in 9 per cent debenture stock in another company. Basic-rate income tax is 30 per cent.

Required:
Show the journal entry for the receipt of a full year's interest on the investment.

	£	£
Dr Interest receivable account (received in cash *(70% × 9% × £120,000)*	7,560	
Dr Income tax due from Revenue account (offset against tax payable, or failing this reclaimed in cash) *(30% × 9% × £120,000)*	3,240	
Cr Profit and loss account (shown as investment income) *(9% × £120,000)*		10,800
	£10,800	£10,800

The credit to the Profit and loss account is the gross amount of the investment income, and is chargeable to corporation tax. The income tax can be found as 3/7ths of the net amount received:

$$£7,560 \times 3/7 = £3,240.$$

10.4 DIVIDEND PAYMENTS

In Section 10.3 above we stated that a dividend payment is called a 'franked payment', since it is shown in a company's Profit and loss account after corporation tax has been charged.

The corporation tax charged in the Profit and loss account is called the company's basic liability. In the absence of any dividend payments each company will have a specific date on which that basic liability must be paid. In general this will be nine months after the end of the accounting period to which the basic liability relates (although longer periods are possible).

However, if the company chooses to pay a dividend to their shareholders, then the Inland Revenue require an advance payment of corporation tax on account of the basic liability. This payment on account is called 'ADVANCE CORPORATION TAX', and is computed as 3/7ths of the dividend paid (3/7ths assumes a 30 per cent basic tax rate. The fraction would be 31/69ths if the basic tax rate were 31 per cent).

The advance corporation tax is paid to the Inland Revenue at the end of each quarter under the quarterly accounting system. The remainder of the basic corporation tax liability is called the 'MAINSTREAM LIABILITY' and would be paid on the normal due date nine (or more) months after the end of the accounting period.

One important point to note is that the advance corporation tax is treated as a payment on account of the basic liability of the period in which the related dividend is paid. It is not necessarily the period in which the advance corporation tax is paid, nor is it necessarily the period in which the dividend is charged in the Profit and loss account. A proposed dividend is paid in the next accounting period and it would be that period in which advance corporation tax on the dividend would be offset.

Example 3

A company has 80,000 25 p ordinary shares in issue. A dividend of 2 p per share is paid. The basic tax rate is 30 per cent.

Required:
Show the journal entry for the payment of the dividend and related advance corporation tax.

	£	£
Dr Profit and loss account – dividend paid (80,000 × £0.02)	1,600	
Cr Cash and Bank account – payment to shareholders		1,600
Dr Corporation tax account – advance payment on account of basic liability (3/7 × £1,600)	686	
Cr Advance corporation tax payable account (paid to Inland Revenue at end of quarter)		686
	£2,286	£2,286

The dividend payment is already a net dividend. The receiving shareholder is deemed to have suffered basic-rate tax on the dividend receipt. This imputed tax credit is equal to the advance corporation tax paid by the company.

10.5 DIVIDEND RECEIPTS

When a company holds an investment of shares in another company and a dividend is paid, then we call the dividend a 'franked payment' in the paying company's books, and a 'franked receipt' in the receiving company's books.

The paying company will have paid advance corporation tax to the Inland Revenue equal to 3/7ths of the dividend. We stated in Section 10.4 that a private individual shareholder is deemed to have suffered basic-rate tax on the receipt. When the shareholder is another company, several points arise:

(a) The dividend receipt, since it is a franked receipt in that it has suffered corporation tax in the paying company's hands, is excluded from taxable profits in the receiving company. It is, however, still included in the investment income and hence the accounts profit.
(b) There is a tax credit attaching to the dividend receipt equal to 3/7ths of the dividend (assuming a 30 per cent basic tax rate).
(c) The tax credit affects the timing of the receiving company's own tax payments in that advance corporation tax on the company's dividend payments are reduced by the tax credit, but the mainstream liability is increased by the same amount. The basic tax liability (mainstream liability plus advance corporation tax together) does not change.
(d) The dividend received is presented in the Profit and loss account together with the tax credit. This 'grossed-up' dividend receipt is called FRANKED INVESTMENT INCOME. The tax credit is then added to the tax charge in the Profit and loss account and described as 'tax suffered on franked investment income'.

It can be seen that the debit and credit for the tax credit are both within the Profit and loss account. The reason for grossing up the investment income is to enable a comparison between dividend income and other forms of gross investment income to be made. The tax charge in the Profit and loss account will now consist of two elements. These are the basic tax liability plus the tax suffered on franked investment income.

Example 4

A company holds an investment of 35,000 50 p ordinary shares in another company. A dividend of 5 p per share is received. The basic tax rate is 30 per cent.

Required:
Show the journal entry to record the dividend receipt and related tax credit presentation.

	£	£
Dr Cash and bank account (dividend received) $(35,000 \times £0.05)$	1,750	
Cr Profit and loss account – investment income $(£1,750 \times \frac{10}{7})$		2,500
Dr Profit and loss account – tax charge $(£1,750 \times \frac{3}{7})$	750	
	£2,500	£2,500

Example 5 – Comprehensive example

The following items are contained in the Trial balance of Millstone Ltd:

	Dr	Cr
Sales		250,000
Operating costs	145,000	
Interest paid:		
Net payment to stockholder	7,000	
Income tax paid to Inland Revenue	3,000	
Interest received:		
Net receipt		700
Income tax reclaimed from Inland Revenue		300
Dividend received from UK company (*net receipt only*)		2,100
Dividend paid to shareholders	25,000	
Advance corporation tax paid	9,814	

The following information is relevant:

(1) Basic rate tax rate is 30 per cent.
(2) The company estimates its basic corporation tax liability at £40,000.

Required:
Prepare the Profit and loss account of Millstone Ltd in as much detail as the information permits, and identify the mainstream liability.

MILLSTONE LTD

Profit and loss account	£
Turnover	250,000
Operating costs	(145,000)
Operating profit	105,000
Investment income (W1)	4,000
Interest payable (W2)	(10,000)
Profit on ordinary activities before taxation	99,000
Tax on profit on ordinary activities (W3)	(40,000)
Profit on ordinary activities after taxation	58,100
Dividends paid	(25,000)
Retained profit for the year	£33,100

Corporation tax account

	£		£
Cash a/c – advance corporation tax paid	9,814	Profit and loss a/c – basic tax liability	
Balance c/f – mainstream liability	30,186	(W3)	40,000
	£40,000		£40,000

WORKINGS

(1) Investment income

Interest received – gross (£700 + 300)	1,000
Dividend received – grossed up (£2,100 × 10/7)	3,000
	£4,000

(2) Interest payable

	£
Interest paid – gross (£7,000 + 3,000)	10,000

(3) Tax on profits on ordinary activities

	£
Basic liability – estimate based on taxable profits	40,000
Tax suffered on franked investment income (£2,100 × 3/7)	900
	£40,900

Exercises to Chapter 10

1. For a basic tax rate of 30 per cent you are required to prepare journal entries for the following transactions:

   (a) payment of a half year's interest on £10,000 6 per cent loan stock;
   (b) receipt of a half year's interest on an investment of £8,000 nominal 5 per cent debenture stock;
   (c) payment of a dividend of £5,000 and payment of related advance corporation tax;
   (d) receipt of a net dividend of £4,200.

2. A company has a brought-forward mainstream liability of £10,000, which was an estimate. This was paid in the year at £10,500, together with advance corporation tax of £6,500 on dividends paid. The basic liability for the current year is estimated at £13,300. You are required to compute the Profit and loss account tax charge and the mainstream tax liability which is carried forward.

CHAPTER 11

PREPARATION OF

PUBLISHED ACCOUNTS

11.1 OBJECTIVE OF PUBLISHED ACCOUNTS

In Chapter 9 we summarised two purposes of financial statements. One purpose was to prepare accounts that will be distributed to shareholders, and a copy placed on public file at Companies House.

The form and minimum content of these 'published' accounts is laid down in the Companies Act 1985. Since these accounts are open to inspection by the general public, who will include competitors, minimum disclosure is generally followed very closely. There is no rule preventing a company from giving more than the minimum, but it will seldom be given without some good reason.

It will be some months after the Balance-sheet date that the accounts will finally be ready, and the directors will arrange the company's annual general meeting (AGM) at which the accounts are considered and finally approved.

11.1.1 The objective summarised

The objective of the published accounts is summarised in the Companies Act 1985. It is that the accounts show a 'true and fair view' of the profit or loss for the year and of the position at the Balance-sheet date. This requirement overrides all other factors. In a case of conflict between two methods of accounting or disclosure, then it is the one that best serves the true and fair view which is followed, even where to do so conflicts with some other rule of law. (In such a case the effect of departing from that other law or accounting rule would be disclosed.)

11.1.2 Contents of published accounts

The contents of the published annual report is as follows:

(a) The accounts:

   (i) Outline balance sheet – shows main headings only
   (ii) Outline Profit and loss account – shows main headings only
   (iii) Funds statement – dealt with in Chapter 29
   (iv) Notes to the accounts – the detailed information behind the Balance sheet and Profit and loss account.

(b) Auditors' report – a report by a qualified accountant, elected at the AGM, giving an opinion as to the truth and fairness of the accounts.

(c) Directors' report – a report by the directors containing certain information which is not in the accounts.

In addition there may be a chairman's statement, photographs, explanations and historical summaries. These are not essential and are not legally regulated.

It can be seen that the normal procedure within these accounts is to show headings only on the face of the Balance sheet and Profit and loss account. All of the detailed points are shown in notes to the accounts which are cross-referenced to the 'face' of the accounts.

11.1.3 The Companies Act formats

The Companies Act 1985 contains certain standard Balance sheet and Profit and loss account formats. Eventually all EEC countries will have similar legislation.

There are two possible Balance-sheet formats. Format 1, a vertical layout, is most widely used, and is strongly recommended for exam purposes. Format 2 is a horizontal layout.

There are four possible Profit and loss account formats. Formats 1 and 2 are vertical, formats 3 and 4 are their horizontal counterparts. Format 1 is recommended for exam purposes. Format 2 gives an alternative presentation of Profit and loss account items; there may be instances when information is given in a form which will suggest use of format 2.

The balance of this chapter adopts format 1 for both Balance sheet and Profit and loss account. Alternative Profit and loss account presentation under format 2 is included for comparison.

11.2 Exam technique

Published accounts questions within an exam give rise to time-pressure problems. It is necessary to establish a technique that ensures a methodical approach which picks up the maximum marks as quickly as possible.

The technique demonstrated below incorporates the working points which were dealt with in Chapter 9 on accounting standards, and Chapter 10, which dealt with taxation. These points often arise as smaller points within a larger question.

The summarised technique is:

Step 1	Prepare face of Profit and loss a/c, using workings where necessary
Step 2	Go back and prepare the detailed disclosure notes to the Profit and loss a/c
Step 3	Prepare detailed disclosure notes to the Balance sheet
Step 4	Summarise the information from Step 3 on to the face of the Balance sheet.

The Profit and loss account can always be prepared independently of the detailed notes, hence step 1. However, the Balance sheet cannot be prepared before the information is summarised in the Balance-sheet notes, hence step 4.

Several workings, dealing with taxation and other calculations, are normally required for the Profit and loss account at step 1, and the referencing system *W1, W2, W3*, etc., should be followed to keep the result neat.

Once the Profit and loss account is complete, the Balance sheet does not normally need any additional workings.

One final tip. Always keep a strict record of entries you have made as adjustments. For example, if you are entering a debit to a Profit and loss account working for depreciation, then make a note of the credit entry against the Accumulated depreciation account. This can be done on the question paper.

11.3 WORKED EXAMPLE

The simplest method of describing the detailed content of published accounts is to take an example, and explain each entry.

The following example shows the accounts, and alongside a summary of the relevant legal requirements.

The resulting presentation is not intended to be an exhaustive checklist of all minor points of legislation, but does cover the generality of examination points.

MODEL PLC

Profit and loss account for the year to 31 December

Reference to notes		19X5 £	19X4 £
2	Turnover	592,163	486,970
	Cost of sales	(435,026)	(349,169)
	Gross profit	157,137	137,801
	Distribution costs	(10,296)	(9,353)
	Administration expenses	(54,678)	(52,946)
3	Other operating charges	(6,512)	–
	Other operating income	5,450	5,225
4	Operating profit	91,101	80,727
5	Income from fixed-asset investments	2,400	2,025
6	Interest payable	(1,750)	(1,750)
	Profit on ordinary activities before taxation	91,751	81,002
7	Tax on profit on ordinary activities	(24,930)	(30,072)
	Profit on ordinary activities after taxation	66,821	50,930
8	Extraordinary items	(10,943)	–
	Profit for the financial year	55,878	50,930
	Dividends – proposed ordinary	(17,500)	(15,400)
	Retained profit for the year	£38,378	£35,530

Comments

This Profit and loss account follows format 1. Comparative figures should be given. Only realised profit should be included in a Profit and loss account.

The items shown in the Profit and loss account may be combined with other items if they are not material, or expanded into more categories.

Note that all revenues are shown positive, and all expenses and appropriations are bracketed. This is not required by law, but helps to minimise the chance of arithmetic mistakes.

206

Statement of retained profits

Reference to notes		19X5 £	19X4 £
At 1 January – as previously reported		138,490	103,920
Prior-year adjustment	9	3,450	2,490
At 1 January – as restated		141,940	106,410
Retained profit for the year		38,378	35,530
At 31 December		£180,318	£141,940

Alternative presentation of 19X5 under format 2:

	£
Turnover	592,163
Increase in stocks of finished goods and in work in progress	1,605
Other operating income	5,450
	599,218
Raw materials and consumables	(134,196)
Other external charges	(69,758)
Staff costs	(254,943)
Depreciation	(42,708)
Other operating charges	(6,512)
Operating profit	91,101

(The remainder of the Profit and loss account is as for format 1.)

MODEL PLC

Balance sheets at 31 December

Reference to notes		19X5 £	19X4 £
	Fixed assets		
10	Intangible assets	20,000	18,000
11	Tangible assets	353,711	275,251
12	Investments	24,000	20,250
		397,711	313,501
	Current assets		
13	Stocks	49,250	46,495
14	Debtors	71,940	62,435
	Investments	30,950	24,420
	Cash at bank and in hand	15,460	10,965
		167,600	144,315
15	Creditors: amounts falling due within one year	(82,930)	(69,426)
	Net current assets	84,670	74,889
	Total assets *less* current liabilities	482,381	388,390
16	Creditors: amounts falling due after more than one year	(15,000)	(15,000)
17	Provisions for liabilities and charges	(10,943)	–
18	Accruals and deferred income	(4,620)	(4,950)
		£451,818	£368,440

Comments

This Balance sheet follows format 1.
Comparative figures must be given.

The items shown in this Balance sheet
constitute the minimum Balance-sheet headings
and must appear unless the amount is nil.

The detail given in the notes to the accounts
may be combined with other items if they are
not material, or expanded into more categories.

Note that all assets are positive and all
liabilities negative. This is not required by
law, but helps to minimise the chance of
arithmetic mistakes.

Reference to notes		19X5 £	19X4 £	Comments
	Capital and reserves			
19	Called-up share capital	200,000	180,000	
20	Share premium a/c	52,000	42,000	
21	Revaluation reserve	15,000	–	
	Other reserves	4,500	4,500	
	Profit and loss a/c	180,318	141,940	
		£451,818	£368,440	

On behalf of the board   I. SCRIBBLER
 A. NOTHER

The Balance sheet must be signed on behalf of the board by two directors.

NOTES TO ACCOUNTS

1 Accounting policies

(a) Accounting convention
The accounts are prepared under the historic cost convention, modified to include the revaluation of certain properties.

(b) Depreciation
Depreciation is provided on the straight-line basis at the following rates:

	%
Land	0
Buildings	1
Plant and machinery	10
Vehicles	25
Goodwill	2½

Comments

Disclose methods of depreciation and rates or useful lives (SSAP 12)

(c) Stocks
Stocks are valued at the lower cost and net realisable value. Cost of raw materials is determined on a first-in-first-out basis.

Lower of cost and net realisable value is required by SSAP 9.

(d) Government grants
Government grants on capital expenditure are transferred to a Deferred credit a/c and released to the Profit and loss a/c over the life of the asset.

One of two acceptable methods under SSAP 4.

					Comments
2 Segment information					Disclose turnover relevant to each geographical market and each class of business.
	Turnover		Operating profit		
	19X5	19X4	19X5	19X4	Disclose profit before tax for each class of business (operating profit will be more straightforward)
	£	£	£	£	
Manufacture of brass nuts	369,420	298,410	40,215	43,925	
Retailing of books	222,743	188,560	50,886	36,802	
	£592,163	£486,970	£91,101	£80,727	

All sales were within the United Kingdom

	19X5	19X4	
3 Other operating charges			
Exceptional item – provision for obsolete stock	£6,512	£ –	Disclosure of exceptional items required by SSAP 6.

4 Operating profit

	19X5	19X4	Comments
This is stated after charging:	£	£	Disclose auditors' fees and expenses, but exclude
Auditors' remuneration	10,000	8,500	charges for accounts or taxation work.
Staff costs:			Staff costs under these three headings.
Wages and salaries	194,500	175,390	Staff includes all employees with a contract of
Social security costs	19,250	17,465	service, including directors.
Pension costs	41,193	44,075	
	£254,943	£236,930	
Average number of employees:	No.	No.	Disclose the number of employees earning over
Manufacturing	16	15	£30,000 in bands of £5,000.
Retailing	13	12	
Directors' remuneration:	£	£	Directors (a): Fees; Other remuneration (salaries,
Fees	10,000	8,000	benefits in kind, pension contributions);
other (including pension contributions)	89,340	78,250	Pensions paid; and Compensation for loss of
	£99,340	£86,250	office are always disclosed (unless nil).
Excluding pension contributions:			Directors (b): If fees + other exceeds £60,000
Chairman	27,500	26,200	or the company is a member of a group, then
Highest paid director	31,950	29,260	deduct pension contributions and disclose
Other directors in the band			chairman, highest-paid, other directors in
£15,001 to £20,000	2	2	bands of £5,000 and waived emoluments.
£5,001 to £10,000	1	1	

	19X5	19X4	Comments
	£	£	*Comments*
5 Income from fixed asset investments			
Listed investments	1,050	925	Disclose income from listed investments
6 Interest payable	19X5	19X4	Disclose interest on loans:
	£	£	
Loan not wholly repayable within 5 years	1,750	1,750	(a) wholly repayable within 5 years and bank loans
			(b) not wholly repayable within 5 years
			and split further by those repayable by instalments.
7 Tax on profits on ordinary activities	19X5	19X4	Indicate basis of charging taxation. Disclose
	£	£	overseas tax and any irrecoverable advance corpor-
UK Corporation tax based on profits (at 35%)	(24,930)	(30,072)	ation tax written off.
8 Extraordinary items	19X5	19X4	Disclose the nature of each item of extraordinary
Extraordinary charge – provision for			income and charges, the net extraordinary profit
redundancy costs on closure of factory	£10,943		or loss, and the tax thereon.
9 Prior-year adjustment			Disclosure of nature and effect required by
Stock valuation. In earlier periods stock has been valued at prime			SSAP 6.

Stock valuation. In earlier periods stock has been valued at prime cost. During the period the basis was changed to include a proportion of overheads as required by SSAP 9. The effect on prior-year profits is disclosed at the foot of the Profit and loss a/c. There is no tax effect.

10 Intangible fixed assets

	Goodwill £	Comments
Cost: At 1 January 19X5	76,000	Disclose cost, accumulated depreciation, net book value and movements.
Increase during year	4,000	
At 31 December 19X5	80,000	
Accumulated depreciation: At 1 January 19X5	(58,000)	Disclose period of write-off of goodwill and reason for that period.
Provided in year	(2,000)	
At 31 December 19X5	(60,000)	
Net book value: At 1 January 19X5	£18,000	
At 31 December 19X5	£20,000	

Depreciation is provided over 40 years, which is the estimated life of the goodwill.

11 Tangible fixed assets

	Freehold Land £	Buildings £	Plant and machinery £	Vehicles £	Total £
Cost or valuation:					
At 1 January 19X5	90,000	57,000	206,332	30,032	383,364
Additions	–	–	93,668	10,500	104,168
Revaluation	10,000	3,000	–	–	13,000
At 31 December 19X5	£100,000	£60,000	£300,000	£40,532	£500,532
Accumulated depreciation:					
At 1 January 19X5	–	(1,450)	(90,814)	(15,849)	(108,113)
Provided in year	–	(550)	(30,000)	(10,158)	(40,708)
Revaluation	–	2,000	–	–	2,000
At 31 December 19X5	–	–	£(120,814)	£(26,007)	£(146,821)
Net book value:					
At 1 January 19X5	90,000	55,550	115,518	14,183	275,251
At 31 December 19X5	£100,000	£60,000	£179,186	£14,525	£353,711

Property was valued on 31 December 19X5 by Messrs Valuers & Co., on an open market basis.

The historic cost of freehold property at 31 December 19X5 is land £90,000, buildings £57,000, and accumulated depreciation on buildings would be £2,000.

Comments

Disclose cost or valuation, accumulated depreciation, net book value and movements.

Classes for division:
Land and buildings
  – freehold
  – leases with over 50 years to run
  – other leases
Plant and machinery
Fixtures, fittings, tools and equipment
Payments on account
Separate depreciable part of land and buildings.

In the year of revaluation disclose:
Name or qualification of valuer
Basis of valuation
Historic cost equivalent information.

12 Investments

	19X5 £	19X4 £	Comments
Listed investments at cost	21,000	16,500	Disclose market value of listed investments where this is not their stated value.
Other investments	3,000	3,750	
	£24,000	£20,250	

Listed investments have a market value of £27,500 (*19X4 £19,300*)

13 Stocks

	19X5 £	19X4 £	Comments
Raw materials	10,250	9,100	Disclose stock under these three headings plus payments on account (if any). Disclose replacement cost if materially different.
Work-in-progress	13,900	12,425	
Finished goods	25,100	24,970	
	£49,250	£46,495	

Replacement cost of stock is not materially different.

14 Debtors

	19X5 £	19X4 £	Comments
Trade debtors	58,920	51,580	In addition, disclose any amounts which are not receivable within one year of the Balance-sheet date (although they are still included within current assets).
Advance corporation tax (*not receivable within one year*)	7,500	6,600	
Prepayments	5,520	4,255	
	£71,940	£62,435	

		19X5	19X4	Comments
15	Creditors: amounts falling due within one year	£	£	
	Trade creditors	22,680	9,096	
	Corporation tax	25,830	30,772	
	Other taxes and Social Security	11,490	9,465	
	Proposed dividend	17,500	15,400	
	Accruals	5,430	4,693	
		£82,930	£69,426	
16	Creditors: amounts falling due after more than one year	19X5	19X4	
		£	£	
	10% debenture stock 19X0/Y3	15,000	15,000	
17	Provisions for liabilities and charges		£	Disclose movements on provisions.
	At 1 January 19X5		–	
	Provision for redundancy costs on closure of factory		10,943	
	At 31 December 19X5		£10,943	
18	Accruals and deferred income	19X5	19X4	
		£	£	
	Deferred government grants	4,620	4,950	

	19X5	19X4	Comments
	£	£	
19 Called-up share capital			Disclose number, aggregate nominal value of authorised and allotted shares of each class. Give details of redeemable shares. For shares allotted in the year, give number, class nominal value, consideration and reason for issue.
Ordinary shares of £1			
Authorised	500,000	500,000	
Allotted, and fully paid	200,000	180,000	

20,000 shares were issued in the year at £1.50 each to provide funds for the purchase of new specialised manufacturing plant.

	£		Comments
20 Share premium account			Disclose movement on all reserves.
At 1 January 19X5	42,000		
Premium on issue of shares	10,000		
At 31 December 19X5	£52,000		

	£
21 Revaluation reserve	
At 1 January 19X5	–
Revaluation of freehold land and buildings	15,000
At 31 December 19X5	£15,000

22 Post-Balance-sheet events

After the year-end one factory was closed. Full provision for costs had been met within the accounts.

Comments: Disclose all post-Balance-sheet events as defined by SSAP 17, including nature and financial effect of non-adjusting events.

218

23 Capital commitments	19X5 £	19X4 £	Disclose capital commitments.
Contracted but not provided	10,000	8,000	
Authorised but not contracted	15,000	12,000	
24 Contingencies	19X5 £	19X4 £	Disclose contingencies as defined by SSAP 18.
Bills of exchange discounted	5,520	4,930	

11.4 DIRECTORS' REPORTS

In addition to the financial statements the Companies Act requires the directors to prepare a directors' report containing specific information.

For ease of learning, the information is described below in the form of a MNEMONIC – 'A RED CARP'.

A – Activities, development over year, and future development.
R – Results. Proposed dividend and transfers to reserves. Charitable and political donations if aggregate exceeds £200. Name of political party if individual donations over £200.
E – Employment of disabled; policy if employees over 250.
D – Directors' names and interests in shares and loan capital at the beginning and end of the year.
C – Capital – details of transactions in the company's own shares.
A – Assets – market value of land and buildings if materially different from Balance-sheet amounts.
R – Research and development activities.
P – Post-Balance-sheet events.

Reference is normally given to the reappointment of auditors, and close company status.

11.5 SMALL AND MEDIUM COMPANIES

All companies are required to prepare full accounts for shareholders. Two classes of company, small and medium, are permitted to file modified accounts at Companies House.

11.5.1 Limits of small and medium

Company must satisfy 2 out of 3 of the following criteria for the current and previous period:	Small	Medium
Turnover not exceeding (note 1)	£1.4 m.	£5.75 m.
Fixed + current assets not exceeding	£0.7 m.	£2. 8m.
Average number of employees not exceeding (note 2)	50	250

Notes

1 Turnover limits are for a 52-week period and are scaled up or down for other periods
2 Employees cover all with a contract of employment.

11.5.2 Content of modified accounts

Item	Small	Medium
Profit and loss a/c	None	Turnover, cost of sales omitted
Balance sheet	Headings only (see face of Balance sheet in Section 11.3)	All
Directors' Report	None	All
Notes to accounts	Limited: (i) Accounting policies (ii) Share capital (iii) Loans with over 5 years before payment.	All, except for turnover

It can be seen that a small company has significant advantages. A medium company has few advantages.

Exercises to Chapter 11

1. A company has six directors, who received the following payments in a period:

	Fees £	Salary £	Pension contributions £
A (Chairman)	5,000	90,000	25,000
B (Managing)	5,000	95,000	30,000
C	5,000	41,000	12,000
D	5,000	10,000	3,000
E	5,000	6,000	1,000
F	5,000	–	–

In addition G, who retired in the previous period, was paid a pension by the company of £14,000.

You are required to draft the directors' emoluments note for inclusion in the notes to the company's accounts.

2. A company made the following payments in relation to its employees:

	£
Net pay to employees	325,600
Income tax deducted and paid to Inland Revenue	68,500
National Insurance contributions:	
– Employee's	16,300
– Employer's	32,600
Pension contributions paid to pension scheme:	
– Employee's	14,200
– Employer's	32,900

You are required to draft the staff-costs note for inclusion in the notes to the company's accounts.

CAPITAL TRANSACTIONS

12.1 ISSUE AND FORFEITURE OF SHARES

In Chapter 8 we considered the concept of nominal value of share capital, the way in which a share premium arises and the various methods by which a company may issue shares.

The purpose of this chapter is to consider the mechanics of and accounting entries relating to an issue of shares.

12.1.1 Legal and practical considerations

(a) Shares may never be issued at a discount.
(b) Payment for shares will normally be in two or more instalments.

These are:

Stage	Instalment
Application	A prospective shareholder will be required to pay the whole share premium and part of the nominal share capital at the stage of application for the shares. This does not guarantee that shares will be allocated on all applications. Excess moneys received on application will be returned.
Allotment	A further proportion (or the balance) of the nominal value may be required at the stage the shares are allocated to shareholders.
Call	The company may not require the full nominal value immediately. When that final element of the nominal value is required a call is made and the shares will finally become fully paid shares.

(c) If a shareholder fails to pay instalments of nominal value by a stipulated date or fails to meet a call, then the company will take steps to secure the shares. These forfeited shares are then available for reissue at a price such that the total received from original shareholder and new shareholder cover at least nominal value.

The original shareholder will not receive any repayment of money paid to the company.

12.1.2 Accounts required

Account	Purpose
Application and allotment a/c	Records cash received, shares issued, premium on shares issued and cash repaid
Forfeited shares a/c	To identify the total received on forfeited shares, and the capital and premium arising on reissue
Call a/c	Similar to the application and allotment account, but used for a call which will occur after the application and allotment is completed.

12.1.3 Double entry

Event	Debit	Credit
Company offers shares to public	–	–
Applications received together with application money	Cash a/c	Application and allotment a/c
Shares allotted to successful applicants	Application and allotment a/c	Share capital a/c (nominal) and Share premium a/c (premium)
Application money returned to unsuccessful applicants	Application and allotment a/c	Cash a/c
Balance of nominal capital is received	Cash a/c	Application and allotment a/c
Certain shares forfeited: (i) Capital and premium thereon allotted	Share capital (nominal) a/c and share premium account (premium)	Forfeited share a/c

(ii) Money due but unpaid	Forfeited share a/c	Application and allotment a/c
(iii) Shares reissued	Forfeited shares a/c	Share capital a/c
(iv) Money received	Cash a/c	Forfeited shares a/c
(v) Balance represents share premium	Forfeited shares a/c	Share premium a/c

Example 1

Expanding Plc, an expanding public company, issues 100,000 £1 ordinary shares to the public, at a price of £1.20 per share. The terms are:

    45 p   (including the premium) payable on application
    50 p   payable on allotment
    25 p   payable on call.

The following events occurred:

  1 Jan   Applications for 120,000 shares received
14 Jan   Allotments for 100,000 shares made
15 Jan   Excess money returned
  1 Feb   Allotment money on 99.000 shares received
16 Feb   1,000 shares forfeited
18 Feb   Forfeited shares reissued at 80 p each, including the allotment instalment but not the call instalment.
10 Aug Call made
31 Aug Call money received in full.

Required:
Record the above transactions in the books of Expanding Plc (Bank and Cash accounts are not required).

Application and allotment account

Date		£	Date		£
14 Jan	Share capital a/c *(100,000 × £0.75)*	75,000	1 Jan	Cash and Bank a/c – applications received *(120,000 × £0.45)*	54,000
	Share premium a/c *(100,000 × £0.20)*	20,000	1 Feb	Cash and Bank a/c	

15 Jan	Cash and Bank a/c – returned applications (20,000 × £0.45)	9,000			allotment money received (99,000 × £0.50)	49,500
				16 Feb	Forfeited shares a/c – (1,000 × £0.50)	500
		£104,000				£104,000

Ordinary share capital account

Date		£	Date		£
16 Feb	Forfeited shares a/c (1,000 × £0.75)	750	14 Jan	Application and allotment a/c (£100,000 × £0.75)	75,000
18 Feb	Balance c/d	75,000	18 Feb	Forfeited shares a/c – reissue (1,000 × £0.75)	750
		£75,750			£75,750
			18 Feb	Balance b/d	75,000
10 Aug	Balance c/d	100,000	10 Aug	Call a/c (100,000 × £0.25)	25,000
		£100,000			£100,000

Share premium account

Date		£	Date		£
16 Feb	Forfeited share a/c (1,000 × £0.20)	200	14 Jan	Application and allotment a/c – (100,000 × £0.20)	20,000
18 Feb	Balance c/d	20,300	18 Feb	Forfeited share a/c – total forfeited plus reissue premium	500
		£20,500			£20,500
			18 Feb	Balance b/d	20,300

Forfeited share account

Date		£	Date		£
16 Feb	Application and allotment a/c – (sums unpaid)	500	16 Feb	Share capital a/c	750
				Share premium a/c	200

16 Feb	Balance c/d – total						
	received and forfeited	450					
		£950					£950
18 Feb	Share capital a/c			16 Feb	Balance b/d		450
	(*1,000 × £0.75*)	750		18 Feb	Cash and Bank a/c		
18 Feb	Share premium a/c –				(*1,000 × £0.80*)		800
	(*balance*)	500					
		£1,250					£1,250

Call account

Date		£		Date		£
10 Aug	Share capital a/c –			31 Aug	Cash and Bank a/c	25,000
	(*100,000 × £0.25*)	25,000				
		£25,000				£25,000

12.2 REDEMPTION AND PURCHASE OF SHARES IN A PUBLIC COMPANY

12.2.1 Legal provisions

(a) A company may issue redeemable ordinary or preference shares, provided it also has irredeemable shares.
(b) Redeemable shares may be redeemed provided they are fully paid.
(c) A company may also purchase any of its own shares provided they are immediately cancelled.
(d) A company may issue new shares (a fresh issue) in order to provide the funds to pay for a redemption or purchase. These new shares may be of a different class to those redeemed or purchased.
(e) The premium payable on redemption or purchase of shares may be written off to Share premium account subject to the following three limits. The lower of the three figures will determine the maximum amount which may be written off:

  (i) The balance on the Share premium account, including the premium on any fresh issue;
  (ii) The share premium originally received on the issue of the shares which are now being redeemed or purchased; and
  (iii) The cash proceeds received from any fresh issue.

  Any premium not written off to Share premium account must be written off to the Profit and loss account.

(f) A transfer from Profit and loss account to a capital redemption reserve is required. The amount of the transfer is equal to the nominal value of shares redeemed or purchased less the cash proceeds of any fresh issue. The purpose of this transfer is to maintain the level of capital and non-distributable reserves. For this reason we say the redemption or purchase is made from profits rather than from capital.

12.2.2 Double entry and technique

Event	Debit	Credit
Fresh issue of shares	Cash and Bank a/c – proceeds	Share capital a/c – nominal. Share premium a/c – premium
Redemption or purchase at a discount	Share capital a/c – nominal	Cash and Bank a/c – cost. Profit and loss a/c – discount
Redemption or purchase at a premium: (i) Compute amount written-off share premium a/c (see (c) above) (ii) Entry	Share capital a/c – nominal Share premium a/c – per working. Profit and loss a/c – balance	Cash and Bank a/c – cost
Transfer to capital redemption reserve to maintain capital: (i) Compute transfer (see (f) above) (ii) Entry	Profit and loss a/c	Capital redemption reserve

Example 2

Public Plc have 100,000 £1 ordinary shares in issue. These were originally issued some years ago at a premium of 20 p per share. The balance on the Share premium account now stands at £15,000 (the remainder having been used to write off preliminary expenses).

The company are to purchase 20,000 shares for cancellation at a price of £1.80 each. This is financed in part by the issue of 10,000 £1 preference shares at £1.70 each.

Required:
Show the journal entries necessary to record the above transactions,
together with workings.

WORKINGS	£

(1) Fresh issue

	£
Preference share capital	10,000
Share premium $(10,000 \times £0.70)$	7,000
Proceeds	£17,000

(2) Purchase

	£
Ordinary share capital	20,000
Premium payable $(20,000 \times £0.80)$	16,000
Cost	£36,000

(3) Premium payable which may be written off to Share premium
account:

(i) Balance on that account $(£15,000 + 7,000\ (WI))$	£22,000
(ii) Original issue premium $(20,000 \times £0.20)$	£4,000
(iii) Proceeds of fresh issue $(W1)$	£17,000
Lower:	£14,000

(4) Transfer to capital redemption reserve

	£
Nominal capital purchased	20,000
Proceeds of fresh issue $(W1)$	(17,000)
	£3,000

Journal entries:	£	£
Cr Cash and Bank account $(W1)$	17,000	–
Cr Preference share capital account	–	10,000
Cr Share premium account	–	7,000
	£17,000	£17,000

Being fresh issue of shares.

	£	£
Dr Ordinary share capital	20,000	–
Dr Share premium account $(W3)$	4,000	–
Dr Profit and loss account (*balance*)	12,000	–
Cr Cash and bank account $(W2)$	–	36,000
	£36,000	£36,000

Being purchase of shares.

Dr Profit and loss account (*W4*)	3,000	–
Cr Capital redemption reserve	–	3,000
Being maintenance of capital.		

12.3 REDEMPTION AND PURCHASE OF SHARES IN A PRIVATE COMPANY

12.3.1 Legal provisions

(a) The points covered in Section 12.2.1 (a) to (e) also apply to a private company. Item (f) does not apply.
(b) A private company may reduce the level of capital and non-distributable reserves, but only after distributable reserves have been fully utilised. We say, therefore, that a private company may make a redemption or purchase of shares out of capital.
(c) The amount by which the capital and non-distributable reserves are reduced is called the 'permissible capital payment'. This is computed by deducting the proceeds of any fresh issue together with the balance of distributable reserves from the cost of shares redeemed or purchased.
(d) A transfer of distributable profits to capital redemption reserve is necessary if the nominal value of shares redeemed or purchased exceeds the proceeds of any fresh issue together with the permissible capital payment.
(e) However, if the nominal value of shares redeemed or purchased is less than the proceeds of any fresh issue together with the permissible capital payment, then the deficit is written off against:

(i) Revaluation reserve or other undistributable reserves;
(ii) Capital redemption reserve;
(iii) Share premium account;
(iv) Share capital account.

No order of priority is specified within the Companies Act 1985, but the above order would be sensible.

12.3.3 Double entry and technique

Event	Debit	Credit
Fresh issue of shares	Cash and Bank a/c – proceeds	Share capital a/c – nominal Share premium a/c – premium
Redemption or purchase at a discount	Share capital a/c – nominal	Cash and Bank a/c – cost Profit and loss a/c – discount
Redemption or purchase at a premium: (i) Compute amount written off Share premium a/c (see 12.2.1 (e) above) (ii) Entry	Share capital a/c – nominal Share premium a/c – per working. Profit and loss a/c – balance	Cash and Bank a/c – cost
Either: Excess of nominal value of shares redeemed or purchased over proceeds of fresh issue plus permissible capital payment	Profit and loss a/c	Capital redemption reserve
Or: Deficit of nominal value of shares redeemed or purchased below proceeds of fresh issue plus permissible capital payment.	Revaluation reserve or Capital redemption reserve or Share premium a/c or Share capital a/c	Profit and loss a/c

Example 3

Private Ltd has the following capital and reserves:

	£
Ordinary shares at 25 p each	80,000
Share premium account	52,000
Revaluation reserve	61,000

Profit and loss account	6,000
	£199,000

The company purchases 30,000 shares for cancellation at 130 p each. There is no fresh issue.

Required:
Show the journal entries necessary to record the above transactions, together with workings.

WORKINGS

(1) Purchase	£
Share capital *30,000 × 25 p*	7,500
Premium payable *30,000 × 105 p*	31,500
Cost	£39,000

Since there is no fresh issue the entire premium payable is written off to Profit and loss account.

(2) Permissible capital payment	£
Cost of shares purchased (*W1*)	39,000
Distributable reserves	(6,000)
Permissible capital payment	£33,000

(3) Deficit to be written off	£
Nominal value of shares purchased	7,500
Permissible capital payment	(33,000)
Deficit	£25,500

Journal entries:	£	£
Dr Ordinary share capital	7,500	
Dr Profit and loss account	31,500	
Cr Cash and Bank account (*W1*)	–	39,000
	£39,000	£39,000

Being purchase of shares.

	£	£
Dr Revaluation reserve	25,500	
Cr Profit and loss account		25,500

Being write-off of deficit created by premium paid on shares purchased.

12.4 REDEMPTION OF DEBENTURES AND USE OF SINKING FUNDS

12.4.1 Issue of debentures

Debenture stock may be issued by a company at a discount, at par, or at a premium. The majority of debenture issues are at a discount so that investors receive a capital gain on redemption as well as interest while held. A discount on issue may be written off against the Share premium account. A premium on issue is not entered in the Share premium account, but is added to distributable reserves.

12.4.2 Creation of a sinking fund

It is normal for a company to make provision for the eventual redemption of debentures over the period during which the debentures are in issue. One method is to create a sinking fund. This involves two separate transfers:

(a) An annual transfer of profits from the Profit and loss account to a Sinking fund account. The Sinking fund account is eventually used to maintain the capital after the debentures have been redeemed.
(b) An equal transfer of cash from the general Cash and Bank account to a sinking fund Bank account. This cash is invested and the investments held to provide the cash necessary for eventual redemption of the debentures. Investment income earned on sinking fund investments is added to the Sinking fund account.

At all times:
Sinking fund account balance = sinking fund investments balance +
sinking fund bank balance.

12.4.3 Double entry for a sinking fund

Event	Debit	Credit
Annual appropriation		
(i) Profits	Profit and loss a/c	Sinking fund a/c
(ii) Cash	Sinking fund bank a/c	General bank a/c

Investment of cash	Sinking fund investment a/c	Sinking fund bank a/c
Investment income	Sinking fund bank a/c	Sinking fund a/c
Sale of investment (i) Proceeds	Sinking fund bank a/c	Sinking fund investments a/c
(ii) Profit (loss) on sale	Sinking fund investment a/c	Sinking fund a/c

12.4.4 Redemption of debentures

Redemption may occur:

(a) At final redemption date at an agreed price. This would normally be par value or at a small premium.
(b) By purchase in the open market prior to final redemption. The debentures purchased may be cancelled or held as an investment. (This would not be possible with shares purchased.)

    An amount called the 'Debenture redemption account' is used to deal with the redemption.

12.4.5 Double entry for redemption of debentures

Event	Debit	Credit
Debentures purchased in open market	Debenture redemption a/c	Sinking fund bank a/c
Transfer nominal value of debentures	Debentures a/c	Debenture re-demption a/c
Balance on Debenture redemption a/c represents discount on redemption	Debenture redemption a/c	Sinking fund A/c
Maintain capital by trans-fer equal to nominal value of debentures redeemed	Sinking fund a/c	Non-distributable reserve (equivalent to capital redemp-tion reserve in a share redemption)

Example 4

Thrifty Plc have in issue £80,000 of debenture stock, which is redeemable in five years' time at par. The company has created a sinking fund, and at 1 January of the current year the balances brought forward were:

Sinking fund account	£45,000
Sinking fund investments	£41,000
Sinking fund bank account	4,000
	£45,000

Debentures are purchased in the open market if an advantageous price can be obtained, for cancellation.

During the current period the following transactions occurred:

1 Annual transfer from profits of £7,000 was made
2 Investments purchased at cost £6,000
3 Investment income totalled £4,500
4 Debentures with a nominal value of £12,000 were purchased in the open market for £10,500
5 Investments with a cost of £9,000 were sold for £9.800.

Required:

Write up these transactions in the Sinking fund account, Sinking fund investments account, Sinking fund bank account and Debenture redemption account.

Sinking fund account

	£		£
Transfer to non-distribu- table reserve	12,000	Balance b/f	45,000
		Profit and loss a/c – annual appropriation	7,000
		Sinking fund a/c – invest- ment income	4,500
		Debenture redemption a/c – discount	1,500
Balance c/f	46,800	Sinking fund investments a/c – profit on sale	800
	£58,800		£58,800

Sinking fund investments account

	£		£
Balance b/f	41,000	Sinking fund bank a/c – proceeds of sale	9,800
Sinking fund bank a/c – purchases	6,000		
Sinking fund a/c – profit on sale (£9,800 – 9,000)	800	Balance c/f	38,000
	£47,800		£47,800

Sinking fund bank account

	£		£
Balance b/f	4,000	Sinking fund investments	
General bank a/c – annual		a/c – purchases	6,000
appropriation	7,000	Debenture redemption a/c	
Sinking fund a/c – invest-		– cost of debentures	10,500
ment income	4,500		
Sinking fund investments		Balance c/f	8,800
a/c – proceeds of sale	9,800		
	£25,300		£25,300

Debenture redemption account

	£		£
Sinking fund bank a/c –		Debentures a/c – nominal	12,000
cost of debentures	10,500		
Sinking fund a/c – discount	1,500		
	£12,000		£12,000

12.5 RECONSTRUCTIONS AND REORGANISATIONS

12.5.1 Terminology

Many different terms are used within the overall subject of capital reorga-
nisations, often indiscriminately. The following explanations are therefore
for guidance:

(a) *Reorganisation*. Any procedure whereby a company's capital structure
or the rights of shareholders or creditors are affected.
(b) *Reconstruction*. A scheme whereby a company's capital is reduced
to eliminate losses, asset deficits or replace debt capital. This chapter
is chiefly concerned with such a scheme of capital reduction.
(c) *Amalgamation or absorption*. The purchase of the net assets of one or
more businesses by another business, which may have been formed
for that purpose. This may be the simplest method of effecting a
reorganisation. A company whose net assets are purchased would
be liquidated.
(d) *Takeover*. The purchase of the majority of equity shares of one company (the subsidiary) by another company (the holding company).
Both subsidiary and holding company continue to trade. The subsidiary
is controlled by the holding company. Periodically, group accounts
are prepared. (See Chapters 17–21.)

(e) *Acquisition*. A takeover where the holding company shareholders become dominant.

(f) *Merger*. A takeover where the shareholders of the subsidiary accept shares in the holding company, and continue to influence the affairs of both companies.

12.5.2 Legal provisions

(a) Companies Act 1985, Section 582

This relates to an amalgamation or absorption. It enables the liquidator of the vendor company to receive shares in another company as consideration for assets sold. These shares may then be distributed to shareholders.

(b) Companies Act 1985, Section 425

This section has wide application. It provides that any scheme (which could include any form of reorganisation, reconstruction, amalgamation or absorption) which is approved by the Courts will be binding on all members and creditors.

(c) Companies Act 1985, Section 135

This relates specifically to a capital reduction. Examples would be:

(i) Cancel uncalled capital
   (e.g. a £1 share 20 p paid up becomes a 20 p share fully paid)
(ii) Return capital to shareholders
(iii) A scheme of capital reduction (see below).

In each case Court authority is required.

12.5.3 Scheme of capital reduction – position

The typical examination position is a company which has suffered a period of decline. It has accumulated losses. The Balance-sheet asset values are overstated. It is unable to meet its debts. Liquidation appears inevitable.

However, the opportunity to secure a prosperous future arises through a new product, or a new contract if the immediate crises can be averted.

12.5.4 Scheme of capital reduction – objectives

The following are general objectives

(a) Elimination of adverse factors;
(b) Secure future;
(c) Fairness to all parties – the ordinary shareholders would be expected to bear the majority of any loss;
(d) All parties (shareholders, creditors) receive a better return than under a liquidation;
(e) The balance sheet reflects valuable assets;
(f) The capital structure is sensible;
(g) The company is able to meet its debts as they fall due.

12.5.5 Scheme of capital reduction – technique

Step 1: Establish the likely liquidation position

This indicates the limiting position of any scheme since all parties require a better return than under a liquidation. If this is not achieved, then agreement of all parties will not be forthcoming.

Step 2: Compute the loss of the going-concern scheme

This involves calculations of:

 (i) Costs of the scheme;
 (ii) Revaluation of all assets;
(iii) Provision for uncertainties.

Step 3: Allocate the loss

The following order should be used:

 (i) Reserves (there are no limitations);
 (ii) Ordinary share capital (each share would be reduced in nominal value);
(iii) Preference share capital ⎫
(iv) Unsecured creditors   ⎬ subject to the results of step 1.
                                                      ⎭

238

Step 4: Determine the need for cash

(i) To cover the costs of the scheme;
(ii) Settle preferential and secured creditors;
(iii) Provide adequate working capital and new plant;
(iv) Reduce unsecured creditors to a reasonable level.

The textbook current ratio – that is, current assets to current liabilities – of 2 to 1 may be used as a target in deciding the balance of items (iii) and (iv).

Step 5: Determine the sources of cash

(i) Sale of surplus or non-trading assets such as investments;
(ii) Sale and leaseback/secure loan mortgage provided that suitable assets exist;
(iii) Issue of new shares to directors (this is always a good indicator of the directors' faith in the scheme!);
(iv) Rights issue of shares.

The balance of share issues and debt finance should give a reasonable capital gearing position. A typical gearing level would be where debt was about 30 per cent of total capital employed.

Step 6: Preparation of projected balance sheet after the scheme is complete.

Example 5

Transformation Ltd, a company engaged in the manufacture of beauty products, has suffered a series of trading losses, leading to the appointment of a receiver. A decision must be made to either liquidate the company or devise a scheme of capital reduction, such that the company could continue to trade. A long-term secure market has been identified providing deodorant in bulk to the armed forces, and negotiations are at an advanced stage.

The Balance sheet of Transformation Ltd is given below, together with details of asset values on a going-concern and a liquidation basis.

	Existing		Going concern value	Liquidation value
	£	£	£	£
Fixed assets				
Intangible assets – Goodwill		15,280		
Tangible – Freehold		80,000	140,000	100,000
– Plant and machinery		65,240	36,100	18,000
– Vehicles		24,500	18,950	16,000
		185,020		
Current assets				
Stocks	54,920		21,540	10,000
Debtors	49,465		35,450	35,000
	£104,385			
Current liabilities				
Trade creditors	(65,425)			
Overdraft	(46,500)			
Debenture interest	(2,500)			
	£(114,425)	(10,040)		
		174,980		
Long-term liabilities				
5% secured debenture stock		(50,000)		
		£124,980		
Capital and reserves				
25 p ordinary shares		100,000		
Share premium account		40,000		
Profit and loss account		(15,020)		
		£124,980		

The following information is relevant:

(1) Costs of a going concern scheme would total £5,000. Costs of a liquidation would total £20,000.
(2) The debenture stock is secured on the freehold. Debenture interest is in arrears, and requires immediate payment
(3) The overdraft is secured by a floating charge on plant and machinery. The bank require immediate repayment, but will be willing to purchase up to £60,000 new debenture stock provided that a rate of 12 per cent is offered, and security provided by a floating charge.
(4) Trade creditors are unsecured.

(5) If a going-concern scheme is approved the company will require additional plant and stocks of £30,000 and £15,000 respectively.

Required:
A scheme of capital reduction which will prove acceptable to all parties.

It must be appreciated that there are many acceptable solutions to such a problem. The following solution attempts to take a reasonable line.

WORKINGS

		£	£
(1) Liquidation position			
Assets at liquidation values:			
Freehold			100,000
Plant and machinery			18,000
Vehicles			16,000
Stocks			10,000
Debtors			35,000
			179,000
Applied to:			
Costs		(20,000)	
Debenture holders		(52,500)	
Overdraft		(46,500)	(119,000)
Available to trade creditors			60,000

Trade creditors will receive $\dfrac{£60,000}{£65,425}$ 91.7 p in the £

Shareholders will receive no return of capital.

	£
(2) Going-concern scheme – loss to be borne	
Costs of scheme	5,000
Deficit on revaluation of assets:	
Goodwill	15,280
Plant and machinery (£65,240 – £36,100)	29,140
Vehicles (£24,500 – £18,950)	5,550
Stocks (£54,920 – £21,540)	33,380
Debtors (£49,465 – £35,450)	14,015
	102,365

Surplus on revaluation of assets
    Freehold (*£140,000 − £80,000*)   (60,000)

	42,365
Profit and loss account – adverse balance	15,020
Provision to meet unknown costs and errors in estimates	
(*rough estimate*)	2,615
	£60,000

To the extent that the provision created is unused it will form a reserve after the scheme is complete.

(3) Going-concern scheme – allocation of loss	£
Share premium	40,000
Ordinary share capital – each share reduced to 20 p each	20,000
	£60,000

(4) Going-concern scheme – cash requirements	£
Costs	5,000
Debenture interest	2,500
Overdraft	46,500
New plant	30,000
New stock	15,000
Reduce trade creditors (*20 p in the £*)	13,085
Provide cash at bank	27,915*
	£140,000

*This figure has been chosen to provide a current ratio of approximately 2:1.

(5) Going-concern scheme – sources of cash	£
Issue of 12 per cent debentures	30,000+
Issue of new 20 p ordinary shares	
– to directors	30,000
– rights issue (*1 for 1*)	80,000
	£140,000

+ This figure has been chosen to provide debt of approximately 30 per cent of total capital.

Projected Balance sheet after the scheme	£	£
Fixed assets		
Freehold		140,000
Plant and machinery (*£36,100 + £30,000*)		66,100

Vehicles		18,950
		225,050

Current assets		
Stocks (£21,540 + £15,000)	36,540	
Debtors	35,450	
Cash at bank	27,915	
	£99,905	

Creditors: amounts falling due within one year		
Trade creditors (£65,425 – £13,085)	(52,340)	
Net current assets		47,565
Total assets *less* current liabilities		272,615
Creditors: amounts falling due after more than one year		
5 per cent Secured debenture stock	(50,000)	
12 per cent Secured debenture stock	(30,000)	
		(80,000)
		£192,615
Capital and reserves		
Ordinary shares of 20 p each		190,000
Reserve arising from scheme		2,615
		£192,615

Current ratio   *£99,905:£52,340 = 1.9:1*

Capital gearing $\dfrac{£80,000}{£272,615}$ *= 29.3 per cent*

Exercises to Chapter 12

1. A company has 100,000 ordinary shares of 25 p each in issue. A further 20,000 shares are to be issued at a price of 40 p each, payable 20 p on application, and a further 20 p on allotment. Applications were received for 30,000 shares. Cash was returned to the unsuccessful applicants. On allotment an applicant to whom 1,000 shares were allotted failed to pay allotment money. The shares were forfeited and reissued as fully paid for 25 p each.

   You are required to prepare journal entries to record:

   (a) Receipt of application money;
   (b) Repayment of excess money;

    (c) Allotment;

    (d) Receipt of allotment money;

    (e) Forfeiture;

    (f) Reissue of forfeited shares.

2. A public company has 50,000 ordinary shares of £1 each in issue. These were originally issued at £1.50 each. The Share premium account stands at £10,000. The company wishes to purchase 10,000 of the shares for cancellation under the following alternatives:

    (a) 10,000 shares purchased for £2.50. No fresh issue.

    (b) 10,000 shares purchased for £2.50. Fresh issue of 5,000 shares at £2.25.

You are required to prepare journal entries to record the purchase, fresh issue and relevant reserve transfers.

PART IV

BUSINESS EXPANSION

BRANCH ACCOUNTS

13.1 AUTONOMOUS BRANCHES

13.1.1 Situation

A sole trader, partnership or company may decide to increase their trade by increasing geographical sales outlets, but without creating a completely new business. One method is a branch. A manager would be appointed to each branch.

An autonomous branch is one which maintains separate accounting records. These are aggregated periodically with those of the head office to produce the total accounts of the combined business. The autonomous branch may purchase all stock from head office or may purchase from outside the business. Where stock is supplied from the head office it will normally be invoiced at a price above cost, i.e. inclusive of some profit element.

13.1.2 Objective

To produce a Trading, profit and loss account and Balance sheet for each of the head office, branch and combined business.

13.1.3 Current account

All transactions between a head office and branch are recorded in a Current account. A version of the Current account is maintained by each of the head office and branch. The following are typical transactions passing through a Current account:

Transactions passing through a current account

Transaction	Entry in head office				Entry in branch			
	Debit		Credit		Debit		Credit	
Stock transferred to branch	Current a/c		Goods sent to Branch a/c		Goods from Head office a/c		Current a/c	
Cash remitted to head office	Cash a/c		Current a/c		Current a/c		Cash a/c	
Administration cost charged by head office to branch	Current a/c		Profit and loss a/c		Profit and loss a/c		Current a/c	
Depreciation on branch fixed assets, recorded in head office accounts	Current a/c		Accumulated de-preciation a/c		Profit and loss a/c		Current a/c	
Branch net profit transferred to head office at end of period	Current a/c		Profit and loss a/c		Profit and loss a/c		Current a/c	

In theory a debit balance on the head office version of the Current account should match a credit balance on the branch version of the same account.

In practice goods and cash still in transit at the end of a period will result in differences. The Current accounts must always be made to balance. By convention any adjustment is made in the head office books.

Adjustments are:

Adjustment	Debit	Credit
Goods in transit	Goods in transit a/c (added to stock in the head office Balance sheet)	Head office current a/c
Cash in transit	Cash in transit a/c (added to cash in the head office Balance sheet)	Head office current a/c

13.1.4 Gross profit equation

In Chapter 5 we considered how gross profit percentage information can be used. This idea can be applied to branches where the head office supplies stock to the branch at a price above cost, and the branch adds further profit to determine selling price.

Example 1

A business which has a head office and one branch purchases all stock centrally. The head office supplies goods to the branch at cost plus 10 per cent. All sales by head office and the branch yield a gross profit of 25 per cent on the original cost.

Required:
Profit equations for sales by head office and the branch.

Sales by head office:

Cost	+	Gross profit	=	Selling price
100	+	25	=	125

Sales by branch:

Cost	+	Profit added by head office	=	Transfer price	+	Profit added by branch	=	Selling price
100	+	10	=	110	+	15	=	125

Example 2

Facts as in Example 1

	£
Sales by head office to customers	80,000
Goods sent to branch (*at transfer price*)	33,000
Sales by branch to customers	35,000

Required:
Compute gross profit of head office, branch and combined business.

Head office gross profit £

(i) on sales to customers $\frac{25}{125}$ × £80,000   16,000

(ii) on sales to branch $\frac{10}{110}$ × £33,000   3,000

          £19,000

Branch gross profit

$\frac{15}{125}$ × £35,000   £4,200

Combined business gross profit

$\frac{25}{125}$ × £(80,000 + 35,000)   £23,000

Note that the combined business gross profit does not equal the head office and branch gross profits together. This is due to branch stock which includes UNREALISED PROFIT.

13.1.5 Unrealised profit

Where the branch holds stock purchased from head office at a price which includes an element of profit added by the head office, then such profit is unrealised profit so far as the combined business is concerned. An adjustment is made in the head office Profit and loss account (debit entry) to eliminate the unrealised profit. The related credit entry appears in the head office Balance sheet called PROVISION FOR UNREALISED PROFIT.

Example 3

Facts as in Examples 1 and 2.
Branch closing stock, valued at transfer price, was £2,200.

Required:
Compute the unrealised profit, and stock at cost.

Unrealised profit $£2,200 \times \dfrac{10}{110} = £200$

	£
Stock at transfer price	2,200
Provision for unrealised profit	(200)
Stock at cost	£2,000

Points arising:

1 No adjustment is required where stock has been sold by the branch.
2 Branch stock is always valued at transfer price in the branch books.
3 Head office and combined business stock are always valued at cost.

13.1.6 Technique for preparation of accounts

Step 1: Compute profit equation.
Step 2: Reconcile Current accounts for goods and cash in transit.
Step 3: Prepare Head office and Branch trading accounts. Compute gross profit as required.
Step 4: Prepare Combined business trading account. Compute gross profit as required.
Step 5: Compute provision for unrealised profit.
Step 6: Prepare Profit and loss accounts.
Step 7: Transfer branch net profit to head office via Current account.
Step 8: Prepare Balance sheets.

Example 4

Jim Jones, a sole trader, has run a successful hardware shop for some years. On 1 January 19X9 he opened a branch and appointed a manager to run the branch and maintain separate accounting records. All stock is purchased at head office and invoiced to the branch at selling price less 20 per cent. The head office purchases the stock at selling price less 25 per cent. The following Trial balances were extracted at 31 December 19X9:

	Head office		Branch	
	Dr	Cr	Dr	Cr
	£	£	£	£
Capital account - 1 January 19X9	–	35,700	–	–
Drawings	8,200	–	–	–
Sales	–	125,000	–	36,000
Purchases	122,500	–	–	–
Stock at 1 January 19X9	11,300	–	–	–
Goods sent to branch	–	34,000	–	–
Goods from head office	–	–	33,200	–
Administration costs	12,500	–	4,200	–
Establishment costs	9,120	–	1,850	–
Fixed assets				
Head office cost	8,800	–	–	–
Accumulated depreciation	–	6,300	–	–
Branch cost	3,000	–	–	–
Accumulated depreciation	–	–	–	–
Current accounts	17,600	–	–	16,300
Trade debtors/creditors	3,420	12,290	950	–
Cash at bank	16,850	–	12,100	–
	£213,290	£213,290	£52,300	£52,300

The following is relevant:

1 Depreciation is to be charged at 10 per cent of cost. The branch fixed assets are recorded in the Head office accounts, but depreciation is to be charged to the branch.
2 At the Balance-sheet date there was stock in transit to the branch with a transfer price of £800 and cash in transit from the branch to the head office of £500.

Required:
Trading, profit and loss accounts and Balance sheets for each of the head office, branch and combined business in a columnar format.

WORKINGS

(1) Profit equations

Head office:	Cost	+	Gross profit	=	Selling price
	75	+	25	=	100

Branch:	Cost	+	Profit of head office	=	Transfer price	+	Profit of branch	=	Selling price
	75	+	5	=	80	+	20	=	100

(2) *Current account – head office version*

	£		£
Balance b/f	17,600	Goods-in-transit a/c	800
		Cash-in-transit a/c	500
		Balance c/d – agreed to	
		branch	16,300
	£17,600		£17,600
Balance b/d	16,300		
Accumulated depreciation			
a/c	300		
Profit and loss a/c –			
branch net profit	850	Balance c/f	17,450
	£17,450		£17,450

N.B. The entry for deprecation and net profit transferred also appear in the branch Current account as credit entries.

(3) Gross profit

		£
Head office (i) Outside $\dfrac{25}{100} \times £125,000 =$		31,250
(ii) Branch $\dfrac{5}{80} \times £34,000$	=	2,125
		£33,375
Branch $\dfrac{20}{100} \times £36,000$	=	£7,200
Combined business $\dfrac{25}{100} \times £161,000$	=	£40,250

(4) Provision for unrealised profit

		£
(i) Branch stock $\dfrac{5}{80} \times £4,400$	=	275
(ii) Goods in transit $\dfrac{5}{80} \times £800$	=	50
		£325

(5) Combined business closing stock

	In hand £	In transit £
Head office accounts	8,175	800
Branch accounts	4,400	–
	12,575	800
Provision for unrealised profit (*W4*)	(275)	(50)
Cost	£12,300	£750

Full trading profit and loss accounts and balance sheet appear on pages 255 and 256.

13.2 FOREIGN BRANCHES

13.2.1 Situation

An autonomous branch as in the previous section, but which operates in a foreign currency and maintains accounting records in a foreign currency. The technique for accounts preparation is:

Step 1: Prepare the branch Trial balance in its local currency;
Step 2: Translate the Trial balance into sterling;
Step 3: Prepare final accounts as in the previous section.

13.2.2 Translation of foreign Trial balance

Since by nature the branch is an extension of the head office trade, we use rates of exchange which were relevant on the dates that each transaction was recorded by the branch, i.e. as if the combined business activities were recorded in sterling as each transaction occurred. This is called the 'temporal method of translation'.

The detailed rates are as follows:

Item	Rate of exchange
(a) Profit and loss account items	
Sales	Average rate for period
Purchases (local)	Average rate for period
Goods from head office	Date of transfer (or internal fixed rate)
Stock	Date of transfer (or internal fixed rate)
Depreciation	Rate used for related asset
Other expenses	Average rate for period

Continued on page 257

Example 4

Trading, profit and loss account for year to 31 December 19X9

	Head office £	Branch £	Combined business £		Head office £	Branch £	Combined business £
Opening stock	11,300	–	11,300	Sales	125,000	36,000	161,000
Purchases	122,500	–	122,500	Goods sent to branch	34,000	–	–
Goods from head office	–	33,200	–	Closing stock – in transit	–	–	750 (*W5*)
Gross profit c/d (*W3*)	33,375	7,200	40,250	– in hand (*balance*)	8,175	4,400	12,300 (*W5*)
	£167,175	£40,400	£174,050		£167,175	£40,400	£174,050
Provision for unrealised profit (*W4*)	325	–	–	Gross profit b/d	33,375	7,200	40,250
Administration costs	12,500	4,200	16,700				
Establishment costs	9,120	1,850	10,970				
Depreciation (*10%*)	880	300	1,180				
Net profit c/d	10,550	850	11,400				
	£33,375	£7,200	£40,250		£33,375	£7,200	£40,250
Current a/c	–	850	–	Net profit b/d	10,550	850	11,400
Capital a/c	11,400	–	11,400	Current a/c	850	–	–
	£11,400	£850	£11,400		£11,400	£850	£11,400

Example 4

Balance sheets at 31 December 19X9

	Head office £	Branch £	Combined business £
Fixed assets			
Cost	11,800	–	11,800
Accumulated depreciation	(7,480)	–	(7,480)
	4,320	–	4,320
Current assets			
Stock in hand	8,175	4,400	12,300
Stock in transit	800	–	750
Current account	17,450	–	–
Trade debtors	3,420	950	4,370
Cash at bank	16,850	12,100	28,950
Cash in transit	500	–	500
	£51,515	£17,450	£51,190

	Head office £	Branch £	Combined business £
Capital a/c			
1.1.X9	35,700	–	35,700
Net profit for year	11,400	–	11,400
	47,100	–	47,100
Drawings	(8,200)	–	(8,200)
31.12.X9	38,900	–	38,900
Current a/c	–	17,450	–
Creditors due within one year			
Trade creditors	12,290	–	12,290
Provision for unrealised profit (W4)	325	–	–
	£51,515	£17,450	£51,190

(b) Balance-sheet items	
Fixed-asset cost	Date of purchase
Accumulated depreciation	Date of purchase
Stock	Date of transfer (or internal fixed rate)
Debtors	Balance-sheet date (closing rate)
Cash	Balance-sheet date
Creditors	Balance-sheet date
Loans	Balance-sheet date
(c) Current a/c items	
Balance b/f	Actual equivalent in head office books
Goods from head office	Date of transfer (or internal fixed rate)
Cash remitted	Amount realised
Net profit	Total of Profit and loss a/c items

Since many different rates have been applied it is not surprising that the sterling Trial balance does not balance. The difference is an EXCHANGE DIFFERENCE and is charged or credited to the branch Profit and loss account.

Example 5

Bella Black is a sole trader operating from a shop in the United Kingdom. On 1 January 19X8 she decided to open a branch in Whiteland, where the currency is the Hue (H). On 31 December 19X8 the following Trial balances were extracted:

	Head Office		Whiteland branch	
	£	£	H	H
Capital account - 1 January 19X8	–	62,580	–	–
Drawings	8,950	–	–	–
Sales	–	136,400	–	354,000
Purchases	125,200	–	78,000	–
Goods sent to branch	–	28,400	–	
Goods from head office	–	–	206,250	–
Current accounts				
Capital transferred	20,000	–	–	200,000
Stock transferred	28,400	–	–	206,250
Cash remitted	–	22,670	203,650	–
Administration costs	12,590	–	17,630	–
Selling costs	10,420	–	16,580	–
Fixed assets, at cost	51,000	–	180,000	–
Accumulated depreciation				
1 January 19X8	–	27,500	–	–
Stock at 1 January 19X8	13,620	–	–	–

	£	£	H	H
Debtors	11,590	–	35,400	–
Creditors	–	10,420	–	2,540
Cash and bank balances	6,200	–	25,280	–
	£287,970	£287,970	H762,790	H762,790

The following information is relevant:

1 Rates of exchange have been:

1 January 19X8	£1	= H10
31 December 19X8		= H8
Average 19X8		= H9.2

2 All goods are transferred at a fixed rate of £1 = H7.5, at cost. The branch additionally buys some stock locally.

3 On 31 December 19X8 there was stock in transit to the branch of £900 at cost. This had been recorded by the head office, but not the branch.

4 Branch fixed assets were acquired on 1 January 19X8. All fixed assets are to be depreciated at 10 per cent on cost.

5 Stock in hand on 31 December 19X8 was:

Head office	£17,650
Branch – all from head office	H32,620

Required:
Sterling trading, Profit and loss accounts for the year and Balance sheets at 31 December 19X8 for each of the head office, branch and combined business.

All workings to the nearest £.

WORKINGS

(1) *Translation of branch Trial balance*

	H	H	Rate	£	£
Sales	–	354,000	Average 9.2	–	38,478
Purchases	78,000	–	Average 9.2	8,478	–
Goods from head office	206,250		Internal 7.5	27,500	–
Closing stock	32,620	32,620	Internal 7.5	4,349	4,349
Current account					
Capital	–	200,000	Transfer 10	–	20,000
Stock	–	206,250	Internal 7.5	–	27,500
Cash	203,650	–	Realised	22,670	–

BELLA BLACK

Trading, profit and loss account for year to 31 December 19X8

	Head office £	Branch £	Combined business £		Head office £	Branch £	Combined business £
Opening stock	13,620	–	13,620	Sales	136,400	38,478	174,878
Purchases	125,200	8,478	133,678	Goods sent to branch	28,400	–	–
Goods from head office	–	27,500	–	Closing stock			
Gross profit c/d	43,630	6,849	50,479	– in transit	–	–	900
				– in hand	17,650	4,349	21,999
	£182,450	£42,827	£197,777		£182,450	£42,827	£197,777
Depreciation	5,100	1,800	6,900	Gross profit b/d	43,630	6,849	50,479
Administration costs	12,590	1,916	14,506	Exchange difference	–	1,655	1,655
Selling costs	10,420	1,802	12,222				
Net profit c/d	15,520	2,986	18,506				
	£43,630	£8,504	£52,134		£43,630	£8,504	£52,134
Current a/c		2,986		Net profit b/d	15,520	2,986	18,506
Capital a/c	18,506		18,506	Current a/c	2,986		
	£18,506	£2,986	£18,506		£18,506	£2,986	£18,506

The balance sheet appears on page 261

Administration	17,630	–	Average 9.2	1,916	–
Selling costs	16,580	–	Average 9.2	1,802	–
Fixed-asset cost	180,000	–	Purchase 10	18,000	–
Depreciation (10%)	18,000	18,000	Purchase 10	1,800	1,800
Debtors	35,400	–	Closing 8	4,425	–
Creditors	–	2,540	Clsoing 8	–	318
Cash and bank	25,280	–	Closing 8	3,160	–
Exchange different			Balance	--	1,655
	H813,410	H813,410		£94,100	£94,100

(2) *Current account per head office books*

	H	£		H	£
Capital transferred	200,000	20,000	Cash remitted	203,650	22,670
Stock transferred	213,000	28,400	Stock in tran-		
			sit	6,750	900
			Balance c/d	202,600	24,830
	H413,000	£48,400		H413,000	£48,400
Balance b/d	202,600	24,830			
Net profit	50,160	2,986	Balance c/f	252,760	27,826
	H252,760	£27,816		H252,760	£27,816

13.3 SELLING AGENCY BRANCHES – FIXED MARK-UP

13.3.1 Situation

Where the head office maintains all accounting records we say that the branch is a selling agency branch. Special accounts are maintained within the head office books to record and control branch stock, cash and debtors and to compute branch profit.

Two separate techniques are used:
(a) where there is a FIXED MARK-UP on all goods supplied to and sold by the branch (dealt with in this section); and
(b) Where there is NO FIXED MARK-UP (dealt with in the next section, 13.4).

13.3.2 Objective

The following statements are prepared:

(a) Head office trading account, including cost of goods sent to the branch;

Balance sheets at 31 December 19X8

	Head office £	Branch £	Combined business £
Fixed assets			
Cost	51,000	18,000	69,000
Accumulated depreciation	(32,600)	(1,800)	(34,400)
	18,400	16,200	34,600
Current assets			
Stock in hand	17,650	4,349	21,999
Stock in transit	900	–	900
Current a/c	27,816	–	–
Debtors	11,590	4,425	16,015
Cash at bank and in hand	6,200	3,160	9,360
	£82,556	£28,134	£82,874

	Head office £	Branch £	Combined business £
Capital a/c			
1.1.X8	62,580	–	62,580
Net profit for year	18,506	–	18,506
	81,086	–	81,086
Drawings 31.12.X8	(8,950)	–	(8,950)
	72,136	–	72,136
Current a/c	–	27,816	–
Creditors	10,420	318	10,738
	£82,556	£28,134	£82,874

(b) Combined Profit and loss accounts showing the head office and branch gross profit and expenses separately; and

(c) Combined Balance sheet.

No branch Trading account is prepared. The branch gross profit is computed from a 'Branch mark-up account'.

13.3.3 Accounts required

Three special accounts are used:

(a) Branch stock account

Balance (debit) represents branch stock in hand valued at selling price;

(b) Branch mark-up account

Balance (credit) represents gross profit on stock in hand.

The net balance of Branch stock account less Branch mark-up account gives branch stock at cost, which is included in the combined Balance sheet.

(c) Goods sent to branch account

To compute the total cost of goods sent to all branches for inclusion in the Head office trading account.

13.3.4 Double entry

Transaction	Debit	Credit
Goods sent to branch	Branch stock a/c (*selling price*)	Goods sent to Branch a/c (*cost price*) Branch mark-up a/c (*gross profit*)
Branch sales (i) Credit (ii) Cash	Debtors' a/c Cash a/c	Branch stock a/c Branch stock a/c
Amounts written-off stock value	Branch mark-up a/c (*gross profit element*) Profit and loss a/c (*cost element*)	Branch stock a/c
Carry forward branch stock at selling price	Branch stock a/c balance	

Carry forward gross profit thereon	Branch mark-up a/c balance	
Balancing figure on branch mark-up account represents branch gross profit earned	Branch mark-up a/c	Profit and loss a/c

Unexplained differences on branch stock account would represent branch stock or cash missing and would be charged to the Profit and loss account.

Example 6

Fred Fogg is a sole trader who owns two shops, one of which is the head office. All purchases are made by the head office and all accounting records are kept at the head office. All sales by the head office and branch yield a gross profit of 25 per cent on cost.

The following Trial balance was prepared at 31 December 19X5:

	Dr £	Cr £
Capital account 1 January 19X5	–	20,500
Drawings	6,950	–
Fixed assets		
Head office at cost	15,000	–
Accumulated depreciation 1.1.X5	–	6,000
Branch at cost	6,800	–
Accumulated depreciation 1.1.X5	–	1,360
Stock at 1 January 19X5		
Head office at cost	6,520	–
Branch at selling price	3,150	–
Gross profit thereon	–	630
Cash and bank balances	7,425	–
Creditors	–	10,865
Sales (all cash)		
Head office	–	48,000
Branch	–	20,000
Purchases	56,400	–
Sundry expenses		
Head office	3,150	–
Branch	1,960	–
	£107,355	£107,355

The following information is relevant:
1 During the year goods with a cost price of £16,800 were sent to the branch.
2 Depreciation is to be provided at 10 per cent on cost.
3 During the year, goods at the branch with a selling price of £200 were scrapped.

Required:
Branch stock and mark-up accounts, a combined Profit and loss account for 19X5, and combined a Balance sheet at 31 December 19X5.

WORKINGS

1 Profit equation

Cost	+	Gross profit	=	Selling price
100	+	25	=	125

Branch stock account

	£		£
Balance b/f	3,150	Sales	20,000
Goods sent from head		Stock scrapped	200
office $(£16,800 \times \frac{125}{100})$	21,000	Balance c/f (*balancing figure*)	3,950
	£24,150		£24,150

Branch mark-up account

	£		£
Gross profit on stock scrapped $(£200 \times \frac{25}{125})$	40	Balance b/f	630
		Gross profit on goods sent from head office	
Profit and loss account – gross profit realised (*balancing figure*)	4,000	$(£16,800 \times \frac{25}{100})$	4,200
Balance c/f $(£3,950 \times \frac{25}{125})$	790		
	£4,830		£4,830

FRED FOGG

Trading, profit and loss account for the year to 31 December 19X5

	£	£
Head office sales		48,000
Opening stock	(6,520)	
Purchases	(56,400)	
	(62,920)	
Goods sent to branch	16,800	
Closing stock (*balancing figure*)	7,720	(38,400)
Head office gross profit ($£48,000 \times \dfrac{25}{125}$)		9,600
Head office expenses		
Depreciation ($£15,000 \times 10\%$)	(1,500)	
Sundry	(3,150)	(4,650)
Head office net profit		4,950

	£	£	£
Branch gross profit		4,000	
Branch expenses			
Depreciation ($£6,800 \times 10\%$)	(680)		
Sundry	(1,960)		
Stock scrapped ($£200 \times \dfrac{100}{125}$)	(160)	(2,800)	
Branch net profit			1,200
Total net profit			£6,150

Balance sheet at 31 December 19X5

	£	£ .
Fixed assets		
Head office at cost	15,000	
Accumulated depreciation	(7,500)	7,500
Branch at cost	6,800	
Accumulated depreciation	(2,040)	4,760
		12,260
Current assets		
Stock at head office	7,720	
Stock at branch ($£3,950 - £790$)	3,160	
Cash at bank and in hand	7,425	

	18,305	
Creditors	(10,865)	
Net current assets		7,440
		£19,700

Capital account	£
At 1 January 19X5	20,500
Net profit for year	6,150
	26,650
Drawings	(6,950)
At 31 December 19X5	£19,700

13.4 SELLING AGENCY BRANCHES – NO FIXED MARK-UP

13.4.1 Assumption

While there are many lines of stock sold, each earning a different gross profit margin, it is assumed that the mix of sales at the head office and branch are similar. This means that the total gross profit can be divided between the head office and branch in sales ratio.

13.4.2 Objective

The following statements are prepared:

(a) Combined Trading account
(b) Combined Profit and loss account showing gross profit and expenses divided between the head office and branch; and
(c) Combined Balance sheet.

13.4.3 Accounts required

Two special accounts are used:

(a) Branch stock account

Balance (*debit*) represents branch stock in hand valued at selling price;

(b) Branch sales account

Balance (*credit*) also represents branch stock in hand valued at selling price. The purpose of this account is to compute branch sales for inclusion in the combined Trading account.

The net balance of Branch stock account and Branch sales account is nil.

13.4.4 **Double entry**

Transaction	Debit	Credit
Goods sent to branch	Branch stock a/c (*selling price*)	Branch sales a/c (*selling price*)
Branch Sales (i) Credit (ii) Cash	Debtors' a/c Cash a/c	Branch stock a/c Branch stock a/c
Amounts written off stock value	Branch stock a/c (*total reduction*) Profit and loss a/c (*cost element*)	Branch stock a/c (*total reduction*) Trading a/c (*cost element*)
Carry forward branch stock at selling price	Branch stock a/c (debit balance)	Branch stock a/c (credit balance)
Branch sales a/c represents branch sales sents branch sales	Branch sales a/c	Trading a/c

Unexplained differences on Branch stock account would represent branch stock or cash missing, and would be charged to the Profit and loss account.

Example 7

Hattie Hogg is a sole trader and owns two shops. All purchases are made at the head office. All sales are for cash and there is no fixed profit mark-up on cost.

The following Trial balance was prepared at 30 June 19X7:

	Dr £	Cr £
Capital account 1 July 19X6	–	31,000
Drawings	11,450	–
Fixed assets		
Head office at cost	21,000	–
Accumulated depreciation	–	9,500
Branch at cost	10,500	–
Accumulated depreciation	–	2,250
Stock at 1 July 19X6		
Head office at cost	9,600	–
Branch cost (*selling price £5,000*)	3,700	–
Cash and bank balances	10,420	–
Creditors	–	4,690
Sales		
Head office	–	75,000
Branch	–	25,000
Purchases	73,200	–
Sundry expenses	–	–
Head office	4,630	–
Branch	2,940	–
	£147,440	£147,440

The following information is relevant:

1 Goods with a selling value of £29,300 were sent to the branch.
2 Depreciation is to be provided at 10 per cent on cost.
3 Cost of goods in stock at 30 June 19X7 was head office £15,100 and branch £6,100.
4 The mix of sales at head office and the branch are similar.
5 During the year goods at the branch with a cost of £300, selling price £400 were scrapped.

Required:
Trading, profit and loss account for the year to 30 June 19X7 and a Balance sheet on that date. The net profit of head office and branch should be identified.

Branch stock account

	£		£
Balance b/f	5,000	Cash a/c – sales	25,000
Branch sales a/c – goods sent from head office	29,300	Branch sales a/c – write-down of stock	400
		Balance c/f (*balance figure*)	8,900
	£34,300		£34,300

Branch sales account

	£		£
Branch stock a/c – write-down of stock	400	Balance b/f	5,000
Trading a/c – branch sales	25,000	Branch stock a/c – goods sent from head office	29,300
Balance c/f	8,900		
	£34,300		£34,300

HATTIE HOGG

Trading, profit and loss account for year to 30 June 19X7

	£	£
Sales – head office		75,000
– branch		25,000
		100,000
Opening stock at cost (*£9,600 + £3,700*)	(13,300)	
Purchases	(73,200)	
	86,500	
Cost of stock written off	300	
Closing stock at cost (*£15,100 + £6,100*)	21,200	(65,000)
Gross profit		£35,000

	Head office	Branch	Combined business
	£	£	£
Gross profit in sales ratio 75:25	26,250	8,750	35,000
Depreciation (*10% × £21,000/£10,500*)	(2,100)	(1,050)	(3,150)

Sundry expenses	(4,630)	(2,940)	(7,570)
Stock written off	–	(300)	(300)
	£19,520	£4,460	£23,980

Balance Sheet at 30 June 19X7

	£	£
Fixed assets		
Head office at cost	21,000	
Accumulated depreciation	(11,600)	9,400
Branch at cost	10,500	
Accumulated depreciation	(3,300)	7,200
		16,600
Current assets		
Stock at cost – head office	15,100	
– branch	6,100	
Cash at bank and in hand	10,420	
	31,620	
Creditors	(4,690)	
Net current assets		26,930
		£43,530
Capital account		
At 1 July 19X6		31,000
Net profit for year		23,980
		54,980
Drawings		(11,450)
At 30 June 19X7		£43,530

Exercises to Chapter 13

1. A head office supplies goods to its branch at cost plus 10 per cent. All sales by head office and the branch are at a fixed selling price.

   (a) If the branch adds 20 per cent to the transfer price to determine the fixed selling price, what is the total percentage of gross profit on cost to the business? and

   (b) If the fixed selling price is found by taking cost to the head office and adding 25 per cent, what is the percentage profit on selling price recorded by the branch alone?

2. The following transactions occurred between a head office and its newly formed autonomous branch.

	£
Goods transferred to branch	50,420
Cash float paid to branch	500
Goods returned by branch	1,210
Cash paid by branch	25,490
Depreciation of branch fixed assets appearing in head office books	5,400
Management charge by head office	2,400

You are required to write up the Current account in the head office books and identify the balance carried forward.

3. A foreign branch reports the following summary of revenues and expenses in its local currency, Dollars.

	£
Sales	100,000
Opening stock	10,000
Transfers from head office	75,000
Closing stock	8,000
Depreciation	5,500
Other overheads	13,200

The relevant rates of exchange are:

Transfer of opening stock	1.80 = £1
Transfer during year	1.75
Transfer of closing stock	1.76
Purchase of fixed asset	1.85
Average rate for year	1.78

You are required to prepare the sterling Profit and loss account of the branch, identifying net profit.

JOINT VENTURES

A joint venture is a temporary trading relationship between two parties. The parties may be individuals, sole traders, partnerships or companies or any combination of these.

Profits and losses arising from the venture are divided in an agreed ratio.

Where a separate set of accounts are opened, normal partnership accounting rules apply (see Chapter 7).

This chapter deals with the recording of the joint-venture transactions in one or both of the venturers' separate business accounts.

14.1 ONE VENTURER RECORDS ALL TRANSACTIONS

14.1.1 Accounts required

Two special accounts are used:

(a) Joint-venture account

This is the Profit and loss account of the venture.

(b) Current account with partner

Records amounts due to or from the partner to the venture.

14.1.2 **Double entry**

Transaction	Debit	Credit
Purchase of goods, expenses incurred		
(i) by recording partner	Joint-venture a/c	Cash/creditors' a/c
(ii) by other partner	Joint-venture a/c	Current a/c
Sale of goods		
(i) by recording partner	Cash/debtors' a/c	Joint-venture a/c
(ii) by other partner	Current a/c	Joint-venture a/c
Cash paid to partner	Current a/c	Cash a/c
Goods transferred to partner	No entry	
Goods taken over		
(i) by recording partner	Purchases a/c	Joint-venture a/c
(ii) by other partner	Current a/c	Joint-venture a/c
Balance on joint-venture account represents profit:		
(i) recording partners' share	Joint-venture a/c	Profit and loss a/c
(ii) other partners' share	Joint-venture a/c	Current a/c
Balance remaining on Current a/c	Final cash balance due to or from partner	

Example 1

Bill and Ben enter a joint venture to buy and sell lawn mowers, sharing profits and losses in the ratio 3:2. The following transactions occurred (all for cash):

1 Jan   Bill purchased two mowers for £50 each.
10 Jan   Bill sold one mower for £80.
11 Jan   Bill sent the other mower to Ben.
12 Jan   Ben sold the mower for £75.
13 Jan   Ben purchased a mower for £60.
14 Jan   Ben sold the mower for £85, but sent the cheque to Bill, as it was made payable to Bill 'A/c Payee'.
15 Jan   Ben purchased a mower for £45, which he sent to Bill, after incurring repair costs of £15.
20 Jan   Bill took over the unsold mower at a valuation of £70.
21 Jan   The venture was terminated and the final cash settlement made.

274

Required:
Write-up the Joint-venture account and Current account with Ben assuming that Bill records all transactions.

Joint-venture account

Date	£	Date	£
1 Jan Cash a/c – purchases	100	10 Jan Cash a/c – sale	80
13 Jan Current a/c – purchase	60	12 Jan Current a/c – sale	75
15 Jan Current a/c – purchase	45	14 Jan Current a/c – sale	85
– repairs	15	20 Jan Purchases a/c – taken	
21 Jan Profit on venture:		over	70
Profit and loss a/c			
(3/5) 54			
Current a/c			
(2/5) 36	90		
	£310		£310

Current account with Ben

Date	£	Date	£
12 Jan Joint-venture a/c – Sale	75	13 Jan Joint-venture a/c – purchase	60
14 Jan Joint-venture a/c – Sale	85	14 Jan Cash a/c – cheque	85
21 Jan Cash a/c (*balance*) – settlement from Bill to Ben	81	15 Jan Joint-venture a/c – purchase	45
		repairs	15
		21 Jan Joint-venture a/c – share of profit	36
	£241		£241

14.2 EACH VENTURER RECORDS OWN TRANSACTIONS

14.2.1 Accounts required

Two special accounts are used:

(a) Joint-venture account with partner
Each partner maintains such an account which records all payments and receipts made by that partner on behalf of the venture, and share of profit and goods taken over (at valuation).

(b) Memorandum joint-venture account
This is a working only, to compute the total profit or loss on the venture, which is then shared between the venturers.

14.2.2 **Double entry**

Transaction	Debit	Credit
Purchase of goods, expenses incurred	Joint-venture a/c	Cash/creditors' a/c
Sale of goods	Cash/debtors' a/c	Joint-venture a/c
Cash paid to partner	Joint-venture a/c	Cash a/c
Goods transferred to partner	No entry	
Share of profit from memorandum Joint-venture a/c	Joint-venture a/c	Profit and loss a/c
Balance remaining on joint venture	Final cash balance due or from partner	

Example 2

Facts as in Example 1, but Bill and Ben each record their own transactions.

Required:
Joint-venture accounts in each of Bill and Ben's books, together with memorandum joint-venture account.

Bill's books: Joint-venture account with Ben

Date	£	Date	£
1 Jan Cash a/c – purchases	100	10 Jan Cash a/c – Sale	80
21 Jan Profit and loss a/c – share of profit (3/5 × £90)	54	14 Jan Cash a/c – cheque from Ben	85
21 Jan Cash a/c – cash balance paid to settle	81	20 Jan Purchases a/c – taken over	70
	£235		£235

276

Ben's books: Joint-venture account with Bill

Date	£	Date	£
13 Jan Cash a/c – purchase	60	12 Jan Cash a/c – sale	75
14 Jan Cash a/c – cheque to Bill	85	14 Jan Cash a/c – sale	85
15 Jan Cash a/c – purchase	45	21 Jan Cash a/c – cash balance received to settle	81
– repairs	15		
21 Jan Profit and loss a/c – share of profit ($2/5 \times £90$)	36		
	£241		£241

Memorandum joint venture account

Date	£	Date	£
1 Jan Purchase	100	10 Jan Sale	80
13 Jan Purchase	60	12 Jan Sale	75
15 Jan Purchase	45	14 Jan Sale	85
15 Jan Repairs	15	20 Jan Taken over by Bill	70
21 Jan Profit on venture	90		
	£310		£310

Exercises to Chapter 14

1. *A* and *B* operate a joint venture, with *A* recording all transactions. The following is a summary of *B*'s transactions.

	£
Opening Current account balance (due from *A* to *B*)	4,210
Sales by *B* (cash retained)	20,490
Expenses incurred by *B*	2,430
Purchases by *B*	14,340
Cash paid by *A* to *B*	3,320
Stock transferred to *A*	500
B's share of venture profit	5,650

You are required to write up the above transactions in the Current account for *B* which appears in *A*'s books and identify the balance carried forward.

2. Facts as in exercise 1, except that each party records their own transactions. You are required to prepare the Joint venture account in *B*'s books and identify the balance carried forward.

CONVERSION OF A BUSINESS TO A LIMITED COMPANY

15.1 CLOSING-OFF THE BOOKS OF THE BUSINESS

The accounting entries to close the books of a partnership were fully described in Chapter 7.5.

The closing of a sole trader's books will require identical accounts and entries except that the Capital account will have one column only.

15.2 VENDORS' ACCOUNT

This account appears in the books of the acquiring company and provides the double entry for assets acquired and consideration given. A typical Vendors' account is given below:

Vendors' account

	£		£
Share capital a/c – nominal value of shares issued	x	Fixed asset a/c – *valuation* of assets acquired	x
Share premium a/c – premium on shares issued	x	Stock a/c – *valuation* of stock acquired	x
Debentures a/c – debentures issued	x	Debtors' a/c – debtors' acquired	x
Creditors' a/c – creditors taken over from partnership	x	Cash a/c – partnership cash balance taken over	x
Cash a/c – payments to partnership, payment of expenses	x	Goodwill a/c – *valuation* of goodwill acquired	x
	x		x

The debit side of the Vendors' account is a mirror entry of the credit side of the Purchasers' account in the old business books. Often this account can be used to compute goodwill as a balancing figure.

Example 1

Aye, Bee & Cee have been in partnership for many years. They decide to incorporate the business as *ABC* Ltd with effect from 1 January 19X9.
The partnership Balance sheet at 31 December 19X8 was as follows:

	£	£
Fixed assets		
Property		35,000
Plant		22,000
		57,000
Current assets		
Stock	12,500	
Debtors	10,250	
Bank	5,690	
	£28,440	
Creditors amounts falling due within one year		
Trade creditors	(8,420)	
Accrued expenses	(1,570)	
	£(9,990)	
Net current assets		18,450
Total assets *less* current liabilities		75,450
Creditors: amounts falling due after more than one year		
Loan from *Bee*		(10,000)
		£65,450
Capital accounts		£
Aye		26,180
Bee		26,180
Cee		13,090
		£65,450

The purchase is effected as follows:

1 *ABC* Ltd will issue 80,000 £1 ordinary shares at a value of £1.25 each. In addition £10,000 loan stock will be issued to satisfy the loan from Bee.
2 *ABC* Ltd will acquire assets at the following values:

	£
Property	58,000
Plant	20,000
Stock	12,000
Debtors	10,000
Goodwill	25,000

3 *ABC* Ltd will assume all liabilities, and pay £800 towards expenses.
4 Any balance of the consideration will be paid in cash.

Required:
The Vendors' account in the books of *ABC* Ltd.

Vendors' account

	£		£
Share capital a/c		Goodwill a/c	25,000
(*80,000 × £1*)	80,000	Property a/c	58,000
Share premium a/c		Plant a/c	20,000
(*80,000 × £0.25*)	20,000	Stock a/c	12,000
Creditors' a/c	8,420	Debtors' a/c	10,000
Accrued expenses a/c	1,570		
Loan stock a/c	10,000		
Bank a/c – expenses	800		
Bank a/c – balance of consideration	4,210		
	£125,000		£125,000

N.B. The company will commence to trade with an overdraft, since no bank balance was taken over from the partnership.

15.3 ALLOCATION OF SHARES BETWEEN PARTNERS

The allocation of shares issued by an acquiring company between the partners may be in a simple ratio, e.g. profit-sharing ratio.

However, the partners who are to become directors may wish to preserve the profit-sharing arrangements between themselves with respect to salaries, interest on capital and balances in profit-sharing ratio.

The allocation is as follows:

1 Award directors salaries equal to partners' salaries.
2 Issue ordinary shares in profit-sharing ratio such that one partner's capital is fully satisfied by the issue of these shares.

The partner who is fully satisfied will be the one with the lowest capital/profit-sharing ratio factor. This is found by dividing each partner's capital balance by profit share.
3 Issue cumulative preference shares to satisfy the remaining capital balances. The preference shares should carry a fixed rate of dividend equal to the interest on capital given by the partnership.

Example 2

Dee, Eee & Eff have been partners sharing profits in the ratio 5:3:2. They receive 10 per cent interest on capital balances and salaries of £8,000 each. On 31 December their capital balances were £100,000, £75,000 and £60,000 respectively. They decide to convert the partnership to a limited company, *DEF* Ltd.

Required:
Devise a scheme of share issue to satisfy the capital of the partners, and preserve their relationship in sharing profits that was enjoyed within the partnership.

Prove the scheme by sharing:

(a) a profit of £50,000; and
(b) a loss of £10,000 between the partners/shareholders.

	Dee £	Eee £	Eff £
Capital balances	100,000	75,000	60,000
Profit-sharing ratio	5	3	2
Capital ÷ PSR	20,000	25,000	30,000

Dee is the lowest, and will receive full capital in ordinary shares.

Profit appropriation:

Partnership

	Total	Dee	Eee	Eff
Salary	24,000	8,000	8,000	8,000
Interest	23,500	10,000	7,500	6,000
Balance – 5:3:2	2,500	1,250	750	500
	£50,000	£19,250	£16,250	£14,500

Company

	Total	Dee	Eee	Eff
Salary	24,000	8,000	8,000	8,000
Preference dividend	3,500	–	1,500	2,000
Ordinary dividend/ retained profit	22,500	11,250	6,750	4,500
	£50,000	£19,250	£16,250	£14,500

Loss appropriation:

Partnership

	Total £	Dee £	Eee £	Eff £
Salary	24,000	8,000	8,000	8,000
Interest	23,500	10,000	7,500	6,000
Balance (loss) 5:3:2	(57,500)	(28,750)	(17,250)	(11,500)
	£(10,000)	£(10,750)	£(1,750)	£ 2,500

Company

	Total £	Dee £	Eee £	Eff £
Salary	24,000	8,000	8,000	8,000
Preference dividend	3,500	–	1,500	2,000
Ordinary retained	(37,500)	(18,750)	(11,250)	(7,500)
	£(10,000)	£(10,750)	£(1,750)	£ 2,500

	Dee	*Eee*	*Eff*
	£	£	£

Scheme of share issue:

1 Directors' salaries	8,000	8,000	8,000
2 Ordinary £1 shares at par	100,000(5)	60,000 (3)	40,000(2)
3 10% Cumulative £1 preference shares			
at par	–	15,000	20,000
	£100,000	£75,000	£60,000

15.4 CONVERSION WITHOUT CLOSING-OFF THE BOOKS OF ACCOUNT

15.4.1 Situation

It may occur that through negligence or ignorance the partnership or sole trader books of account are not closed-off, and the company's transactions are recorded within the same accounting records. At the next Balance-sheet date appropriate entries will be needed to deal with the closing of Capital accounts, valuation of assets and issue of shares.

15.4.2 Accounts required

Two special accounts are used:

(a) Capital/Realisation account

Capital accounts are run on to deal with issue of shares, assets and liabilities to be taken and settled by the partners, and revaluation of assets including goodwill. This account has a single total-column only.

(b) Directors' loan accounts

Any balances due to or from the new directors in respect of the dissolution of the old business are entered to a Directors' loan account until settled in cash.

N.B. There is no Purchasers' account or Vendors' account.

15.4.3 **Double entry**

Transaction	Debit	Credit
Shares issued	Capital/Realisation a/c	Share capital a/c – nominal Share premium a/c – premium
Goodwill at valuation	Goodwill a/c	Capital Realisation a/c
Assets to be taken over by partners, but collected by company	Capital/Realisation a/c	Directors' loan a/c
Liabilities to be borne by partners, but paid by company	Directors' loan a/c	Capital/Realisation a/c
Expenses paid: – borne by partnership – borne by company	Capital/Realisation a/c Preliminary expenses a/c	Cash a/c Cash a/c

N.B. No entries are necessary for assets and liabilities taken over by the company.

Example 3

Aitch, Eye & Jay are in partnership sharing profits in the ratio 5:3:2. They decide to incorporate the business as *HIJ* Ltd from 1 April 19X8, in which each will be a director. However, new books of account have not been opened for the company, and all transactions recorded in the partnership books. The following Trial balance was extracted at 31 December 19X8

	Debit £	Credit £
Capital accounts 1 January 19X8		
– Aitch		25,000
– Eye		20,000
– Jay		15,000
Drawings for year		
– Aitch	8,620	
– Eye	7,480	
– Jay	7,960	

	£		£
Tangible fixed assets at cost	70,200		
Accumulated depreciation 31 December 19X8			26,000
Net profit for year			72,760
Stock at 31 December 19X8	25,350		
Debtors	83,640		
Creditors (trade)			71,670
Bank balance	27,180		
	£230,430		£230,430

The following information is relevant:

1 Net profit for the year accrued evenly. Directors' salaries of £12,000 each per annum have been neither provided nor paid. Drawings accrue evenly and should be dealt with as a payment on account of salaries for the latter nine months.

2 Ordinary share capital of 100,000 £1 shares was issued at par in profit-sharing ratio.

3 A loan to the partnership of £12,000 was to be cleared by the partners, but was in fact cleared by the company in August 19X8.

4 Goodwill was valued, and acquired by the company.

Required:
Balance sheet of *HIJ* Ltd at 31 December 19X8, showing any balances due to or from the directors.

WORKINGS

(1) *Capital/Realisation account*

	£		£
Drawings to 31.3.X8		Capital a/c – *Aitch*	25,000
Aitch (3/12)	2,155	– *Eye*	20,000
Eye (3/12)	1,870	– *Jay*	15,000
Jay (3/12)	1,990	Net profit to 31.3.X8	
Share capital a/c	100,000	(3/12 × £72,760)	18,190
		Directors' loan a/c – loan	
		repaid	12,000
		Goodwill a/c – balance	15,825
	£106,015		£106,015

(2) *Directors' loan accounts*

	£		£
Capital/realisation a/c –		Profit and loss a/c –	
loan repaid	12,000	salaries *(3 × 9/12*	
Drawings		*× £12,000)*	27,000
Aitch (9/12)	6,465	Balance c/f	3,045
Eye (9/12)	5,610		
Jay (9/12)	5,970		
	£30,045		£30,045

(3) *Profit and loss account*

	£
Net profit for 9 months to 31.12.X8	
(9/12 × £72,760)	54,570
Directors' salaries *(W2)*	(27,000)
	£27,570

HIJ LIMITED

Balance sheet at 31 December 19X8

	£	£
Fixed assets		
Intangible – goodwill *(W1)*		15,825
Tangible – cost	70,200	
– accumulated depreciation	(26,000)	44,200
		60,025
Current asset		
Stock	25,350	
Debtors	83,640	
Directors' loan accounts *(W2)*	3,045	
Bank	27,180	
	139,215	
Creditors: amounts falling due within one year		
Trade creditors	(71,670)	
Net current assets		67,545
		£127,570
Capital and reserves		
Called-up share capital – £1 ordinary shares		100,000
Reserves – Profit and loss account *(W3)*		27,570
		£127,570

Exercises to Chapter 15

1. *A*, *B* & *C*, who have been partners, together decide to transfer their business to a limited company. Agreed values of assets are:

	£
Freehold	60,000
Furniture	5,230
Machinery	10,450
Vehicles	21,420
Debtors	13,490
Cash at bank	2,430

Creditors of £10,320 are to be taken over. Consideration is to 100,000 shares of 25 p each valued at £1.30. In addition the company will meet dissolution costs of £800.

You are required to prepare the Vendors' account in the company's books and identify the amount of goodwill.

2. *X*, *Y* & *Z* are partners and decide to convert their business to a company. Capital accounts after entering all surpluses and deficits arising from the dissolution are £20,000, £15,000 and £10,000 respectively. The partners have been entitled to 10 per cent interest on capital and have shared profits in the ratio 2:2:1. No salaries have been paid.

You are required to devise a scheme of share issue in satisfaction of capital which preserves the partners' rights in the distribution of profits, and which maximises the number of ordinary shares in issue. The scheme should be proved by sharing the distribution of a profit of £10,000 as partners and as shareholders.

INVESTMENT ACCOUNTS

16.1 NATURE OF AN INVESTMENT

A company may purchase shares and debentures of other companies or government stocks. The reason may be:

(a) In order to generate income, e.g. a holding of ordinary shares which is below 20 per cent of the total ordinary shares, or any purchase of preference shares, debenture stock or government stock. Such an investment may be in conjunction with a sinking fund.
(b) In order to participate in or control another company's trading operations, e.g. a holding of ordinary shares totalling 20 per cent or more or the investee company's total ordinary shares. A holding of 20–50 per cent is generally called an 'associate company', and a holding in excess of 50 per cent is generally called a 'subsidiary'.

This chapter is concerned with the recording of the investment in the investor company's accounts. In the following chapters the preparation of consolidated accounts involving subsidiary and associate companies is considered in depth.

16.2 INVESTMENT ACCOUNT

A purchase of shares or debentures is recorded in an Investment account. This has three columns to show:

(a) nominal value of stock or number of shares
(b) income received
(c) capital carrying value.

16.2.1 **Purchase of investment**

Dr   Investment a/c   (*capital column*)
    Cr   Cash a/c
with cost of investment

Enter nominal value/number of shares purchased to debit side of account.

16.2.2 **Bonus issue on shares held**

This does not affect the capital column. Enter number of shares only received to debit side of numbers column.

16.2.3 **Rights issue on shares held**

(a) Rights taken up
Entries as for purchase of investment above.
(b) Rights sold nil paid
Dr   Cash a/c
    Cr   Investment a/c   (*capital column*)
   with proceeds received.

No change is made to the number of shares.

16.2.4 **Determining average cost**

When two or more purchases have occurred the average cost is found by dividing the aggregate nominal value/number of shares into the aggregate capital column cost.

16.2.5 **Sale of investments**

The entry is in three stages:

(a) Dr   Cash a/c
      Cr   Investment a/c   (*capital column*)
   with sale proceeds.

Enter nominal value/number of shares sold to credit side of account.

(b) Carry forward the closing nominal value/number of shares and average cost thereof in the capital column.

(c) Balancing figure in the capital column represents profit or loss on sale, which is transferred to the Profit and loss account.

16.2.6 **Receipt of income**

(a) Receipt of dividends/interest:
  Dr Cash a/c
    Cr Investment a/c (*income column*)
  with amount received.

(b) At end of period:
  Dr Investment a/c (*income column*)
    Cr Profit and loss a/c
  with total income received in the period.

Example

Diverse Plc prepares accounts on the 31 December. During 19X2 the company entered into the following transactions in 25 p ordinary shares of Object Plc.

1 Feb   Purchased 1,000 shares at £4 each.
1 Mar   Received a 1-for-4 bonus issue.
1 Apr   Object Plc made a 1-for-10 rights issue. Diverse Plc sold 75 shares nil paid for £1 each, and took up 50 shares at £2.10 each.
1 May   Sold 500 shares for £7 each.
30 Jun   Received a 10 per cent dividend on the shares held.
1 Aug   Purchased 200 shares for £3.60 each.
1 Oct   Sold 400 shares for £3.75 each.
31 Dec   Received a 20 per cent dividend on the shares held.

Required:
Record the transactions in the Investment account in the books of Diverse Plc.

Investment account

Date		Number	Income £	Capital £	Date		Number	Income £	Capital £
1 Feb	Cash a/c – purchase	1,000	–	4,000	1 Apr	Cash a/c – rights sold	–	–	75
1 Mar	Bonus issue	250	–	–	1 Apr	Balance c/d	1,300	–	4,030
1 Apr	Cash a/c – rights taken up	50	–	105					
		1,300		£4,105			1,300		£4,105
1 Apr	Balance b/d (*Average £3.10*)	1,300	–	4,030	1 May	Cash a/c – sale	500	–	3,500
1 May	Profit and loss a/c – profit on sale	–	–	1,950	1 May	Balance c/d (*at £3.10*)	800	–	2,480
		1,300	–	£5,980			1,300	–	£5,980
1 May	Balance b/d	800	–	2,480	30 Jun	Cash a/c – dividend (*800 × £0.25 × 10%*)	–	20	–
1 Aug	Cash a/c – purchase	200	–	720	1 Aug	Balance c/d	1,000	–	3,200
1 Aug	Balance c/d	–	20	–					
		1,000	£20	£3,200			1,000	£20	£3,200
1 Aug	Balance b/d (*Average £3.20*)	1,000	–	3,200	1 Aug	Balance b/d	–	20	–
1 Oct	Profit and loss a/c Profit on sale	–	–	220	1 Oct	Cash a/c – sale	400	–	1,500
31 Dec	Profit and loss a/c – income	–	50	–	31 Dec	Cash a/c – dividend (*600 × £0.25 × 20%*)	–	30	–
					31 Dec	Balance c/f (*at £3.20*)	600	–	1,920
		1,000	£50	£3,420			1,000	£50	£3,420

Exercises to Chapter 16

A company has entered into various transactions in the shares of *A* Plc, as follows:

1 Jan Purchased 500 shares at £2 each.

1 Feb Took up all shares available under a 1-for-5 rights issue at £1.80.

1 Mar Received a 1-for-12 bonus issue.

1 Apr Sold one-half of the holding for net proceeds of £2.50 per share.

1 May Purchased a further 425 shares for £2.40 per share.

1 June Sold one-third of the holding for net proceeds of £2.60 per share.

You are required to write up the Investment account, and identify the final balance carried forward, assuming sales are dealt with on an average basis.

PART V

GROUP ACCOUNTS

CONSOLIDATED BALANCE SHEET — DIRECT SUBSIDIARY

17.1 INTRODUCTION

17.1.1 Consolidated accounts

In Chapter 16 we examined the technique of accounting for an investment of shares in another company.

In the situation where the investment represents a controlling interest, such as a holding of more than 50 per cent of shares, then a special relationship exists. The term 'subsidiary' is used. In the separate accounts of the investor the rules set out in Chapter 16 will apply. However, in addition, a consolidated Balance sheet and consolidated Profit and loss account will be prepared, showing the position of both companies added together; that is, as if they were a single entity.

17.1.2 Definitions

(a) *Group* – a holding company together with its subsidiaries.
(b) *Holding company* – a company is a holding company of another if that other company is its subsidiary as defined below.
(c) *Subsidiary* – is a company (i) in which another company either holds more than half the nominal value of equity shares or is a member of it and controls the composition of the board of directors; or (ii) which is a subsidiary of a subsidiary.
(d) *Direct subsidiary* – a subsidiary by reason of a direct shareholding by the holding company.
(e) *Indirect subsidiary* – a subsidiary by reason of shares held by another subsidiary of the ultimate holding company. There may or may not be a direct holding of shares in an indirect subsidiary.

17.1.3 Objective of a consolidated Balance sheet

To show the position of the holding company as if it had acquired the net assets of the subsidiary rather than the shares.

The terms 'consolidated' implies that a single Balance sheet is prepared for all companies within a group.

17.2 BASIC TECHNIQUE

To deal thoroughly with the technique of preparing a consolidated Balance sheet, we will start with a simple example and gradually build in additional features until a realistic standard is attained. We will then be able to set out an exam technique which deals effectively and efficiently with a typical exam question.

17.2.1 Basic example

We will refer to the holding company as H, and the subsidiary as S throughout.

Example 1	*H*	*S*
Balance sheets at 31 December 19X1	£	£
Fixed assets	1,000	400
Net current assets	600	250
Investment in shares of S	750	–
	£2,350	£650
Ordinary shares of £1	1,100	500
Reserves	1,250	150
	£2,350	£650

H has purchased 100 per cent of the shares of S.

The following points are relevant:

1 If H had purchased the net assets of S (£650) for £750, then we would say that the excess of £100 represented goodwill. In a consolidated Balance sheet the goodwill also arises, but is called 'goodwill on consolidation'. It is found by comparing the investment (from H Balance sheet) with the share capital and reserves of S (from S Balance sheet).

2 To find the consolidated fixed assets and net current assets, we add together the figures for H and S.
3 Only the share capital of H appears in the consolidated Balance sheet.
4 Only the reserves of H appear in the consolidated Balance sheet.

The CONSOLIDATED BALANCE SHEET will appear thus:

	£
Goodwill on consolidation $(£750 - (500 + 150))$	100
Other fixed assets $(£1,000 + 400)$	1,400
Net current assets $(£600 + 250)$	850
	£2,350
Ordinary shares of £1 (H *only*)	1,100
Reserves (H *only*)*	1,250
	£2,350

*This will be adapted in more complex examples.

17.2.2 Pre- and post-acquisition reserves

In Example 1 we dealt with a consolidation at the same date that the shares were purchased. All of the reserves of S had been earned before the acquisition, and were taken into the goodwill calculation. We call these 'pre-acquisition reserves'. In general all pre-acquisition reserves are treated in this way.

When a subsidiary increases its reserves after acquisition, then these reserves are added to those of the holding company in the consolidated Balance sheet. We call these reserves 'post-acquisition reserves'.

It is always necessary to split subsidiary reserves into pre-acquisition and post-acquisition.

Example 2

Facts as in Example 1, except that H had purchased the shares of S in an earlier period when S reserves were £100.

The following points are relevant:

1 Out of the S reserves total of £150 we are told that £100 are earned pre-acquisition. These are taken together with the S share capital and

compared with the investment in *H* Balance sheet to find the goodwill on consolidation.

2 The balance of *S* reserves, £50, are earned post-acquisition, and can be treated as reserves in the consolidated Balance sheet.

The CONSOLIDATED BALANCE SHEET will appear thus:

	£
Goodwill on consolidation (*£750 − (500 + 100)*)	150
Other fixed assets (*£1,000 + 400*)	1,400
Net current assets (*£600 + 250*)	850
	£2,400
Ordinary shares of £1 (H *only*)	1,100
Reserves (*£1,250 + 50*)	1,300
	£2,400

17.2.3 Minority interests

Examples 1 and 2 both deal with a 100 per cent holding of shares by *H* in *S*. When *H* acquires less than 100 per cent (but more than 50 per cent), then the remaining shareholders are referred to as 'the minority shareholders'.

Example 3

Facts as in Example 2, except that *H* acquired 80 per cent of the shares of *S* at a cost of £750, when *S* reserves were £100.

The following points are relevant:

1 Fixed assets and net current assets will continue to be the total of *H* and *S* added together.

2 Share capital of *H* only will continue to be shown in the Balance sheet.

3 The share capital of *S* will be divided in two parts. *H* share only is taken to the goodwill calculation. The minority share is the first part of the 'minority shareholders interests'.

4 The reserves of *S* will be divided into three parts. The minority share of the total is the second part of the 'minority shareholders interests'. *H* share of the pre-acquisition reserve is taken to the goodwill calculation. *H* share of the post-acquisition reserve is added to *H* reserves in the consolidated Balance sheet.

5   The total of minority shareholders interests will appear as a credit item in the consolidated Balance sheet, beneath the share capital and reserves.

The CONSOLIDATED BALANCE SHEET will appear thus:

	£
Goodwill on consolidation (£750 − (80% × 500) − (80% × 100))	270
Other fixed assets (£1,000 + 400)	1,400
Net current assets (£600 + 250)	850
	£2,520
Ordinary shares of £1 (H *only*)	1,100
Reserves (£1,250 + (80% × £50))	1,290
	2,390
Minority interests (20% × £500) + (20% × £150))	130
	£2,520

17.2.4 Organising the workings

We have now reached the stage where we need to consider a structured form of workinngs. In practice, columnar workings are normally used. For exam purposes it is always safer to use T accounts.

Four T accounts are used:

Name of account	Purpose	Balance represents
S Reserves a/c	Divide S reserves into three parts	No balance remains
Consolidated Reserves a/c	To add together H reserves and H share of S post-acquisition reserves	Credit balance is the reserves figure for the consolidated Balance sheet
Adjustment a/c	To compare the investment with H share of S share capital and pre-acquisition reserves	Debit balance is goodwill on consolidation
Minority a/c	To add together minority share of S share capital and total reserves	Credit balance is the minority shareholders' interests

The double entry to the T accounts can be summarised thus:

Step	Technique
1	Transfer investment from H Balance sheet to debit side of Adjustment a/c
2	Transfer S share capital in two parts: (a) H share to credit side of Adjustment a/c (b) Minority share to credit side of Minority a/c
3	Transfer H reserves to credit side of consolidated Reserves a/c
4	Transfer S reserves to credit side of S Reserves a/c

5	Double entry for S reserves in three parts:
	(a) Dr S Reserves a/c
	    Cr Minority a/c
	    with Minority share of total
	(b) Dr S Reserves a/c
	    Cr Adjustment a/c
	    with H share of pre-acquisition
	(c) Dr S Reserves a/c
	    Cr Consolidated Reserves a/c
	    with H share of post-acquisition

6	Calculate balances to carry down in: (a) Consolidated Reserve a/c (b) Minority a/c (c) Adjustment a/c

Using the figures in Example 3 the workings would appear thus:

S Reserves account

	£		£
Minority a/c (*20% × 150*)	30	Balance b/f	150
Adjustment a/c (*80% × 100*)	80	(*pre-acq. 100*)	
Consolidated reserves a/c		(*post-acq. 50*)	
(*80% × 50*)	40		
	£150		£150

Consolidated reserves account

	£		£
		Balance b/f – H	1,250
		S Reserves a/c	40
Balance c/f	1,290		
	£1,290		£1,290

Adjustment account

	£		£
Investment	750	S share capital	
		(*80% × 500*)	400
		S Reserves a/c	80
		Balance c/f – goodwill	
		on consolidation	270
	£750		£750

Minority account

	£		£
		S share capital	
		(*20% × 500*)	100
		S Reserves a/c	30
Balance c/f	130		
	£130		£130

Each of the balances carried forward can be traced to the consolidated Balance sheet. No workings are normally necessary for the fixed assets, net current assets or *H* Share capital.

17.2.5 Reserve on consolidation

The balance which arose on the Adjustment account above was a debit balance, and was described as goodwill on consolidation. It is quite possible, although it occurs less frequently, for a credit balance to arise. In that case the balance is called a 'reserve arising on consolidation'. It is kept separate from other reserves, but is included in the reserves part of the Balance sheet. It represents a non-distributable reserve.

17.2.6 Preference shares in the subsidiary

Where a subsidiary has both ordinary shares and preference shares the holding company may own a percentage of each type of share.

The following points arise:

1 It is the holding of a majority of ordinary shares which determines subsidiary status. The holding in preference shares may be less than 50 per cent of the total preference shares.

2 The cost of both ordinary and preference shares held is debited to the Adjustment account.

3 The nominal value of both ordinary and preference shares is divided between the Adjustment account and the Minority account according to the percentage held in each.

4 Subsidiary reserves are divided using the ordinary shareholding percentages.

5 A single balance of goodwill on consolidation is carried forward in the Adjustment account.

6 A single balance of minority shareholders' interests is carried forward in the Minority account.

17.2.7 Debentures or loan stock in the subsidiary

In addition to shares the holding company may hold stock in a subsidiary. As with preference shares the percentage held does not affect subsidiary status, and may be less than 50 per cent of the total stock.

The following points arise:

1 The cost of stock held is debited to the Adjustment account.

2 The holding company's share of the nominal value of stock is credited to the Adjustment account.

3 The remainder of the nominal value of stock appears in the consolidated Balance sheet. This is because it is a creditor of the group, and not part of minority shareholders' interests. In this respect the treatment differs from preference shares.

Example 4

	H	S
Balance sheets at 31 December 19X1	£	£
Fixed assets	1,000	700
Net current assets	600	350
Investment in S:		
– Ordinary shares	750	–
– Debenture stock	300	–
Debenture stock	–	(400)
	£2,650	£650

Ordinary shares of £1	1,100	500
Reserves	1,550	150
	£2,650	£650

H purchased 80 per cent of the shares of *S* and 60 per cent of the debenture stock when *S* reserves where £100.

Required:
A consolidated Balance sheet of *H* and its subsidiary with workings.

Adjustment account

	£		£
Cost of investments:		Nominal value of *S*	
Shares	750	Shares (*80%*)	400
Debentures	300	Debentures (*60%*)	240
		S Reserves a/c	80
		Balance c/f – goodwill	330
	£1,050		£1,050

Minority account

	£		£
		Nominal value of *S*	
		shares (*20%*)	100
Balance c/f	130	*S* Reserves a/c	30
	£130		£130

Consolidated reserves account

	£		£
		Balance b/f – H	1,550
Balance c/f	1,590	*S* Reserves a/c	40
	£1,590		£1,590

Subsidiary reserves account

	£		£
Minority a/c (*20% × £150*)	30	Balance b/f – *S*	150
Adjustment a/c (*80% × £100*)	80		
Consolidated reserves a/c			
(*90% × (£150 − 100)*)	40		
	£150		£150

H and its subsidiary
Consolidated Balance sheet at 31 December 19X1

	£
Goodwill on consolidation	330
Other fixed assets *(£1,000 + 700)*	1,700
Net current assets *(£600 + 350)*	950
	2,980
Debentures *(40% × £400)*	(160)
	£2,820
Ordinary shares of £1	1,100
Reserves	1,590
	2,690
Minority shareholders' interests	130
	£2,820

17.2.8 Treatment of goodwill

In each example considered we have shown goodwill in the Balance sheet as an asset. This treatment now requires modification.

In practice there are two acceptable treatments of goodwill. These are:

(a) Compute the goodwill in the Adjustment account, and reserves in the consolidated Reserves account. On the consolidated Balance sheet the goodwill is then eliminated by deduction from the reserves. Only the net amount of reserves will then be carried forward into the future.
(b) Record the goodwill as an intangible fixed asset, and provide depreciation over the useful life of the goodwill.

The first of these two treatments is simpler, and will therefore be used exclusively in this text. (The same treatment is also the most commonly used in practice.)

17.3 CONSOLIDATION ADJUSTMENTS

Having considered the basic double-entry consolidation technique we now consider the various adjustments which may arise in the course of a consolidation. Each is explained in turn, and an illustration of a typical exam mixture is then given at the end of the section.

17.3.1 Elimination of inter-company balances

Since the holding company and subsidiaries are separate legal entities, they are able to trade with each other. Their separate Balance sheets will reflect debtor and creditor balances from inter-company transactions.

In theory the debtor in one Balance sheet should be matched by an equal creditor in another Balance sheet.

In practice the balances may not be equal since goods and cash may still be in transit at a Balance-sheet date, and therefore, not recorded by the receiving company.

On consolidation the following steps are taken:

1. Goods and cash in transit are recorded by the holding company (regardless of whether they were the sender or receiver). The entry is:

    Dr Stock in transit (*Balance sheet*) or
            Cash in transit (*Balance sheet*)
    Cr Inter-company account in holding company's books.

2. The inter-company accounts should now be equal and opposite, and should be cancelled.

The effect is that only third-party debtors and creditors appear in the consolidated Balance sheet.

Example 5

At 31.12.X1 the Balance sheet of H showed a debtor due from S of £5,500. The Balance sheet of S showed a creditor due to H of £4,250. On investigation it transpired that there was stock in transit from H to S at an invoice price of £850, and cash in transit from S to H of £400.

The consolidation adjustments will be:

(a) Stock in transit
        Dr Stock a/c   £850
        Cr Current a/c in H books   £850

(b) Cash in transit

        Dr Cash a/c   £400
        Cr Current a/c in H books   £400

(c) Cancel reconciled balances

> Dr Current a/c in *S* books £4,250
> Cr Current a/c in *H* books   £4,250

N.B. Bank accounts – where one group company has a favourable bank balance, and another has an overdraft, then the two are not netted off unless the balances are at the same bank, and the bank has the right of set-off.

17.3.2 Bills of exchange

A bill of exchange is a piece of paper which the creditor (acceptor of the bill) signs to say that a given sum of money will be paid to the holder of the bill on a specified date (a legal definition is given in Chapter 28)

Once accepted the creditor balance in the paying company's books is changed to a bill payable. The debtor balance in the receiving company is changed to a bill receivable of an identical amount.

The bill payable cannot be reduced other than by paying it.

The bill receivable is a valuable asset and can be sold (less a percentage commission). When a bill receivable is sold we say it is 'discounted'.

When a holding company and subsidiary have used bills of exchange to settle their balances, then on consolidation:

1. Identify how much of the total bills RECEIVABLE in both holding company and subsidiary books (i.e. the total NOT discounted) relates to other group companies.
2. Cancel this amount against BOTH bills receivable and bills payable.

The effect is that an amount equal to the bills discounted will continue to appear as a bill payable, since this is the group's liability to third parties.

Example 6

At 31.12.X1 the Balance sheet of *H* showed bills payable of £6,500, of which £3,500 were to *S*.

On the same date the Balance sheet of *S* showed bills receivable of £4,200, of which £2,000 were from *H*.

The consolidation adjustment will be:

(a) Amount of bills receivable which are inter-company is £2,000 (the additional balance of £1,500 which *H* shows as payable must have been discounted by *S* and so cannot be cancelled).

(b) Cancel inter-company bill

Dr	Bills payable in *H* books	£2,000	
Cr	Bills receivable in *S* books		£2,000

(c) On consolidation:

Bills receivable are now	£2,200 (*i.e.* £4,200–2,000)
Bills payable are now	£4,500 (*i.e.* £6,500–2,000)

17.3.3 Unrealised profit on stock

Transactions between group companies will almost certainly include some profit to the selling company. This is quite normal. However if, at the date of consolidation, there remains unsold stock which has been purchased from another group company at a profit, then that stock is not at cost to the group, and the profit is an unrealised profit so far as the group is concerned.

The steps to eliminate the profit are:

1. Calculate the unrealised profit in the unsold stock (ignore stock which has now been sold outside the group).
2. Eliminate the profit against consolidated reserves:
   Dr   Consolidated reserves a/c
   Cr   Stock a/c.

Elimination against consolidated reserves is one of three acceptable methods, but is recommended as the simplest and the most prudent.

Example 7

At 31.12.X1 *S* holds stock which was purchased from *H* at cost to *H* plus 25 per cent. The invoice price was £5,000.

The consolidation adjustment will be:

(a) Calculate unrealised profit

$$£5,000 \times \frac{25}{125} = £1,000$$

(N.B. Profit percentage calculations were dealt with in Chapter 5.)

(b) Eliminate profit

Dr	Consolidated reserves a/c	£1,000
Cr	Stock a/c	£1,000

17.3.4 Subsidiary proposed dividends

Where a subsidiary has proposed dividends at a Balance-sheet date it is important that the minority shareholders' share appears under 'Creditors: amounts falling due within one year' and not as part of the long-term minority shareholders' interest in capital and reserves.

Such minority dividends are in addition to the holding company's own proposed dividends.

In the consolidated workings the technique is:

1. Open a Dividend elimination account.
2. If the subsidiary has provided for its dividends, then transfer the proposed dividend to the credit side of the Dividend elimination account.
3. If the subsidiary has not provided for its dividends then:
   Dr S Reserves a/c
   Cr Dividend elimination a/c with the proposed dividend.
4. If the holding company has taken credit for its share of the dividend, then transfer the dividend receivable to the debit side of the Dividend elimination account.
5. If the holding company has not taken credit for its share of the dividend, then:

   Dr Dividend elimination a/c
   Cr Consolidated reserves a/c with the holding company's share of the dividend.
6. The balance on the Dividend elimination account represents the minority dividends, and is shown in the consolidated Balance sheet in the creditor section.
7. The balance on S Reserves account represents retained reserves only, and is now available for sharing out in the usual manner.

Example 8

At 31.12.X1 S has not provided for ordinary dividends of £8,000. H, which holds 80 per cent of S ordinary shares, has not taken credit for its share of the dividend.

Required:

Write up the Dividend elimination account.

Dividend elimination account

	£		£
Consolidated reserves a/c – dividend receivable (*80% × 8,000*)	6,400	S Reserves a/c – proposed dividend	8,000
Balance c/f – minority dividends	1,600		
	£8,000		£8,000

17.3.5 Dividends from pre-acquisition profits

When a subsidiary pays a dividend to the holding company the normal entry is for the holding company to credit its Profit and loss account.

However, when a dividend is paid AFTER acquisition, but charged by the subsidiary to the profits of a period earned BEFORE acquisition, then the net assets of the subsidiary at the date of acquisition will have been reduced. The value of the subsidiary's shares will consequently also be reduced. The holding company must check the amount at which the investment in the subsidiary is stated in its Balance sheet. No investment should ever be stated at an amount higher than its long-term value.

Two points arise:

1 Double entry for the receipt of the dividend
   (a) If the dividend does not reduce the value of shares in the subsidiary below their stated value:
       Dr Cash a/c
       Cr *H* Profit and loss a/c

   (b) If the dividend does reduce the value of those shares:

       Dr Cash a/c
       Cr Investment in shares of *S* a/c

It is quite possible for a split to occur in the credit entry.

2 The balance of subsidiary reserves at the date of acquisition which is used in dividing the subsidiary reserves between pre- and post-acquisition, should be adjusted so that it is AFTER paying the dividend.
   There is no double entry for this, since the figure of reserves at acquisition is used in the workings only.

Example 9

At 31.12.X1 *H* purchased 70 of *S* ordinary shares for £85,000 cum-div. On that date, S profit and loss account showed a balance of £26,000. Subsequently, *S* declared and paid a dividend of £10,000 out of the profits of 19X1. The shares in *S* will fall in value by the amount of the dividend.

Required:
Entries for receipt of the dividend by *H*.

(a) Entry for dividend is:
     Dr Cash a/c   £7,000
     Cr Cost of investment in *S* a/c
          (*70% × £10,000 = £7,000*)   £7,000

(b) Adjust *S* pre-acquisition reserves:

	£
Balance on 31.12.X1	26,000
Dividend declared subsequently	(10,000)
Adjusted pre-acquisition reserves	£16,000

17.3.6 Revaluation of subsidiary assets

When a holding company purchases a controlling interest of shares in a subsidiary, the consolidated accounts will show the position just as if a 'purchase' has occurred. The consolidated Balance sheet will show the 'cost to the group' of the subsidiary's assets. This will be the value placed upon these assets by the holding company.

In most cases the holding company will require the subsidiary to revalue its assets to their 'fair value'. It follows that depreciation in the subsidiary and consolidated accounts will be that charged after acquisition only, and based on the revalued amount. Where this revaluation has been made, then no problems arise.

However, where a subsidiary has not revalued its assets to fair value at the date of acquisition, then adjustments will be necessary on consolidation. The effect of the adjustments will be to show the position as if the subsidiary had revalued the assets.

The required adjustments are:

1 Compare the fair value of subsidiary assets at acquisition with their net book value on the same date.
2 Enter the pre-acquisition revaluation surplus (*deficit*) by:

Dr   Asset cost a/c with surplus (*deficit*)
Cr   Adjustment a/c with holding company %
Cr   Minority a/c with minority %.

3 Compare charges for depreciation after acquisition based on fair value with actual charges.
4 Enter the post-acquisition depreciation increase (*write back*) by:

Dr   Subsidiary profit and loss a/c
Cr   Accumulated depreciation a/c.

5 Identify the subsidiary accumulated depreciation at acquisition and eliminate by:

Dr   Accumulated depreciation a/c
Cr   Asset cost a/c

Example 10

The Balance sheet of S includes the following fixed assets:

	£
Cost on 1.1.X1	10,000
Depreciation to 31.12.X3	(3,000)
Net book value on 31.12.X3	7,000
Depreciation for 19X4	(1,000)
Net book value on 31.12.X4	£6,000

On 31.12.X3 *H* purchased 80 per cent of the ordinary shares in *S*, valuing the fixed asset at £9,000 on that date with a ten-year remaining life. No revaluation was recorded by *S*.
On consolidation the adjustments will be:

(a) Compute pre-acquisition revaluation surplus

	£
Fair value at 31.12.X3	9,000
Net book value at 31.12.X3	7,000
Surplus	£2,000

(b) Enter surplus

Dr	Fixed-asset cost a/c	£2,000	
Cr	Adjustment a/c (*80% × £2,000*)		£1,600
Cr	Minority a/c (*25% × £2,000*)		400

(c) Compute post-acquisition depreciation adjustment

	£
Charge for 19X4 on fair value (*10% × £9,000*)	900
Actual charge	1,000
Over provision	£100

(d) Write-back over provision

Dr	Accumulated depreciation a/c	£100	
Cr	*S* Reserves a/c		£100

(e) Eliminate depreciation at acquisition

Dr	Accumulated depreciation a/c	£3,000	
Cr	Fixed asset cost a/c		£3,000

The adjusted figures are now:

	£
Fixed asset cost a/c (*£10,000 + 2,000 – 3,000*)	9,000
Accumulated depreciation a/c (*£4,000 - 100 – 3,000*)	(900)
Adjusted net book value at 31.12.X4	£8,100

17.3.7 Piecemeal acquisition

A piecemeal acquisition occurs when the holding company acquires its investment in the subsidiary as two or more smaller purchases.

The following points are relevant:

1 Cost of shares taken to Adjustment account is the total of the costs of the separate purchases.
2 Nominal value of subsidiary shares is divided between Adjustment account and Minority account on the basis of the final shareholding at the Balance-sheet date.

3 Subsidiary reserves are split on a piecemeal basis:

  (i) Minority a/c: Total reserves × final shareholding.
  (ii) Adjustment a/c: Reserves at each purchase date × % purchased
       at each date.
  (iii) Consolidated reserves a/c: The simplest method is to take the
        balance on the subsidiary reserves account.

The Adjustment account posting from the Subsidiary Reserves account
is the trickiest part. The piecemeal treatment is applied as soon as the
total shares held exceeds 20 per cent (not 50 per cent).

Example 11

H acquires S in two stages. 30 per cent of shares were purchased when S
reserves were £10,000, and a further 45 per cent of shares when S reserves
were £12,000. The S reserves are £15,000 at the Balance-sheet date.
Required:
Show the division of S reserves.

S reserves account

	£		£
Minority a/c		Balance b/f	15,000
(25% × £15,000)	3,750		
Adjustment a/c			
(30% × £10,000) +			
(45% × £12,000)	8,400		
Consolidated reserves a/c			
(balance)	2,850		
	£15,000		£15,000

17.4 EXAM TECHNIQUE – SUMMARY

The approach to a consolidated Balance sheet should be:

Step 1: Calculate the shareholding percentages of H and minority in
         ordinary shares, preference shares and debentures.
Step 2: Open T account workings.
Step 3: Deal with consolidation adjustments in a systematic double-
         entry fashion.

Step 4:   Main consolidation:
- cost of shares of *S* held by *H*
- *S* nominal value
- *S* reserves
- carry-down balances.

Step 5:   Cross-cast remaining balances to establish the consolidated Balance sheet.

Example 12 – typical exam question

The following are the draft Balance sheets of Hold Plc and its subsidiary Sub Ltd on 31 December 19X5

	£	£	£	£
Plant at cost	114,000		63,500	
Accumulated depreciation	(32,400)	81,600	(24,250)	39,250
Fixtures at cost	34,000		9,450	
Accumulated depreciation	(10,500)	23,500	(4,600)	4,850
Investment in Sub Ltd		75,000		
		180,100		44,100
Stock at cost	26,000		23,900	
Trade debtors	28,400		32,450	
Current account with Sub Ltd	4,750			
Cash at bank			3,200	
	£59,150		£59,550	
Trade creditors	(22,120)		(28,410)	
Corporation tax	(9,520)		(6,480)	
Current account with Hold Plc			(3,250)	
Overdraft	(2,850)			
Proposed ordinary dividends	(10,000)		(6,000)	
	£(44,490)		£(44,140)	
		14,660		15,410
		£194,760		£59,510
Ordinary shares of £1		100,000		40,000
Profit and loss account		94,760		19,510
		£194,760		£59,510

The following information is relevant:

1 Hold Plc acquired 60 per cent of the shares in Sub Ltd on 31 December 19X2 when that company's Profit and loss account was £9,500; and a further 25 per cent of the shares on 31 December 19X3 when the Sub Ltd Profit and loss account stood at £12,000.

2 At 31.12.X1 there was cash in transit from Sub Ltd to Hold Plc of £1,500.
3 Included in the stock of Hold Plc are goods purchased from Sub Ltd for £8,000. This represents a transfer price of cost plus $33\frac{1}{3}$ per cent.
4 Goodwill is to be eliminated against reserves.

Required:
Prepare a consolidated Balance sheet at 31 December 19X5, together with relevant workings.

HOLD PLC AND ITS SUBSIDIARY CONSOLIDATED BALANCE SHEET AT 31 DECEMBER 19X5

	£	£
Fixed assets – tangible		
Plant at cost	177,500	
Accumulated depreciation	(56,650)	120,850
Fixtures at cost	43,450	
Accumulated depreciation	(15,100)	28,350
		149,200
Current assets		
Stock at cost (£26,000 + 23,900 − 2,000)	47,900	
Trade debtors	60,850	
Cash at bank	3,200	
Cash in transit	1,500	
	£113,450	
Creditors: amounts falling due within one year		
Trade creditors	(50,530)	
Corporation tax	(16,000)	
Overdraft	(2,850)	
Proposed dividends – Hold Plc	(10,000)	
– Minority (W6)	(900)	
	£(80,280)	
Net current assets		33,170
Total assets *less* current liabilities		£182,370

	£
Capital and reserves	
Called-up share capital	100,000
Profit and loss account (W4)	73,443
Minority interests (W3)	8,927
	£182,370

WORKINGS

(1) Shareholdings

		%
Hold Plc	– 31.12.X2	60
	– 31.12.X3	25
		85
Minority		15
		100

(2) *Adjustment account*

	£		£
Investment	75,000	Nominal value	34,000
		(85% × £40,000)	
		S Reserves a/c	8,700
		Consolidated reserves a/c	
		– goodwill eliminated	32,300
	£75,000		£75,000

(3) *Minority account*

	£		£
		Nominal value	6,000
		(15% × £40,000)	
Balance c/f	8,927	S Reserves a/c	2,927
	£8,927		£8,927

(4) *Consolidated reserves account*

	£		£
Stock a/c – provision for unrealised profit		Balance b/f – Hold plc	94,760
		Dividend elimination a/c	
$(\dfrac{33.1/3}{133.1/3} \times £8,000)$	2,000	– dividend receivable	5,100
		S Reserves a/c	7,883
Adjustment a/c – goodwill eliminated	32,300		
Balance c/f	73,443		
	£107,743		£107,743

(5) *Sub Ltd reserves account*

	£		£
Minority a/c		Balance b/f – Sub Ltd	19,510
(15% × £19,510)	2,927		
Adjustment a/c			
(60% × £9,500) + (25%			
× £12,000)	8,700		
Consolidated reserves a/c			
(balance)	7,883		
	£19,510		£19,510

(6) *Dividend elimination account*

	£		£
Consolidated reserves a/c		Proposed dividend	6,000
(85% × £6,000)	5,100		
Balance c/f – minority			
dividend	900		
	£6,000		£6,000

Exercises to Chapter 17

1. *H* purchased 80 per cent of the ordinary shares of *S* for £72,000.
S's total ordinary share capital is £65,000 and total reserves are currently £25,000. At the date of acquisition *S*'s total reserves were
£10,000. *H*'s total reserves are currently £48,000.

   You are required to compute:

   (a) the goodwill on consolidation of *S*;
   (b) the minority interests in *S*; and
   (c) the consolidated reserves before elimination of goodwill.

2. H has a subsidiary, *S*, with which *H* trades. At the Balance-sheet date
H had bills payable of £8,500, of which £6,000 were to *S*. *H* also had
bills receivable of £3,300, of which £2,500 were from *S*. *S* had bills
payable of £3,800, of which £3000 were to *H*. *S* also had bills receivable of £7,200, of which £4,800 were from *H*. You are required to compute the amount of bills receivable and bills payable that will appear in
the consolidated Balance sheet.

3. S sells stock to its holding company H. At the year end, £15,000 of stock at transfer price from S was included in H's stock. All stock sold by S to H is at cost plus 20 per cent.

You are required to prepare a journal entry to eliminate the unrealised profit in stock.

4. H acquired S as follows:

30 per cent when S reserves were £10,000;
25 per cent when S reserves were £15,000
20 per cent when S reserves were £20,000.

S reserves are now £28,000.
You are required to allocate S reserves between:

(a) group pre-acquisition;
(b) group post-acquisition; and
(c) minority shareholders.

CONSOLIDATED BALANCE
SHEET — INDIRECT
SUBSIDIARY

18.1 VERTICAL AND MIXED GROUPS

In Section 17.1.2 we defined an indirect subsidiary as a subsidiary by reason of shares held by another subsidiary of the ultimate holding company.

Two such situations can arise (Figure 18.1).

fig 18.1 *examples of vertical and mixed group structures*

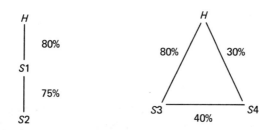

Both $S1$ and $S3$ are direct subsidiaries of H. $S2$ is an indirect subsidiary of H, since it is a direct subsidiary of $S1$, which is a direct subsidiary of H. H controls $S1$, which in turn controls $S2$.

$S4$ is neither a direct subsidiary of H nor $S3$. But it is a subsidiary of H, since H can control 70 per cent of the votes of $S4$: 30 per cent by a direct shareholding, plus a further 40 per cent due to the controlling holding in $S3$. It does not matter that H owns less than 100 per cent of $S3$. Indeed, 51 per cent would be adequate to give H CONTROL of $S3$.

18.2 TECHNIQUE

18.2.1 Subsidiary proposed dividends

As with the basic technique in Chapter 17, proposed dividends of each subsidiary must be fully dealt with before consolidation commences. When dealing with an indirect subsidiary the key is to allocate dividends on the basis of DIRECT shareholdings. This is best done by drawing a picture and following the percentages shown.

A Dividend elimination account is again used, with the objective of showing a final balance of subsidiary dividends which will be paid to outside shareholders.

Example 1

fig **18.2** *group structure*

All holdings are in ordinary shares. *S1* has a proposed dividend of £10,000, and *S2* of £8,000. There is a minority interest of 30 per cent in *S1* (being shares not held by *H*), and 35 per cent in *S2* (being shares not held by *H* or *S1*).

H will take credit for 70 per cent of *S1* dividends, and 25 per cent of *S2* dividends. If *H* has not already done this in its own accounts, then it is done as a consolidation adjustment by crediting consolidated reserves.

S1 will take credit for 40 per cent of *S2* dividends (either in its own accounts, or by crediting *S1* Reserves account as a consolidation adjustment).

The balance on Dividend elimination account will be 30 per cent of *S1* dividends together with 35 per cent of *S2* dividends.

Dividend elimination account

	£		£
Consolidated reserves a/c		Proposed dividends:	
– receivable from *S1*		*S1*	10,000
(*70% × £10,000*)	7,000	*S2*	8,000
– receivable from *S2*			
(*25% × £8,000*)	2,000		
S1 Reserves a/c – receivable			
from *S2* (*40% × £8,000*)	3,200		
Balance c/f – due to			
minority shareholders	5,800		
	£18,000		£18,000

The balance due to minority shareholders represents £3,000 from *S1* (*30% × 10,000*), plus £2,800 from *S2* (*35% × £8,000*).

18.2.2 Consolidation

The consolidation stage involves the compilation of indirect percentages (Figure 18.3).

Example 2

fig 18.3 *group structure*

The relevant percentages are:

	S1	*S2*
	%	%
H interest		
direct	80	–
indirect (*80 × 75*)	–	60
Minority interests (*balance*)	20	40
	100	100

322

Figure 18.4 is constructed by taking direct holdings by *H*, a proportion of indirect holdings (by reference to the percentage in the subsidiary holding shares), and then inserting the minority interests as the balancing figure.

Example 3

fig 18.4 *group structure*

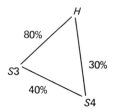

The relevant percentages are:

	S3	S4
	%	%
H interest:		
direct	80	30
indirect (*80 × 40*)	–	32
	80	62
Minority interests (*balance*)	20	38
	100	100

In both Examples 2 and 3 the resulting minority interests are composite direct plus indirect interests. Only the total identified will be used.

The consolidation proceeds as follows:

(a) Allocate cost of shares in subsidiaries between Adjustment account (debit) and Minority account (debit), using the percentages relevant to the company HOLDING THE SHARES.
(b) Allocate nominal value of subsidiary share capital between Adjustment account (credit) and Minority account (credit), using the percentages relevant to THAT SUBSIDIARY.
(c) Allocate subsidiary reserves in the normal way, using the percentages relevant to THAT SUBSIDIARY.

For Example 2 the entries will be:

Item	Adjustment a/c		Minority a/c		Consolidated reserves	
	Debit	Credit	Debit	Credit	Debit	Credit
	%	%	%	%	%	%
Cost of shares held by H in S1	100	–	–	–	–	–
Cost of shares held by S1 in S2	80	–	20	–	–	–
S1 share capital	–	80	–	20	–	–
S2 share capital	–	60	–	40	–	–
S1 reserves	–	80 pre-acq.	–	20	–	80 post-acq.
S2 reserves	–	60 pre-acq.	–	40	–	60 post-acq.

For Example 3 the entries will be:

Item	Adjustment a/c Debit	Adjustment a/c Credit	Minority a/c Debit	Minority a/c Credit	Consolidated reserves Debit	Consolidated reserves Credit
	%	%	%	%	%	%
Cost of shares held by H in S3	100	–	–	–	–	–
Cost of shares held by H in S4	100	–	–	–	–	–
Cost of shares held by S3 in S4	80	–	20	–	–	–
S3 share capital	–	80	–	20	–	–
S4 share capital	–	62	–	38	–	–
S3 reserves	–	80 pre-acq.	–	20	–	80 post-acq.
S4 reserves	–	62 pre-acq.	–	38	–	62 post-acq.

Example 4

The balance sheets of *H*, *S1* and *S2* at 31 December 19X6 are:

	H £	S1 £	S2 £
Fixed assets			
Tangible	95,400	82,150	56,930
Investments in: S1 (60%)	85,000		
S2 (75%)		45,000	
Current assets			
Stocks	42,130	29,460	21,210
Debtors	36,965	31,645	24,900
Cash at bank	2,400	16,965	
Creditors: amounts falling due within one year			
Trade creditors	(19,990)	(23,420)	(21,950)
Bank overdraft			(4,690)
Proposed dividends	(20,000)	(12,000)	(8,000)
	£221,905	£169,800	£68,400
Ordinary shares of £1	150,000	100,000	50,000
Profit and loss account	71,905	69,800	18,400
	£221,905	£169,800	£68,400

The following information is relevant:

1 *H* acquired its 60 per cent holding in *S1* when that company's reserves were £32,000. On the same date *S1* acquired its 75 per cent holding in *S2* when that company's reserves were £10,000.
2 The stock of *S1* includes stock purchased from *S2* and includes a profit of £1,000.
3 Goodwill should be eliminated against reserves.

Required:
The consolidated Balance sheet of *H* and its subsidiaries, together with workings.

H AND ITS SUBSIDIARIES

CONSOLIDATED BALANCE SHEET AT 31 DECEMBER 19X6

	£	£
Fixed assets – tangible (*£95,400 + 82,150 + 56,930*)		234,480
Current assets		
Stocks (*£42,130 + 29,460 + 21,210 – 1,000*)	91,800	
Debtors (*£36,965 + 31,645 + 24,900*)	93,510	
Cash at bank (*£2,400 + 16,965*)	19,365	
	£204,675	
Creditors: amounts falling due within one year		
Trade creditors (*£19,990 + 23,420 + 21,950*)	(65,360)	
Bank overdraft	(4,690)	
Proposed dividends		
H	(20,000)	
Minority shareholders (*W6*)	(6,800)	
	£(96,850)	
Net current assets		107,825
Total assets *less* current liabilities		£342,305
Capital and reserves		£
Called-up share capital		150,000
Profit and loss account (*W3*)		102,365
		252,365
Minority interests (*W2*)		89,940
		£342,305

WORKINGS

(1) *Adjustment account*

	£		£
Cost of shares:		Nominal value:	
Held by *H* in *S1* (*100%*)	85,000	*S1* (*60%*)	60,000
Held by *S1* in *S2* (*60%*)	27,000	*S2* (*45%*)	22,500
		S1 Reserves a/c	19,200
		S2 Reserves a/c	4,500
		Consolidated reserves a/c	
		– goodwill eliminated	5,800
	£112,000		£112,000

(2) *Minority account*

	£		£
Cost of shares held by		Nominal value:	
S1 in S2 (*40%*)	18,000	S1 (*40%*)	40,000
Balance c/f	89,940	S2 (*55%*)	27,500
		S1 Reserves a/c	30,320
		S2 Reserves a/c	10,120
	£107,940		£107,940

(3) *Consolidated reserves account*

	£		£
Stock a/c – unrealised		Balance b/f – *H*	71,905
profit	1,000	Dividend elimination	
Adjustment a/c – goodwill		a/c	7,200
eliminated	5,800	S1 Reserves a/c	26,280
Balance c/f	102,365	S2 Reserves a/c	3,780
	£109,165		£109,165

(4) *S1 Reserves account*

	£		£
Minority a/c		Balance b/f – *S1*	69,800
(*40% × £75,800*)	30,320	Dividend elimination a/c	6,000
Adjustment a/c			
(*60% × £32,000*)	19,200		
Consolidated reserves a/c			
(*balance*)	26,280		
	£75,800		£75,800

(5) *S2 Reserves account*

	£		£
Minority a/c		Balance b/f – *S2*	18,400
(*55% × £18,400*)	10,120		
Adjustment a/c			
(*45% × £10,000*)	4,500		
Consolidated reserves a/c			
(*balance*)	3,780		
	£18,400		£18,400

328

(6) *Dividend elimination account*

	£		£
Consolidated reserves a/c		Proposed dividends:	
(*60% × £12,000*)	7,200	*S1*	12,000
S1 Reserves a/c		*S2*	8,000
(*75% × £8,000*)	6,000		
Balance c/f –			
minority dividends	6,800		
	£20,000		£20,000

(7) Picture of shareholdings (see Figure 18.5)

fig **18.5** *group structure*

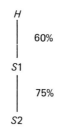

(8) Chart of shareholdings

	S1	*S2*
H interest:	%	%
direct	60	–
indirect (*60 × 75*)	–	45
Minority interest (balance)	40	55
	100	100

(N.B. It is irrelevant that this minority percentage is over 50 per cent since the chain of control *H — S1 — S2* exists.)

Exercises to Chapter 18

1. *H* acquired an 80 per cent holding in *S* when *S*'s reserves were £40,000 at a cost of £92,000. On the same date *S* acquired a 75 per cent holding in *T* at a cost of £67,000. *T*'s reserves on that date were £30,000. *S* and *T*'s share capital is £60,000 and £50,000 respectively.

You are required to compute the goodwill on *H*'s consolidation of *S* and *T*.

2. *H* has a 90 per cent interest in *S* and a 40 per cent interest in *M*. *S* also has a 30 per cent interest in *M*. *S* proposed to pay a £20,000 dividend and *M* proposed to pay a £15,000 dividend.

You are required to prepare a Dividend elimination account to identify the total dividends owing to minority shareholders.

CONSOLIDATED PROFIT AND LOSS ACCOUNT

19.1 BASIS OF CONSOLIDATION

19.1.1 Principles

The principle of consolidation involves adding together (aggregating) the separate accounts of the holding company and its subsidiaries.

Within a Profit and loss account there are three items in particular which will require adjustment from a simple aggregation. They are:

(a) *Inter-company sales.* The whole amount of sales from any group company to any other is excluded from the consolidated turnover. This adjustment is to avoid double counting the sale of one item of stock by two companies: the first time within the group and the second outside the group. As a result of the adjustment only sales outside the group are included in consolidated turnover. It follows that an identical deduction must be made in arriving at consolidated cost of sales, since a sale by one group company will be a purchase to the recipient of the goods.

(b) *Provision for unrealised profit.* In exactly the same way as we adjusted for unrealised profit on unsold stock in consolidated Balance-sheet workings we will adjust the consolidated Profit and loss account workings. The reduction in profit appears as an addition to the consolidated cost of sales.

(c) *Inter-company dividends.* All inter-company dividends, whether paid or proposed, preference or ordinary, are excluded from consolidated investment income.

19.1.2 Pro-forma consolidated Profit and loss account

Below is a typical consolidated Profit and loss account, with a description of how each figure is made up. The holding company is abbrieviated to H, and the subsidiary to S.

TYPICAL COMPANY

CONSOLIDATED PROFIT AND LOSS ACCOUNT FOR YEAR TO 31 DECEMBER

	£	Comments
Turnover	1,519,468	100% H + 100% S – inter-company sales
Cost of sales	(829,350)	100% H + 100% S – inter-company purchases + pro-vision for unrealised profit
Gross profit	690,118	Subtotal
Distribution costs	(52,930)	100% H + 100% S
Administration costs	(141,264)	
Operating profit	495,924	Subtotal
Investment income	26,300	100% H + 100% S – inter-company dividends and interest
Interest payable	(36,900)	100% H + 100% S – inter-company interest
Profit on ordinary activities before tax	485,324	Subtotal
Tax on profit on ordinary activities	(200,420)	100% H + 100% S
Profit on ordinary activities after tax	284,904	Subtotal
Minority interests	(32,100)	Minority share of S profit after tax
Attributable to members of holding company	252,804	Subtotal
Extraordinary items	22,390	100% H + H share of S
Profit for the financial year	275,194	Subtotal
Dividends	(50,000)	100% H only
Retained profit for year	225,194	Subtotal
Retained profit brought forward	562,930	100% H + H share of S post-acquisition only
Retained profit carried forward	£788,124	Total

Points arising:

1 Inter-company interest on stock is cancelled against both investment income and interest payable.
2 The minority share of the profit after tax of the subsidiary is shown as a deduction after the tax charge, but before extraordinary items.
3 Prior to the minority deduction 100 per cent of items relating to the subsidiary were aggregated. After the minority deduction only the group share of items related to the subsidiary are aggregated.
4 Dividends shown are those of the holding company only.
5 Retained profit is that of the holding company, plus the group share of the subsidiary's retained profit earned after acquisition only.
6 The final amount of retained profit carried forward should agree to the balance on the consolidated reserves account in the Balance-sheet workings.

19.2 EXAM TECHNIQUE

Having examined the structure and content of a consolidated Profit and loss account, we now need to establish an exam technique.

The most convenient form is a columnar working which requires:

(a) one column for the holding company
(b) one column for each subsidiary
(c) one column to show cancellations of sales and interest
(d) a total column which represents the final consolidated Profit and loss account figures.

The technique is best illustrated with an example.

Example 1

H Plc acquired 80 per cent of the ordinary, and 25 per cent of the preference shares of *S* Plc when the retained profits of *S* Plc were £10,000. In addition *H* Plc owns 30 per cent of the loan stock of *S* Plc. The following are their draft Profit and loss accounts for the year to 31 December 19X5:

	H Plc	S Plc
	£	£
Turnover	962,212	227,383
Cost of sales	(621,679)	(169,463)
Gross profit	340,533	57,920
Distribution costs	(21,460)	(2,460)
Administration costs	(46,293)	(13,940)
	272,780	41,520
Investment income	16,900	2,400
Interest on loan stock	–	(4,000)
	289,680	39,920
Taxation	(121,340)	(13,920)
	168,340	26,000
Extraordinary items	21,500	6,000
	189,840	32,000
Dividends	(40,000)	(10,000)
Retained profits for year	149,840	22,000
Retained profit brought forward	30,000	12,000
	£179,840	£34,000

The following information is relevant:

1 Turnover of *H* included £100,129 of goods sold to *S*.
2 The stock of *S* includes an unrealised profit of £3,400.
3 The dividends of *S* are £6,000 ordinary and £4,000 preference.
4 The investment income of *H* includes £4,800 of *S* ordinary dividend, £1,000 of *S* preference dividend and £1,200 of *S* loan stock interest.

Required:
A working to support the consolidated Profit and loss account.

	H Plc	S Plc	Adjustments	Consolidated Profit and loss account
	£	£	£	£
Turnover	962,212	227,383	(100,129)	1,089,466
Cost of sales				
(i) Per question	(621,679)	(169,463)		
(ii) Provision	(3,400)	–		
(iii) Subtotal	(625,079)	(169,463)	100,129	(694,413)
Gross profit	337,133	57,920		395,053
Distribution costs	(21,460)	(2,460)		(23,920)
Administration costs	(46,293)	(13,940)		(60,233)

Operating profit	269,380	41,520		310,900
Investment income				
(*excludes* S *dividends*)	11,100	2,400	(1,200)	12,300
Interest payable	–	(4,000)	1,200	(2,800)
Profit on ordinary activities				
before taxation	280,480	39,920		320,400
Tax on profit on ordinary				
activities	(121,340)	(13,920)		(135,260)
Profit on ordinary activities				
after taxation	159,140	26,000		185,140
Minority interests				
(i) Preference dividend (*25%*)	1,000	(4,000)	(3,000) (*75%*)	–
(ii) Balance for ordinary				
shareholders		22,000	(4,400)	(7,400)
(iii) Minority shares		(*20%*) (4,400)		
Transfer ordinary dividends	4,800	(4,800)		–
	164,940	12,800		177,740
Extraordinary items	21,500	4,800		26,300
	186,440	17,600		204,040
Dividends	(40,000)	–		(40,000)
Retained profit for year	146,440	17,600		164,040
Retained profit brought				
forward	30,000	1,600*		31,600
Retained profit carried				
forward	£176,440	£19,200		£195,640

* 80% × £12,000 − 10,000 = £1,600.

Points arising:

1 The minority calculation was dealt with in two stages:
  (a) Preference dividends. The total is deducted from the S column. H's share is added to the H column and the minority share is deducted from the total column.
  (b) The balance remaining in S column is all attributable to ordinary shareholders. S ordinary percentage is deducted from the S column and the total column.

  By leaving a balance in the S column the working provides an arithmetic check throughout.
2 H share of S dividends are transferred from S column to H column without affecting the total column.

19.3 DISCLOSURE POINTS

19.3.1 Published accounts points

In Chapter 11 we examined the special disclosure requirements of a published Profit and loss account.

When dealing with a consolidated published Profit and loss account the following points should be observed:

1	Auditors' remuneration –	$100\% H + 100\% S$.
2	Depreciation and hire of plant –	$100\% H + 100\% S$.
3	Directors'remuneration –	Disclose only the directors of H, but show the amounts paid to them by both H and S. (Other directors' remuneration is charged but not disclosed.)
4	Investment income –	From third parties only.
5	Interest payable –	To third parties only.

19.3.2 Exemption from publishing holding company Profit and loss account

Group accounts are normally made up of four statements:
(a) Consolidated Balance sheet.
(b) Holding company Balance sheet.
(c) Consolidated Profit and loss account.
(d) Holding company Profit and loss account.

However, the holding company Profit and loss account need not be given provided one additional piece of information is given in the consolidated Profit and loss account.

That is the amount of group profit (normally after extraordinary items) which is dealt with in the separate books of the holding company.

In Example 1 this amount is £186,440. It can be found from the holding company's column of the columnar working immediately following the extraordinary items.

19.4 ACQUISITION DURING AN ACCOUNTING PERIOD

Where a subsidiary is acquired during an accounting period the following principles apply:

(a) The subsidiary's results are consolidated from the date of acquisition; no sooner and no later.
(b) The date of acquisition is defined as the earlier of:
   (i) the date consideration passes; or
   (ii) the date an offer for the controlling shares becomes unconditional.

(c) In the columnar working the subsidiary's results are apportioned so that only the post-acquisition results are included.
(d) Dividends paid by the subsidiary, and received by the holding company for the year of acquisition will be partly from pre-acquisition profits, and partly from post-acquisition profits. However, within the columnar working, only the post-acquisition element appears, since all amounts are apportioned. The remaining element, paid from pre-acquisition profits is received by the holding company, but does not appear in the columnar working. It is dealt with in Chapter 17, Subsection 17.3.5.

Example 2

Facts as in Example 1, except that *H* Plc acquired all its investments in *S* Plc on 1 October 19X5. The extraordinary item of *S* Plc occurred after acquisition. The inter-company sales all occurred after acquisition.

Required:
A working to support the consolidated Profit and loss account.

	H Plc	*S* Plc	Adjustments	Consolidated Profit and loss account
	£	£	£	£
Turnover	962,212	56,846	(100,129)	918,929
Cost of sales				
(i) Per question	(621,679)	(42,366)		
(ii) Provision	(3,400)			
(iii) Subtotal	(625,079)	(42,366)	100,129	(567,316)
Gross profit	337,133	14,480		351,613
Distribution costs	(21,460)	(615)		(22,075)
Administration costs	(46,293)	(3,485)		(49,778)
Operating profit	269,380	10,380		279,760
Investment income				
(excludes *S* dividends)	11,100	600	(300)	11,400
Interest payable		(1,000)	300	(700)
Profit on ordinary activities before taxation	280,480	9,980		290,460

Tax on profits on ordinary activities	(121,340)	(3,480)		(124,820)
Profit on ordinary activitites after taxation	159,140	6,500		165,640
Minority interests				
(i) Preference dividend	(25%) 250	(1,000)	(75%) (750)	
(ii) Balance for equity shareholders		5,500		
(iii) Minority share	(20%)	(1,100)	(1,100)	(1,850)
Transfer ordinary dividends	1,200	(1,200)		
	160,590	3,200		163,790
Extraordinary items	21,500 (80%)	4,800		26,300
	182,090	8,000		190,090
Dividends	(40,000)			(40,000)
Retained profit for year	142,090	8,000		150,090
Retained profit brought forward	30,000			30,000
Retained profit carried forward	£172,090	£8,000		£180,090

Points arising:

1 The extraordinary item of S Plc was not apportioned since it occurred after acquisition.
2 The retained profit of S Plc brought forward is all pre-acquisition, and is therefore excluded.
3 In a situation where preference shares had been held in the subsidiary prior to the ordinary (controlling) shares being acquired, then the preference dividends relating to the pre-acquisition period would be introduced to the holding company's column as investment income.

Exercises to Chapter 19

1. H owns 70 per cent of the shares of S. Results for the past year have been:

	H	S
Sales	52,950	41,430
Cost of sales	31,960	20,570

Included in the above are sales of £8,300 by S to H. The goods, which included a £500 profit margin, are still held by H.

You are required to compute the consolidated turnover and cost of sales. sales.

2. The following is a summary of the directors' emoluments of H and its subsidiary, S.

	H	S
Mr A	11,000	–
Mr B	19,000	12,000
Mr C	18,000	10,000
Mr D	–	21,000

You are required to compute the total emoluments disclosed in the consolidated accounts of H.

ASSOCIATED COMPANIES

20.1 DEFINITION

An associated company is in essence an investment which falls short of a controlling interest (which would be a subsidiary) but is of sufficient size to give some influence. Typically a holding of 20 per cent to 50 per cent of equity shares will give that influence, which would include nominating one or more members of the board of directors.

The Companies Act 1985 uses the term 'related company' to describe such an investment.

The full definition of an associated company is contained in Statement of Standard Accounting Practice 1 and is as follows:

An associated company is a company not being a subsidiary of the investing group or company in which

(a) the interest of the investing group or company is effectively that of a partner in a joint venture or consortium and the investing group or company is in a position to exercise a significant influence over the company in which the investment is made; or

(b) the interest of the investing group or company is for the long term and is substantial and, having regard to the disposition of the other shareholdings, the investing group or company is in a position to exercise a significant influence over the company in which the investment is made.

Significant influence over a company essentially involves participation in the financial and operating policy decisions of that company (including dividend policy) but not necessarily control of those policies. Representation on the board of directors is indicative of such participation, but will neither necessarily give conclusive evidence of it nor be the only method by which the investing company may participate in policy decisions.

Where the interest of the investing group or company is not effectively that of a partner in a joint venture or consortium but amounts to 20 per cent or more of the equity voting rights of a company, it should be presumed that the investing group or company has the ability to exercise significant influence over that company unless it can clearly be demonstrated otherwise. For example, there may exist one or more other large shareholdings which prevent the exercise of such influence.

Where the interest of the investing group or company is not effectively that of a partner in a joint venture or consortium and amounts to less than 20 per cent of the equity voting rights of a company it should be presumed that the investing group or company does not have the ability to exercise significant influence unless it can clearly demonstrate otherwise. Unless there are exceptional circumstances, this demonstration should include a statement from the company in which the investment is made that it accepts that the investing group or company is in a position to exercise significant influence over it.

Where different companies in a group hold shares in a company, the investment in that company should be taken as the aggregate of the holdings of the investing company together with the whole of those of its subsidiaries but excluding those of its associates in determining wheter or not significant influence is presumed to exist.

20.2 THE EQUITY METHOD

Associated companies are dealt with by investing groups using the 'equity' method of accounting. The principle features of the method are as follows:

(a) Balance sheet
The investment still appears as a fixed-asset investment, but is valued using the underlying net assets of the associate, rather than cost or market value.
(b) Profit and loss account
The investment income (i.e. dividends) is replaced with a share of profit or loss, which is included within the total operating profit (since the investing company are deemed to have had influence in earning the profit).

The profits of the associate, however, are not realised profits of the investing company. For this reason the equity method is used for an associate within consolidated accounts, but not in the investing company's own accounts. Consolidated accounts will only be prepared where the investing company has subsidiaries.

Where an investing company has an associate, but no subsidiaries, then no consolidated accounts exist. In this case the equity method will be used in either supplementary accounts of the investing company, or in notes to the investing company's own accounts.

We can summarise the three methods of accounting for investments as follows:

Method	Investment	Equity	Consolidation
Balance sheet	Investment at cost or market value	Investment based on underlying net assets	Separate assets and liabilities are aggregated
Profit and loss a/c	Dividends shown as investment income	Share of earnings included in operating profit	Separate revenues and expenses are aggregated
Underlying principle	Cash-flow basis (*cost = cash paid, market value = present value of future cash flow, dividends = cash received*)	Earnings/net assets, in which the investing company participates	Separate transactions, as if the group were a single entity
Suitable situations	Small or temporary holding (*under 20%*)	Influence, but without control (*20–50%*)	Controlling holding (*over 50%*)

20.3 PROFIT AND LOSS ACCOUNT

20.3.1 Objective

By definition an associate is a company in which the investing company participates in the financial and operating policy decisions.

This is reflected in the investing company's consolidated Profit and loss account by introducing a share of the associates profits or losses. The total profit disclosed thus measures the results of all of the investing groups' operations.

20.3.2 Detailed accounting points

The specific amounts that are introduced to the consolidated Profit and loss account together with relevant disclosure are given below:

Amount included	Disclosure
Investing group's share of associate 'profit on ordinary activities before taxation'	Appears on the face of the consolidated Profit and loss a/c immediately before the total operating profit
Investing group's share of associate 'tax on profits on ordinary activities'	Added to total of 'tax on profits on ordinary activities' in the notes to the consolidated Profit and loss a/c
Investing group's share of associate 'extraordinary items'	Added to total of 'extraordinary items' in the notes to the consolidated Profit and loss a/c
Investing group's share of transfers to reserves	Added to total of 'transfers to reserves'

–	The consolidated retained profit for the year is divided between
	
	                          £
	Investing company x
	Subsidiaries x
	Associates x
	                         x

Investing group's share of associate post-acquisition Profit and loss a/c brought forward	Added to total of retained profits brought forward

20.3.3 Technique

For exam purposes the columnar consolidated Profit and loss account working is again useful, but requires adaptation. Two further columns are added to the right of the consolidated total column:

(a) the first additional column is used to display the investing groups' share of the relevant associate figures. (N.B. the first of these is profit on ordinary activities before taxation.)
(b) The second additional column becomes the revised consolidated Profit and loss account.

Example 1

H Plc has one subsidiary *S* Plc, and one associate *A* Plc. *H* Plc purchased 90 per cent of the ordinary shares of *S* Plc when that company's Profit and loss account stood at £6,000. *H* Plc purchased 40 per cent of the ordinary shares of *A* Plc when that company's Profit and loss account stood at £5,000.

The draft Profit and loss accounts for the year ended 31 December 19X5 are given below.

	H Plc £	*S* Plc £	*A* Plc £
Turnover	100,000	60,000	40,000
Cost of sales	(75,000)	(45,000)	(30,000)
Gross profit	25,000	15,000	10,000
Distribution costs	(4,500)	(2,300)	(1,100)
Administration costs	(8,200)	(3,400)	(2,400)
Operating profit	12,300	9,300	6,500
Investment income (*from third parties*)	400	320	240
Interest payable	(1,200)	(670)	(720)
Profit before tax	11,500	8,950	6,020
Tax	(4,750)	(3,450)	(2,770)
Profit after tax	6,750	5,500	3,250
Extraordinary items	2,130	(1,500)	1,100
Profit for the financial year	8,880	4,000	4,350
Ordinary dividends proposed	(4,000)	(1,800)	(1,500)
Retained profit for year	4,880	2,200	2,850
Retained profit brought forward	13,720	8,500	7,450
	£18,600	£10,700	£10,300

The following information is relevant:

1 *H* Plc has not taken credit for any dividends due from *S* Plc or *A* Plc in respect of the current year.
2 There have been no inter-company transactions in the period.
3 There are no preference shares in issue.

Required:
The consolidated Profit and loss account for the *H* Plc group, together with a consolidation schedule.

H Plc

Consolidated Profit and loss account for year to 31 December 19X5

	£
Turnover	160,000
Cost of sales	120,000
	40,000
Distribution costs	(6,800)

Administration costs		(11,600)
		21,600
Share of associate profit before tax		2,408
Operating profit		24,008
Investment income		720
Interest payable		(1,870)
Profit on ordinary activities before taxation		22,858
Tax on profit on ordinary activities		(9,308)
		13,550
Minority interests		(550)
Attributable to the member of *H* Plc		13,000
Extraordinary items		1,200
Profit for the financial year		14,220
Ordinary dividend proposed		(4,000)
Retained profit for the year		10,220
Retained by	£	
H Plc (*W1*)	7,100	
Subsidiary (*W1*)	1,980	
Associate (*W1*)	1,140	
	£10,220	
Retained profit brought forward		16,950
Retained profit carried forward		£27,170

WORKINGS

1. Consolidated schedule

	H Plc £	*S* Plc £	Consolidated £	*A* Plc £ (40%)	Total £
Turnover	100,000	60,000	160,000		
Cost of sales	(75,000)	(45,000)	(120,000)		
Gross profit	25,000	15,000	40,000		
Distribution costs	(4,500)	(2,300)	(6,800)		
Administration costs	(8,200)	(3,400)	(11,600)		
Operating profit	12,300	9,300	21,600		
Investment income	400	320	720		
Interest payable	(1,200)	(670)	(1,870)		
Profit before tax	11,500	8,950	20,450	2,408	22,858
Tax	(4,750)	(3,450)	(8,200)	(1,108)	(9,308)
Profit after tax	6,750	5,000	12,250	1,300	13,550
Minority interests	–	(10%) (550)	(550)	–	(550)
		4,950	11,700		13,000

Transfer ordinary dividends					
(*90% × £1,800*)	1,620	(1,620)			
(*40% × £1,500*)	600		600	(600)	
	8,970	3,330	12,300	700	13,000
Extraordinary items	2,130	(*90%*) (1,350)	780	(*40%*) 440	1,220
	11,100	1,980	13,080	1,140	14,220
Ordinary dividend	(4,000)		(4,000)		(4,000)
Retained profit for year	7,100	1,980	9,080	1,140	10,220
Brought forward	13,720				
(*90% × £8,500–6,000*)		2,250	15,970		
(*40% × £7,450–5,000*)				980	16,950
Carried forward	£20,820	£4,230	£25,050	£2,120	£27,170

2. Shareholdings

	S Plc	A Plc
	%	%
H Plc – direct	90	40
Minority	10	
	100	

(N.B. It is meaningless to show a minority percentage for an associate.)

20.4 BALANCE SHEET

20.4.1 Objective

As the group share of associate profits are recognised the consolidated reserves accumulate the group share of associate post-acquisition reserves (*credit*). The investment disclosed in the consolidated Balance sheet matches this accumulation (*debit*). The resulting amount carried in the investment will therefore be:

Cost of shares + group share of post-acquisition retained reserves.

This amount will always be equal to:

Group share of associate net assets + premium on acquisition
(*alias goodwill*)

The premium on acquisition arises in the same way as goodwill on the consolidation of a subsidiary. It is normally treated in the same way, i.e. eliminated against the consolidated reserves.

Step 1: Compute group share of associate net assets. This will be the group shareholding percentage, multiplied by the associate total capital and reserves at the Balance-sheet date.

Step 2: Compute the premium on acquisition and eliminate against consolidated reserves. This calculation can be done using a familiar Adjustment account, which will compare:

	£
Cost of shares	x
Group share associate nominal capital	(x)
Group share associate pre-acquisition reserves	(x)
Premium on acquisition	x

(N.B. If the result were negative it would represent a discount on acquisition, and would be added to consolidated reserves.)

Step 3: Compute the group share of post-acquisition associate retained reserves and add to consolidated reserves.

Example 2

The draft Balance sheets of the *H* group and *A* Plc at 31 December 19X3 are given below:

	H Group (Consolidated)		*A* Plc	
	£	£	£	£
Fixed assets				
Tangible assets		82,000		40,000
Investments – share in				
A Plc at cost		11,000		
		93,000		
Current assets	56,500		32,500	
Creditors: amounts falling				
due within one year	(21,300)		(18,800)	
Net current assets		35,200		13,700
Total assets *less* current				
liabilities		128,200		53,700

Creditors: amounts falling due after more than one year	(5,000)	(3,000)
	£123,200	£50,700
Capital and reserves		
Called-up share capital	40,000	10,000
Reserves	83,200	40,700
	£123,200	£50,700

The following information is relevant:

1 The *H* group Balance sheet includes various wholly-owned subsidiaries.
2 *H* Plc acquired 30 per cent of *A* Plc shares when *A* Plc reserves were £22,000.

Required:
The consolidated Balance sheet including *A* Plc on the equity basis.

H GROUP

Consolidated Balance sheet at 31 December 19X3

	£	£
Fixed assets		
Tangible assets		82,000
Investments – Associated company at share of net assets (*W1*)		15,210
		97,210
Current assets	56,500	
Creditors: amounts falling due within one year	(21,300)	
Net current assets		35,200
Total assets *less* current liabilities		132,410
Creditors: amounts falling due after more than one year		(5,000)
		£127,410
Capital and reserves		
Called-up share capital		40,000
Reserves (*W3*)		87,410
		£127,410

WORKINGS

(1) Share of *A* Plc net assets
      Net assets   £50,700
      30% thereof   £15,210

(2) Premium on acquisition   £
      Cost of shares   11,000
      Share of nominal capital – (*30% × £10,000*) (3,000)
      Share of pre-acquisition reserves – (*30% × £22,000*) (6,600)

      Premium on acquisition   £1,400

(3) Consolidated reserves   £
      Per draft   83,200
      Share of *A* Plc post-acquisition reserves
        (*30% × (£40,700 – 22,000*)   5,610
      Premium on acquisition eliminated (*W2*) (1,400)

                £87,410

20.5 ADVANCED POINTS

20.5.1 Inter-company transactions

There is no need to eliminate sales between a group and associate in the consolidated Profit and loss account. This is because associate turnover is not included in the total turnover.

However, where there is unrealised profit in stock remaining unsold at the Balance-sheet date, this will require elimination, but only for the group share of the unrealised profit.

The double entry will depend on the direction of sales.

	Debit	Credit
Sale by group to associate	Cost of sales	Share of net assets in associate (*investment in Balance sheet*)
Sale by associate to group	Share of associate profit before tax	Stock (*in Balance sheet*)

20.5.2 Revaluation at date of acquisition

As with subsidiaries the net assets of an associate should be revalued to their fair value at the date of acquisition.

Where this is possible it should be reflected in the consolidated accounts by:

(a) recognising fair value of assets in determining group share of associate net assets; and
(b) increasing (or decreasing) consolidated reserves by an equal amount (the change represents the effect of the revaluation on goodwill in the associate, which it is assumed is eliminated).

Since the holding in the associate is below 51 per cent (i.e. control) this type of adjustment will often not be possible, since the investing company will not be able to gain the necessary information.

Exercises to Chapter 20

The profit and loss of A includes the following:

	£
Turnover	429,300
Cost of sales	(310,290)
	119,010
Administration costs	(92,120)
	26,890
Interest payable	(1,140)
	25,750
Taxation	(10,500)
	15,250
Extraordinary item	4,750
	£20,000

You are required to compute the figures to be included in the consolidated Profit and loss account of H, who hold 40 per cent of the shares of A.

FOREIGN SUBSIDIARIES

21.1 NET INVESTMENT CONCEPT AND THE CLOSING-RATE METHOD

In Chapter 13 we considered the situation of a company operating through a branch which was located in a foreign country, and traded in a foreign currency. We stated that a branch was an extension of the head office trade, and the method of translation, called the 'temporal method', achieved the same result as if each transaction was translated and recorded by the head office as it occurred.

We now consider the situation of a subsidiary operating in a foreign country, and trading in a foreign currency. The parent company will have purchased shares in the subsidiary. The following observations can be made:

(a) the subsidiary did not necessarily come into existence when the parent company purchased the shares. It may well have been in existence before that time;

(b) the subsidiary is a separate legal entity;

(c) the holding company's interest in the subsidiary is recorded as an investment;

(d) the subsidiary will pay a dividend to the parent, which will be investment income in the hands of the parent;

(e) the subsidiary may raise loans locally;

(f) the subsidiary may have its own autonomous management;

(g) the subsidiary will prepare its own local currency accounts to comply with local regulations;

(h) the only reason for translating the subsidiary's accounts is to prepare consolidated accounts. Thus the translation has nothing to do with the holding company's own accounts.

From these observations we can see that the reasons for translating a foreign subsidiary's and a foreign branch's accounts are quite different. The prime objective in translating a foreign subsidiary's results will therefore be to provide figures for consolidation, which occurs once each year. We do not take account of how individual transactions occurred as we did with foreign branches.

This approach to translation of foreign subsidiary accounts is called the NET INVESTMENT CONCEPT, because the subsidiary is a separate entity in which the parent has invested. The investment is represented on consolidation by assets and liabilities less any minority share. The method of translation which results is called the 'closing-rate method'.

21.1.2 Objective of closing-rate method

The objective of the closing-rate method is to translate the Balance sheet and Profit and loss account of the foreign subsidiary with the minimum of distortion. For most items this is achieved by applying a single rate of exchange, which is the rate ruling at the Balance-sheet date. The sterling translation should then show the same ratios between various items in the foreign subsidiary's accounts as existed in the foreign currency version of those accounts.

21.2 RATES OF TRANSLATION AND TECHNIQUE

The closing-rate method can be broken down into three separate stages. These are Profit and loss account, net assets and shareholders' funds.

21.2.1 Profit and loss account

The idea of the net investment method is that the subsidiary is separate, and incurs revenues and expenses which generate cash flows in its local currency. The resulting net profit is therefore translated at a single rate. However, two approaches are acceptable. The simplest is to use the closing rate on the grounds that it will preserve the ratio of return on capital employed through the translation. The other approach is to argue that since the net profit was earned over a period, an average rate of exchange for that period should be used. Whichever of these two approaches is used, it would be stated as an accounting policy. In an exam situation the closing rate should be chosen as the simpler of the two.

The rates for all items are therefore:

Items	Rate
Sales, all other revenues, expenses, taxes, extraordinary items (all items down to profit for the financial year)	Closing rate (or average rate if chosen as an accounting policy)
Dividends paid	Rate on date paid
Dividends proposed	Closing rate

21.2.2 Net assets

No problems arise, since the closing rate is applied to all assets and liabilities:

Items	Rate
Fixed-asset cost, valuation and accumulated depreciation All current assets All liabilities and provisions	Closing rate

21.2.3 Shareholders' funds

Shareholders' funds relates to share capital and reserves. The method of translating these items is less precise than the Profit and loss account and net assets. This is because the share capital and reserves of a subsidiary are absorbed into the consolidated workings. As a result a number of techniques exist, each having good points. In general the following technique is the most straightforward:

Items	Rate
Share capital	Rate at date of acquisition by holding company
Reserves which existed at acquisition (pre-acquisition reserves)	Rate at date of acquisition by holding company
Increase in reserves since acquisition (post-acquisition reserves)	Balancing figure in £ trial balance after translating net assets, share capital and pre-acquisition reserves

If the exchange difference for the year is required then the post-acquisition reserves must be analysed as follows:

	Foreign currency	Rate	£
Post-acquisition reserves at closing Balance-sheet date	x	As above	x
Post-acquisition reserves at opening Balance-sheet date	(x)	As they appeared in previous translation	(x)
Increase in reserves	x		x
Retained profit for year	(x)	Per Profit and loss account	(x)
Exchange difference for year	nil		£x

Further analysis of exchange differences is possible, but is not within the objective scope of this book.

Example

Yewkay Plc is a company trading in the United Kingdom. Several years ago it purchased a controlling interest in a subsidiary, Foren S.A., which trades autonomously in the country where the currency is the franc. The following are the accounts of Foren S.A.:

Profit and loss account for year ended 30 June 19X5	Francs
Sales	2,168,000
Cost of sales	(1,324,500)
Gross profit	843,500
Distribution costs	(126,350)
Administration costs	(321,490)
Operating profit	395,660
Tax	(120,450)
	275,210
Extraordinary items	(52,750)
	222,460
Proposed dividend	(80,000)
Retained profit	Fr 142,460

Balance sheet at 30 June 19X5

Fixed assets	Francs	Francs
Tangible assets – cost		612,000
Accumulated depreciation		(156,000)
		456,000
Current assets		
Stocks	342,900	
Debtors	216,400	
Cash at bank and in hand	98,520	
	657,820	

Creditors: amounts falling due within one year

Trade creditors	(195,320)	–
Local tax	(120,450)	–
Proposed dividend	(80,000)	–
	(395,770)	–
Net current assets		262,050
Total assets *less* current liabilities		Fr 718,050
Capital and reserves		
Called-up share capital		100,000
Profit and loss account		618,050
		Fr 718,050

The following information is relevant:

1 Yewkay Plc purchased its holding in Foren S.A. when the reserves of Foren S.A. were Fr 200,000. The rate of exchange was £1 = Fr 10.0.
2 On 30 June 19X4 the translation showed post-acquisition reserves of £37,716.
3 On 30 June 19X5 the exchange rate was £1 = Fr 8.0.

Required:
A sterling translation of the accounts of Foren S.A. in a form suitable for consolidation, and a working to identify the exchange difference for the year.

Translation of Profit and loss account

	Franc	Rate	£
Sales	2,168,000	Closing 8.0	271,000
Cost of sales	(1,324,500)	”	(165,563)
Distribution costs	(126,350)	”	(15,794)
Administration costs	(321,490	”	(40,186)
Tax	(120,450)	”	(15,056)
Extraordinary item	(52,750)	”	(6,594)
Profit for the financial year	222,460	–	27,807
Proposed dividend	(80,000)	Closing 8.0	(10,000)
Retained profit	Fr 142,460	–	£17,807

(N.B. The sterling column would be included in a consolidated Profit and loss account working, illustrated in Chapter 19.)

Translation of Balance sheet

	Franc	Franc	Rate	£	£
Fixed asset – cost	612,000	–	Closing 8.0	76,500	–
Accumulated depreciation	–	156,000	"	–	19,500
Stocks	342,900	–	"	42,863	–
Debtors	216,400	–	"	27,050	–
Cash at bank and in hand	98,520	–	"	12,315	–
Trade creditors	–	195,320	"	–	24,415
Local tax	–	120,450	"	–	15,056
Proposed dividend	–	80,000	"	–	10,000
Share capital	–	100,000	Acquisition 10.0	–	10,000
Reserves:					
Pre-acquisition	–	200,000	"	–	20,000
Post-acquisition	–	418,050	Balance	–	59,757
(Fr 618,050–200,000)					
	Fr1,269,820	Fr 1,269,820		£158,728	£158,728

(N.B. The sterling figures would be included in consolidated workings, illustrated in Chapter 17. The total reserves are £79,757 (£20,000 + 59,759), of which £20,000 are pre-acquisition. Cost of shares will appear in the holding company's Balance sheet, and is already denominated in sterling.)

356

Identification of exchange difference

	Francs	£
Post-acquisition reserves:		
30 June 19X5	418,050	59,757
30 June 19X4 (*Fr 418,050 – 142,460*)	(275,590)	(37,716)
Increase in current year	142,460	22,041
Retained profit	(142,460)	(17,807)
Increase due to exchange differences	nil	£4,234

21.3 TREATMENT OF EXCHANGE DIFFERENCES

The treatment of exchange differences arising follows the underlying concept. In the situation of the closing-rate method the underlying concept is that the net investment has changed because it is now translated at a different rate. The difference is therefore treated as if it were a revaluation surplus or deficit and is taken directly to a separate reserve, and does not appear in the Profit and loss account. The term 'exchange reserve' would be acceptable for this reserve. In exam questions it is unlikely that such a reserve would need to be identified.

This treatment differs from the treatment of exchange differences for foreign branches in Chapter 13. In that case exchange differences were an integral part of direct transactions by the head office in a foreign currency, and were therefore included within the Profit and loss account as part of the operating profit or loss.

Exercises to Chapter 21

Hot Company operates in Hotland, whre the currency is the Temp. A U.K. company purchased a 75 per cent holding in Hot Company when that company's Balance sheet was:

	Temps
Net assets	100,000
Share capital	80,000
Reserves	20,000
	T 100,000

The rate of exchange was 10 Temps = £1. During the next year the reserves and net assets of Hot Company increased by 30,000 Temps.

On the closing Balance-sheet date the rate of exchange was 8 Temps = £1.

You are required to translate the closing Balance sheet of Hot Company and identify the movements on consolidated reserves.

PART VI

SPECIAL TRANSACTIONS

HIRE-PURCHASE

22.1 INSTALMENT CREDIT TRANSACTIONS

Whenever an examination syllabus refers to 'hire-purchase transactions' the exact meaning is somewhat wider, and could more accurately be described as 'instalment credit transactions'. There are three types of instalment credit transaction, and they are described briefly below.

22.1.1 Rental (or operating lease)

This is a simple hiring arrangement. Legal title remains with the hirer (or lessor) throughout, and the goods are returned by the hiree (or lessee) at the end of the agreed period.

22.1.2 Hire-purchase

This is a contract for hire which contains a provision for eventual purchase of goods. The legal title passes to the purchaser only after all instalments have been paid, and the purchaser has taken up an 'option to purchase'. This may require a further nominal payment. The instalments in a typical hire-purchase agreement would cover two or three years.

22.1.3 Credit sale

This is a contract for purchase of goods, legal title passing immediately, but paid for by instalments. The instalments in a typical credit sale agreement would not exceed one year (Figure 22.1).

Fig 22.1 *comparison of legal alternatives*

	Use of asset	Legal ownership
Rental (operating lease)	Period of lease only	Never passes
Hire-purchase	Life of asset	Passes after all payments completed
Credit sale	Life of asset	Passes imediately

22.2 RENTAL TRANSACTIONS (operating leases)

22.2.1 Accounting basis

Since legal title never passes to the lessee the asset leased is never recorded in the accounts of the lessee. It remains as a fixed asset in the accounts of the lessor, i.e. an asset used by that business to generate revenue. The lessor may be the manufacturer of the asset; a dealer who also sells this type of asset; or a finance company providing finance to a distributor of this type of asset.

22.2.2 Recording the fixed asset

Two points arise:

1 *Cost*. The fixed asset is recorded at cost to the lessor. In the case of a manufacturer this would be the cost of production. In the case of a dealer it would be the cost of purchase. In the case of a finance company it would be the amount paid to the distributor.
2 *Depreciation*. As with any fixed asset with a finite life the cost must be allocated over the asset's estimated useful life on a fair basis. The estimated useful life of a leased asset will be determined by the period or periods in which it will be leased. A single asset may be leased to many lessees over its life, and between periods of use there may be periods of idleness. During these idle periods the asset's value may still be falling due simply to the passing of time. However, the main consumption of asset value will occur during the periods of use, and a method of depreciation based on usage would be the most appropriate, e.g. a motor-car could be depreciated on a mileage basis.

22.2.3 Accounting for rentals

The lessor would credit rentals to income on a receivable basis. The lessee would charge rentals to income on a payable basis.

Example 1

A Plc purchases a coach for £10,000 for the purpose of hiring out. The coach has a total life of 200,000 miles before it is scrapped. Hire terms are £150 per week. In the first year the coach was hired out for a total of 42 weeks, and covered a total of 80,000 miles.

In the Profit and loss account of A Plc for the first year:

	£
Rental income credited $(42 \times £150)$	6,300
Depreciation charged $(\frac{80,000}{200,000} \times £10,000)$	(4,000)
Net profit from hiring of coach	£2,300

In the balance sheet of A Plc at the end of the first year:

	£
Tangible fixed assets	
Cost	10,000
Accumulated depreciation	(4,000)
Net book value	£6,000

22.3 HIRE-PURCHASE TRANSACTIONS

22.3.1 Accounting basis – the substance over form concept

Where the reality of a transaction (substance) differs from the legal position (form), then it is the reality of the transaction which is reflected in the accounts. In the case of a hire-purchase agreement the legal title does not pass until the end of the agreement period. However, the purchaser has the use of the asset throughout the contract period, and ultimately intends to purchase. The purchaser also has a liability to pay instalments to the legal owner. For accounting purposes, therefore, the purchaser shows the asset as a fixed asset, and also shows its liability to pay instalments as a creditor.

The recording of such an asset in the books of the purchaser was dealt with in Chapter 4, Section 5. This chapter considers the books of the dealer selling the asset.

22.3.2 Books of a dealer

We are considering in this subsection a dealer who sells particular assets in the normal course of trade, but who also offers the same assets under hire-purchase terms. The total money received under hire-purchase terms would be higher to reflect hire-purchase interest charged.

Example 2

C Plc sells a standard video-recorder. Each recorder is purchased for £400. Cash selling price is £500, and hire-purchase terms are a deposit of £140, followed by 36 monthly instalments of £12 each. The two types of sale can be compared:

	£
Cash sale:	
Selling price	500
Cost	(400)
Profit	£100

This profit represents a gross profit from trading.

	£
Hire-purchase sale:	
Deposit	140
Instalments *(36 × £12)*	432
Total selling price	572
Cost price	(400)
Profit	£172

The total selling price (£572) is called the hire-purchase selling price. The profit can be divided into two components:

	£
Gross profit from trading (as for cash sale)	100
Hire-purchase interest	72
Total profit	£172

Since the hire-purchase sale is to be dealt with as a sale by the dealer it will be the cash selling price (£500 in the above example) which is included in sales in the Trading account. The additional hire-purchase interest is credited to a separate account. The balance on this account is then released to the Profit and loss account over the duration of the contract, as if it were interest on an investment. The total included in sales, together with the hire-purchase interest, represent the total due from the purchaser or hire-purchase debtor.

The double entry in the dealer's books can be summarised thus:

Transaction	Debit	Credit
At outset of contract	Hire-purchase debtors' a/c – with total instalments and deposit	Trading a/c (Sales) – with cash selling price Finance profit a/c – with hire-purchase interest
Receipt of deposit and instalments	Cash a/c	Hire-purchase debtors' a/c
At end of each accounting period	Finance profit a/c – with proportion of hire purchase interest (see Chap. 22, Sec. 3.3, below)	Profit and loss a/c

For the facts in Example 2, and assuming that twelve instalments are received in the first accounting period, then the Hire-purchase debtors' account will appear thus:

Hire-purchase debtors' account

	£		£
Trading a/c – cash selling price	500	Cash a/c – deposit	140
Finance profit a/c – hire-purchase interest	72	– twelve instalments in first year (*12 × £12*)	144
		Balance c/f (at end of first year)	288
	£572		£572
Balance b/f	288	Cash a/c – twelve instalments in second year	144
		Balance c/f (at end of second year)	144
	£288		£288

Balance b/f	144	Cash a/c – twelve instalments in third year	144
	£144		£144

22.3.3 Calculation of finance profit

Two methods are possible within an examination context:

(a) Straight-line method

This is the simpler of the two. The total hire-purchase interest is divided by the total number of instalments to find an equal amount per instalment.

The amount credited to the Profit and loss account of each period is the hire-purchase interest per instalment multiplied by the number of instalments received in that period.

The balance carried forward on the Finance profit account will be the hire-purchase interest per instalment multiplied by the number of instalments receivable in the future.

For the facts in Example 2, and assuming that twelve instalments out of a total of thirty-six are received in the first accounting period, then the Finance profit account will appear thus:

Finance profit account

	£		£
Profit and loss a/c (year 1) $(\frac{12}{36} \times £72)$	24	Hire-purchase debtors' a/c – hire purchase interest	72
Balance c/f (at end of year 1) $(\frac{24}{36} \times £72)$	48		
	£72		£72
Profit and loss a/c (year 2) $(\frac{12}{36} \times £72)$	24	Balance b/f	48
Balance c/f (at end of year 2) $\frac{12}{36} \times £72)$	24		
	£48		£48
Profit and loss a/c (year 3) $(\frac{12}{36} \times £72)$	24	Balance b/f	24
	£24		£24

(b) Rule of 78 (or sum of digits) method

The object of this method is to spread the hire-purchase interest as if it were interest on a loan, where the loan is gradually being repaid. A greater proportion of the profit is taken in the earlier part of the contract than in the later part.

The technique is to assign a digit to each instalment. The first will be equal to the number of instalments, and the last equal to one.

Instalment	Digit
First	36
Second	35
Third	34
Fourth	33
.	.
.	.
.	.
.	
Thirty-fifth	2
Thirty-sixth	1

The hire-purchase interest credited to the Profit and loss account in any period will be

$$\text{Total hire-purchase interest} \times \frac{\text{Sum of digits of instalments received in that period}}{\text{Sum of digits of total instalments}}$$

The balance carried forward on the Finance profit account will be:

$$\text{Total hire-purchase interest} \times \frac{\text{Sum of digits of future instalments}}{\text{Sum of digits of total instalments}}$$

The calculations are often odd fractions and will need rounding. For the facts in Example 2 the Finance profit account will appear thus:

Finance profit account

	£		£
Profit and loss a/c (year 1)		Hire-purchase debtors' a/c	
$(£72 \times \frac{366 \,(W1)}{666 \,(W2)})$	40	– hire purchase interest	72

Balance c/f (at end of year 1)		
$(£72 \times \dfrac{300 \ (W3)}{666 \ (W2)})$	32	
	£72	£72
Profit and loss a/c (year 2)		Balance b/f 32
$(£72 \times \dfrac{222 \ (W4)}{666 \ (W2)})$	24	
Balance c/f (at end of year 2)		
$(£72 \times \dfrac{78 \ (W5)}{666 \ (W2)})$	8	
	£32	£32
Profit and loss a/c (year 3)		Balance b/f 8
$(£72 \times \dfrac{78 \ (W5)}{666 \ (W2)})$	8	
	£8	£8

WORKINGS

(1) Sum of digits 25 − 36 = 366
(2) Sum of digits 1 − 36 = 666
(3) Sum of digits 1 − 24 = 300
(4) Sum of digts 13 − 24 = 222
(5) Sum of digits 1 − 12 = 78

N.B. The sum of the digits 1 to n is always $\dfrac{n\,(n+1)}{2}$. Hence 1 to 36 is $\dfrac{36 \times 37}{2} = 666$

22.3.4 Accounts disclosure

In the Balance sheet the Hire-purchase debtors' account balance and the Finance profit account balance are netted off within current assets.

For the facts in Example 2, and using the rule-of-78 calculations, the Trading, profit and loss accounts and Balance sheet siwll appear thus:

Trading profit and loss account (*extract*)	Year 1	Year 2	Year 3
	£	£	£
Sales	500	–	–
Cost of sales	(400)	–	–
Gross profit	100	–	–
Finance profit – hire-purchase interest	40	24	8
Net profit	£140	£24	£8

Balance sheet (*extract*)

Current assets			
Hire-purchase debtors	288	144	–
Finance profit allocation to future periods	(32)	(8)	–
	£256	£136	£–

22.3.5 Books of a hire-purchase finance company

Frequently a dealer will not provide hire-purchase finance directly, but will pass the business to a specialist hire-purchase finance company. The dealer collects a deposit from the purchaser, and the balance of the normal cash selling price is paid to the dealer by the finance company. The finance company becomes the legal owner of the asset, and collects instalments directly from the purchaser. The instalments cover the amount paid to the dealer, together with hire-purchase interest added. The finance company does not trade, and so does not prepare a Trading account. There is, therefore, only one type of profit, i.e. hire-purchase interest, to consider in the Profit and loss account.

At the outset of the contract this hire-purchase interest is credited to a Finance profit account. The ensuing double entry, and methods of calculating hire-purchase interest credited to the Profit and loss account are exactly the same as for a dealer. It is likely that the straight-line method would be too simple for a finance company, and would therefore never be used. The double entry for a finance company can be summarised thus:

Transaction	Debit	Credit
At outset of contract	Hire-purchase debtors' a/c – total instalments	Cash a/c – amount paid to dealer Finance profit a/c – hire-purchase interest
Receipt of instalments	Cash a/c	Hire-purchase debtors' a/c
At end of each accounting period	Finance profit a/c – with proportion of interest calculated on rule-of-78 basis (see Chap. 22, Sec. 3.3, above)	Profit and loss a/c

22.3.6 Repossessions

In the event of a customer failing to meet the instalments due, the hire-purchase contract will give the dealer or finance company the right to re-possess the goods. The purchaser forfeits all payments made to that date. In the books of the dealer or finance company the repossessed goods will either be added back to stock for resale, or sold immediately. Goods added back to stock are treated as a purchase, and are added to purchases at an arm's length value. The double entry arising can be summarised thus:

(a) Open a Repossession account
(b) Transfer instalments not paid to the Repossession account:
  Dr Repossession account
    Cr Hire-purchase debtors' account
(c) Transfer hire-purchase interest on unpaid instalments to the Repossession account
  Dr Finance profit account
    Cr Repossession account
(d) Charge expenses of repossession and repair to the Repossession account:
  Dr Repossession account
    Cr Cash/Creditors' account
(e) If taken into stock:
  Dr Purchases account
    Cr Repossession account with the value of the goods; or
(f) If sold immediately:
  Dr Cash or Debtors' account
    Cr Repossession account with the proceeds of sale.
(g) Balance on the Repossession account represents the loss on repossession:
  Dr Profit and loss account
    Cr Repossession account.

22.3.7 Early settlements

Occasionally a customer may wish to clear all future instalments by the payment of a single lump sum. The dealer or finance company would agree a lump sum which would be lower than the total instalments, since the cash is available to the dealer or finance company immediately.
 The double entry arising can be summarised thus:

(a) Open an Early settlements account
(b) Transfer instalments not paid to the Early settlements account:

    Dr Early settlements account
        Cr Hire purchase debtors' account

(c) Transfer hire-purchase interest on instalments unpaid to Early settlements account:

    Dr Finance profit account
        Cr Early settlements account

(d) Lump sum cash received:

    Dr Cash account
        Cr Early settlements account

(e) Balance on the Early settlements account represents hire-purchase interest waived:

    Dr Profit and loss account
        Cr Early settlements account.

22.3.8 Options to purchase fees

A hire-purchase contract may require the payment of a nominal sum at the end of the contract to signify the passing of the legal title.

The double entry for the option to purchase fees is thus:

(a) At the outset of the contract	Dr Hire-purchase debtors' account Cr Option to Purchase fee account

(b) When received at the end of the contract	Dr Cash account
	    Cr Hire purchase debtors' account
	Dr Option to purchase fee account
	    Cr Profit and loss account

The Balance sheets prepared throughout the period of the contract will show the balance on the option to Purchase fee account as a deduction from the Hire-purchase debtors' account (as with the Finance profit account).

22.4 CREDIT SALES

22.4.1 Accounting basis

Legal title passes to the purchaser immediately. This is reflected in the accounts of the dealer by recognising the normal gross trading profit immediately.

However, the additional credit sale interest added to the selling price will be spread over the contract period to reflect the receipt of cash by instalments, as if they were loan repayments.

22.4.2 Accounting

The double entry methods of calculation of interest and disclosure are as for a hire-purchase contract in Section 22.3, above.

22.5 ADVANCED POINTS

(a) The actuarial method of dealing with the calculation of finance profit is not discussed in this chapter, since it is unsuitable within a financial accounts examination context, and would never be set. In practical terms it is a more accurate method than the sum of digits method, although the result would be similar.

(b) Finance leases

Since finance leases are normally dealt with in an advanced accounting syllabus only, they are not specifically referred to in this chapter. The treatment, double entry and methods of calculating finance profit would, however, be similar to that for a hire-purchase contract. One area of difference would arise where taxation was a material factor, affecting the calculation of finance profit.

Exercises to Chapter 22

1. A business sells goods for cash and on hire-purchase terms. Cash selling price for a particular item is £600. Hire-purchase terms require a deposit of £200, followed by twenty-four instalments of £20 each.
    You are required to:

    (a) compute the total finance profit on hire-purchase sales;
    (b) compute the finance profit in the first year, assuming that six instalments are received and that profit is taken on the straight-line method; and
    (c) alternatively, compute the finance profit in the first year, assuming that six instalments were received and that profit is taken on the sum-of-digits method.

2. A hire-purchase finance company repossessed certain goods which were the subject of a hire-purchase agreement. Instalments outstanding at the date of repossession totalled £150, and £30 of the Finance profit

account balance related to this contract. After repair costs of £25 had been spent on the goods they were sold for £132.

You are required to prepare a Repossessions account and identify the loss arising on the repossession.

CHAPTER 23

GOODS ON SALE

OR RETURN

23.1 RECOGNITION OF PROFIT

A sale-or-return agreement involves stock sent out on approval from one party, A, to another, B. B attempts to sell such stock, but has the right to return unsold stock to A.

So far as A is concerned the stock cannot be considered as sold to B, and hence any profit realised, until it is certain that B will not return the stock. This will normally be at the date on which B sells the stock.

23.2 BOOKS OF THE VENDOR

In the accounts of A the entry recording the sale will be:
  Dr   Sales ledger control account (and B's account in the Sales ledger)
       Cr   Sales account.

This entry must not be made until it is certain that B will not return the stock. However, a record of stock sent out on sale or return will be required since the cost must be included in any stock valuation.

The normal solution is to maintain a separate ledger called the 'Sale-or-return ledger'. Details of stock sent out and returned are entered. Once the sale is confirmed, double entry is made as described above. Goods sent out but neither sold nor returned at a Balance-sheet date are valued at cost and included in closing stock.

23.3 BOOKS OF THE PURCHASER

In the accounts of B the stock will not be considered as purchased until it is certain that the stock will not be returned to A. A record of stock held on a sale or return basis is kept, but such stock will not be included in the stock of B.

CHAPTER 24

CONSIGNMENT ACCOUNTS

24.1 BASIS OF AGREEMENT

A consignment of stock is sent from a principal to an agent. The stock remains the property of the principal while in the hands of the agent. The agent sells stock on the principal's behalf in return for a commission. Unsold stock is included in the Balance sheet of the principal at cost, which includes all costs involved in transporting stock to the agent. There is no sale between the principal and agent. In this respect a consignment agreement differs from a sale or return agreement.

24.2 ACCOUNTS OF THE PRINCIPAL

24.2.1 Accounts required

Two special accounts are used. These are:

Account	Purpose
Consignment a/c	To determine any profit or loss on the consignment
Agent's a/c	To determine any balance due from the agent

24.2.2 Double entry

Transaction	Debit	Credit
Goods sent to agent at cost	Consignment a/c	Trading a/c (*shown as a deduction from cost of sales*)
Costs incurred by principal	Consignment a/c	Cash/Creditors' a/c

Costs incurred by agent (*including commission*)	Consignment a/c	Agents' a/c
Sales by agent	Agent's a/c	Consignment a/c
Cash remitted to principal	Cash a/c	Agent's a/c
Closing stock with agent valued at cost with agent	Balance carried forward on consignment account. Include in Balance sheet	
Balancing figure on consignment account = profit on consignment	Consignment a/c	Profit and loss a/c
Balance on Agent's a/c	Balance due from agent = Debtor in Balance sheet	

24.2.3 Determining cost of stock with agent

Closing stock with the agent is valued at cost which includes transit to the agent. It is determined thus:

	£
Material cost to principal	x
Transport to agent	x
Customs duties (where agent is abroad)	x
Insurance in transit	x
Handling in transit	x
Total cost of goods shipped	x

This is divided by total units to determine the cost per unit.
Storage costs at the agent's premises are excluded.

24.3 ACCOUNTS OF THE AGENT

24.3.1 Accounts required

One special account is used. It is:

Account	Purpose
Principal's a/c	To determine any balance due to the principal

24.3.2 **Double entry**

Transaction	Debit	Credit
Goods received from principal	–	–
Costs incurred by agent	Principal's a/c	Cash/Creditors' a/c
Goods sold	Cash/Debtors' a/c	Principal's a/c
Cash remitted to principal	Principal's a/c	Cash a/c
Balance on Principal's a/c	Balance due to principal = creditor in balance sheet	

The Principal's account in the agent's books is a mirror image of the agent's account in the principal's books.

24.3.3 *Del Credere* **agreement**

Under a *del credere* consignment agreement the agent accepts all bad-debt risks in return for a higher rate of commission. Debtors for sales are then maintained in the agent's books, and not in the principal's books. The agent accounts to the principal for all sales.

Example

Prince, a sole trader, sent goods on consignment to his agent, Pauper. Pauper is entitled to a commission of 5 per cent on all sales made by him. The following cash transactions occurred in the first period of trading.

	£
Cost of goods sent to Pauper (1,000 units)	10,000
Costs borne by Prince:	
Transport	400
Insurance in transit	150
Bank charges	80
Costs borne by Pauper:	
Handling	450
Advertising	420
Rent of warehouse	530
Sales by Pauper (800 units)	12,000
Cash remitted by Pauper	8,500

At the end of the period 200 units remained with Pauper for sale in the next period.

Record the above transactions in the books of Prince.

Consignment account

	£		£
Trading a/c – cost of goods sent to agent	10,000	Agents a/c – sales	12,000
Cash a/c – transport	400		
– insurance	150		
– bank charges	80		
Agent's a/c – handling	450		
– advertising	420		
– rent	530		
– commission	600		
Profit and loss a/c – profit on consignment	1,570	Balance c/f (stock) (*W1*)	2,200
	£14,200		£14,200

Agents account – Pauper

	£		£
Consignment a/c – sales	12,000	Consignment a/c – handling	450
		advertising	420
		rent	530
		commission (*5% × £12,000*)	600
		Cash a/c – remittance	8,500
		Balance c/f (*debtor*)	1,500
	£12,000		£12,000

WORKINGS

(1) Valuation of closing stock	£
For 1,000 units:	
Material cost	10,000
Transport	400
Insurance	150
Handling	450
	£11,000
Per unit	£11
For 200 units	£2,200

Exercises to Chapter 24

A business sent goods on consignment to an agent and the following summary of transactions occurred:

	£
Cost of goods consigned	10,000
Transport costs borne by principal	1,500
Costs borne by agent	2,500
Sales by agent	15,000
Cash paid by agent to principal	6,500
Cost of goods with agent, unsold	1,400

You are required to:

(a) prepare a Consignment account and identify the profit arising on the consignment; and
(b) prepare an Agent's account and identify the sum due from the agent.

ROYALTIES

25.1 ROYALTY AGREEMENT

25.1.1 What is a royalty?

A charge made by the owner of a monopoly or privilege in respect of:

(a) the use of a patent;
(b) the reproduction of copyright books, plays and music; and
(c) the extraction of minerals from the ground.

25.1.2 The royalty agreement

A legal contract drawn between the owner (LANDLORD) and user (TENANT) which will specify:

(a) royalty payment per unit;
(b) any minimum payment required;
(c) recovery of excess payments made where output fell below minimum payment (called SHORTWORKINGS); and
(d) right of tenant to enter an agreement to sublet production to a sub-tenant.

25.2 ACCOUNTS OF THE LANDLORD - ROYALTIES RECEIVABLE

25.2.1 Accounts required

Three special accounts are used. These are:

Account	Purpose
Royalties receivable a/c	To determine the amount credited to the Profit and loss a/c as royalty income. This equals the tenant's production multiplied by the royalty per units.
Tenant's a/c	To determine any balance due from the tenant for royalties receivable, adjusted for shortworkings. Such a balance is a debtor in the landlord's Balance sheet.
Shortworkings allowed a/c	Where the tenant's production fell below the minimum specified, the excess of the minimum payment over that based on production is called a 'shortworking'. It is usual to permit an offset of such shortworkings against future royalty payments (subject to the minimum), but within a time limit. This account maintains the balance of shortworkings still available for future offset.

25.2.2 Double entry

Transactions	Debit	Credit
Tenant's production × Royalty per unit	Tenant's a/c	Royalty receivable a/c
Where balance on Tenant's a/c is below minimum, enter deficit	Tenant's a/c	Shortworkings allowed a/c
Where balance on Tenant's a/c exceeds minimum, offset any shortworkings brought forward from previous period, subject to minimum payment	Shortworkings allowed a/c	Tenant's a/c
Close-off accounts	(a) Royalties receivable a/c – credit balance to Profit and loss a/c (b) Tenant's a/c – debtor in Balance sheet (c) Shortworkings allowed a/c – shown as a deduction from the Tenant's a/c in Balance sheet.	

25.3 ACCOUNTS OF THE TENANT – ROYALTIES PAYABLE

25.3.1 Accounts required

Three special accounts are used. These are:

Account	Purpose
Royalties payable a/c	To determine the amount charged to: (i) manufacturing account where production based; or (ii) Trading a/c where sales based
Landlord's a/c	To determine any balance due to the landlord. This will be a mirror version of the Tenant's a/c in the Landlord's a/c
Shortworkings recoverable a/c	To maintain the balance of shortworkings recoverable against future payments. This will be a mirror version of the shortworkings allowed account in the Landlord's a/cs

25.3.2 Double entry

Transaction	Debit	Credit
Tenant's production × Royalty per unit	Royalties payable a/c	Landlord's a/c
Where balance on Landlord's a/c is below minimum, enter deficit	Shortworkings recoverable a/c	Landlord's a/c
Where balance on Landlord's a/c exceeds minimum, offset any shortworkings brought forward from previous period, subject to minimum payment	Landlord's a/c	Shortworkings recoverable a/c
Payment to landlord	Landlord's a/c	Cash a/c
Close off accounts	(a) Royalties payable a/c – debit balance to manufacturing or Trading a/c (b) Landlord's a/c – credited in Balance sheet (c) Shortworkings recoverable a/c – shown as a deduction from the Landlord's a/c in the Balance sheet.	

25.4 TENANT WITH A SUBTENANT

The tenant may be permitted by the royalty agreement to enter a further agreement with a subtenant. The tenant also becomes an intermediate landlord.

The following points arise:

1 The tenant may charge the subtenant a higher royalty per unit than the tenant pays to the landlord.
2 The tenant pays royalties to the landlord for both the tenant's and sub-tenant's production.
3 The tenant maintains six accounts.
Dealing with landlord (described in Section 25.3 above):

  (i) Royalties payable account
  (ii) Landlord's account
  (iii) Shortworkings recoverable account
Dealing with sub-tenant (described in Section 25.2, above):

  (iv) Royalties receivable account
  (v) Subtenant's account (entries as for Tenant's account in land-lord's books)
  (vi) Shortworkings allowable account.

Example

Trendytogs, a manufacturer of jeans, enters a royalty agreement with Smoothlines, designers of clothes, whereby Trendytogs pay £1 to Smoothlines for each pair of jeans manufactured by them under a Smoothlines design. The agreement commenced on 1 January 19X1, and royalties are payable on 30 April of each year following production. The agreement requires a minimum royalty of £1,000. Shortworkings are recoverable within one year, but after that time are forfeited. Production for the first three years were 19X1 700 pairs, 19X2 1,200 pairs, 19X3 1,400 pairs.

Required:
Record the entries in the books of Trendytogs for the three years.

Royalties payable account

19X1	£	19X1	£
Landlord's a/c	700	Manufacturing a/c	700

19X2		19X2	
Landlord's a/c	1,200	Manufacturing a/c	1,200
19X3		19X3	
Landlord's a/c	1,400	Manufacturing a/c	1,400

Shortworkings recoverable account

19X1	£	19X1	£
Landlord's a/c	300	c/d	300
19X2		19X2	
b/d	300	Landlord's a/c	200
		Profit and loss a/c	100
	£300		£300
19X3		19X3	

Landlord's account

19X1	£	19X1	£
c/d	1,000	Royalties payable a/c	700
		Shortworkings recoverable a/c	300
	£1,000		£1,000
19X2		19X2	
Cash a/c	1,000	b/d	1,000
Shortworkings a/c	200	Royalties payable a/c	1,200
c/d	1,000		
	£2,200		£2,200
19X3		19X3	
Cash a/c	1,000	b/d	1,000
c/d	1,400	Royalties payable a/c	1,400
	£2,400		£2,400
19X4		19X4	
Cash a/c	1,400	b/d	1,400

Points arising:

1 In 19X1 the production fell short of the minimum 1,000. The £300 shortfall was shown as a shortworking recoverable carried forward.
2 In 19X2 £200 of the shortworking was recovered, but the balance of £100 was no longer available for recovery and was written off.

Exercises to Chapter 25

A business owns the extraction rights of a particular mineral. They enter an agreement whereby they will receive £50 per ton of mineral extracted by a tenant, subject to a minimum payment of £50,000 each year. Short workings may be recovered in either of the next two years. Settlement is made in the month following the Balance-sheet date. Extraction in the first two years was 900 tons and 1,400 tons respectively.

You are required to prepare the relevant accounts to determine payments received by the landlord following the Balance-sheet date of the first two years.

CONTAINERS

26.1 RETURNABLE CONTAINERS

26.1.1 Accounting objectives

Where a business sells its product in a returnable container it will require accounting records in order to:

(a) Determine the carrying value of containers owned for inclusion as an asset in the Balance sheet;
(b) Determine the liability to customers for credit due when containers are returned, and
(c) compute any profit or loss from container operations.

26.1.2 Pricing structure

Four prices are relevant:

Price	Relevance
Cost	Purchase price of new containers.
Depreciated value	The value at which containers are carried in the accounts.
Charging-out price	The amount charged to a customer for a container.
Credit-back price	The credit given to a customer when a container is returned.

The excess of the charging-out price over the credit-back price is called the 'hire profit'.

26.2 ACCOUNTING FOR CONTAINERS

26.2.1 Accounts required

Three special accounts are used:

Account	Purpose
Containers Stock a/c	To determine book value of all containers owned.
Containers Suspense a/c	To determine liability to customers for containers not yet returned, and within time limit. This will be the credit back price of all such containers.
Containers Profit and loss a/c	To determine net profit or loss on container operations.

26.2.2 Double entry

Transaction	Debit	Credit	Relevant price
Purchase new containers	Containers Stock a/c	Cash/Creditors' a/c	Cost
	Containers Profit and loss a/c	Containers Stock a/c	Cost less depreciated value
Container hired out to customer	Customers' a/c	Containers Suspense a/c	Charging out
	Containers Suspense a/c	Containers Profit and loss a/c	Hire profit
Container returned by customer within time limit	Containers Suspense a/c	Customers' a/c	Credit back
Time limit expires – assume container lost	Containers Suspense a/c	Containers Profit and loss a/c	Credit back
	Containers Profit and loss a/c	Containers Stock a/c	Depreciated value
Repair of containers	Containers Profit and loss a/c	Cash a/c	–
Sale of containers	Cash a/c	Containers Profit and loss a/c	Proceeds

	Containers Profit and loss a/c	Containers Stock a/c	Depreciated value
Balances carried forward	(a) Containers Stock a/c – containers owned at depreciated value. (b) Container Suspense a/c – containers with customers at credit back price. (c) Containers profit and loss a/c – net profit or loss transferred to general Profit and loss a/c		

EXAMPLE

Krates Plc sell their products in returnable containers which are priced as follows:

	£
Cost	20
Depreciated value	8
Charge out price	15
Credit back price	11

During one period the following transactions occurred:

	No.	£
Opening stock of containers:		
– with customers	400	3,200
– in hand	600	4,800
Hired to customers	10,000	–
Returned from customers	8,000	–
Retained by customers	1,500	–
Purchase of new containers	1,800	–
Repair costs	–	500
Proceeds of containers scrapped	50	250

Required:
Record the transactions in the books of Krates Plc.

Containers stock account

	Units	Per Unit £	£		Units	Per unit £	£
Balance b/f	1,000	8	8,000	Containers Profit and loss a/c – retained	1,500	8	12,000

	Units	Per unit £	£		Units	Per unit £	£
Cash a/c				Containers Profit and loss a/c – depreciation		12	21,600
purchases	1,800	20	36,000	Containers Profit and loss a/c – scrapped	50	8	400
				Balance c/f	1,250	8	10,000
	2,800		£44,000		2,800		£44,000

Containers suspense account

	Units	Per unit £	£		Units	Per unit £	£
Containers Profit and loss a/c – hire profit	–	4	40,000	Balance b/f	400	11	4,400
Customers' a/c – returned	8,000	11	88,000	Customers' a/c – hired	10,000	15	150,000
Containers Profit and loss a/c – retained	1,500	11	16,500				
Balance c/f	900	11	9,900				
	10,400		£154,400		10,400		£154,400

Containers Profit and loss account

	£		£
Containers Stock a/c – retained	12,000	Containers Suspense a/c – hire profit	40,000
Containers Stock a/c – depreciation	21,600	Containers Suspense a/c – forfeited by customers	16,500
Cash a/c – repairs	500		

		Cash a/c – proceeds	
Containers Stock		of containers	
a/c – scraped	400	scrapped	250
General Profit and			
loss a/c – profit	22,250		
	£56,750		£56,750

Exercises to Chapter 26

A business hires out returnable containers in which their products are held until consumption by customers. The following is a summary of the first year of operation:

	No.	£
Cost of containers purchased (at cost)	500	5,000
Hired to customers (at charge-out price)	400	6,000
Returned from customers (at credit-back price)	300	3,900

Customers notified that ten containers had been damaged and would not be returned. Depreciated value is £8 per container.

You are required to:

(a) prepare a Containers stock account and identify the containers owned;

(b) prepare a Containers suspense account and identify the amount due to customers; and

(c) prepare a Containers profit and loss account and identify the profit and loss arising.

CONTRACTS

27.1 NATURE OF A CONTRACT

This chapter deals with the accounting implications of one business (the contractor) entering a contract with some other person (the customer) to supply or construct a single substantial asset or to provide a service.

The duration of the contract, that is the period of construction or provision of the service, may be very short, or may exceed a year, possibly running into several accounting periods.

The particular techniques and problems of accounting for contracts arise both in companies whose main business is contracting such as the construction industry, or a company who have entered a contract outside their normal mode of business.

27.1.1 Types of contract

Two major types of contract exist:

(a) *Fixed price contract*. The total sales value of the contract is fixed and written into the contract. The contractor will wish to keep total costs below this fixed price in order to show a profit on the contract as a whole. If total costs exceed the fixed price, then the contractor will show a loss. For this reason a fixed price contract is also called a 'risk contract'.

(b) *Cost plus contract*. There is no fixed sales value. The customer agrees to bear all direct costs-plus overheads at an agreed recovery rate plus profit at an agreed percentage of the total cost.

   The contractor makes a guaranteed profit, which will normally be modest in relation to the cost; 5 per cent would be typical. A cost-plus contract is also called a 'non-risk contract'. Since exam questions generally involve fixed-price contracts, the balance of this chapter is restricted to that type of contract.

27.1.2 Terminology

Set out below are the terms applied as a fixed price contract proceeds from birth to conclusion.

Stage of contract	Terms used
Customer invites several prospective contractors to bid for the contract	Tender – each contractor tenders a price for the contract.
Customer accepts one bid, and contract is signed	–
Work commences	Costs to date – the contractor accumulates all costs incurred on the contract. Value of work done – the sales value (proportion of total) of the work completed to date.
Customer certifies the work done	Cost certificate – a piece of paper given by the customer agreeing the work done to date. Work certified – the sales value of the work which has been certified.
Contractor raises sales invoice for a proportion of the total fixed price	Progress payment – a cash payment by the customer to the supplier based on the value of work certified less retentions. Retentions – an amount withheld by the customer for an agreed period in case of faults arising in the work done.
Contractor takes credit for profit	Profit taken – the contractor will estimate the profit that will arise on the contract, and will attempt to spread the profit over the periods when the work is done.
Contractor provides for a loss	Loss provided – if the contractor foresees a loss at any stage of the contract, a full provision would be made.

27.2 STATEMENT OF STANDARD ACCOUNTING PRACTICE 9 (SSAP 9)

In Chapter 9 we dealt with that part of SSAP 9 covering the valuation of stock and work in progress. In addition SSAP 9 also deals with long-term contract work in progress.

27.2.1 Definitions

(a) *Long-term contract*. A contract entered into for manufacture or building of a single substantial entity or the provision of a service where the time taken to manufacture, build or provide is such that a substantial proportion of all such contract work will extend for a period exceeding one year.

By exception, a contract which is shorter than this will be a short-term contract.

(b) *Attributable profit*. That part of the total profit currently estimated to arise over the duration of the contract (after allowing for likely increases in costs so far as not recoverable under the terms of the contract) which fairly reflects the profit attributable to that part of the work performed at the accounting date. (There can be no attributable profit until the outcome of the contract can be assessed with reasonable certainty.)

(c) *Foreseeable losses*. Losses which are currently estimated to arise over the duration of the contract (after allowing for estimated remedial and maintenance costs, and increases in costs so far as not recoverable under the terms of the contract). This estimate is required irrespective of:

(i) whether or not work has yet commenced on such contracts;
(ii) the proportion of work carried out at the accounting date;
(iii) the amount of profits expected to arise on other contracts.

27.2.2 Accounting points

(a) Profit on a long-term contract should be spread over the periods of the contract, subject to prudent provisions.

(b) Losses on a long-term contract should be fully provided as soon as foreseen.

(c) Short-term contracts should be valued at the lower of cost and net realisable value, i.e. as normal stock and work in progress as in Chapter 9. No profit would thus be taken on a short-term contract until that contract is complete.

27.2.3 Disclosure

(a) *Balance sheet*. Long-term contract work in progress is stated as part of stocks within current assets. A note will be needed to disclose:

	£
Costs to date plus attributable profits (if any)	
less foreseeable losses (if any)	x
Less: Progress payments received and receivable	(x)
Amount added to stocks	x

If the net result is negative as a result of foreseeable losses written off, then that negative should be redisclosed under 'provisions for liabilities and charges'.

(b) *Profit and loss account*. Any profit or loss taken to Profit and loss account on a long-term contract will be included in results from ordinary activities. If the amount is material, then it would be disclosed as an exceptional item (see Chapter 9).

27.3 ACCOUNTS AND DOUBLE ENTRY

Four special accounts are required:

Account	Purpose
Contract a/c (*Debit balance*)	Accumulates the costs to date, the attributable profit taken less foreseeable losses provided.
Certificates a/c (*Credit balance*)	Accumulates the value of work certified (normally used as the turnover figure).
Customers' a/c (*Debit balance*)	Debtor a/c – sums due from customer.
Retentions a/c (*Debit balance*)	Maintains the balance withheld by the customer.

The balance on the Certificates account less the balance on the Retentions account is the figure of 'progress payments received and receivable' required for the Balance-sheet disclosure in Subsection 27.2.3 above

The double entry required will be:

Transaction	Debit	Credit
Costs incurred (materials delivered, labour paid, hire of plant, site expenses paid)	Contract a/c	Cash/Creditors' a/c
Central overheads allocated to contract	Contract a/c	Overhead recovery a/c
Depreciation of assets	Contract a/c	Accumulated depreciation a/c
Materials unused at end of period	Carry forward as balance of Stock on contract a/c	
Work certified	Customers' a/c	Certificates a/c
Retention imposed (reverse when released)	Retentions a/c	Customers' a/c
Profit taken	Contract a/c	Profit and loss a/c
Loss provided	Profit and loss a/c	Contract a/c

The following balances are then extracted:

Contract account –   Costs to date plus attributable profit *less* foreseeable losses

Certificates account
less Retentions
   account –   Progress payments received and receivable
Customers' account –   Debtors

Example 1

Builders Plc entered a contract on 1 January 19X1 to construct an office building. The fixed selling price is £4,000,000. Work is expected to take three years. The transactions for the first year of construction are given below:

	£
Materials purchased and delivered to site	729,540
Payments to labour force	362,490
Site expenses paid	142,970
Value of work certified on 31 December 19X1	1,500,000
Materials unused at 31 December 19X1	13,540
Site expenses incurred but not yet paid	5,495
Attributable profit calculated, and taken	145,985

No progress payments have yet been received. Work certified less a 10% retention is receivable on 1 March in the following period.

Required:
Record the above transactions in the accounts of Builders Plc for the year to 31 December 19X1, and show how the figure would appear in the Balance sheet at 31 December 19X1.

Contract account

	£		£
Cash a/c			
– materials	729,540		
– labour	362,490		
– site expenses	142,970		
Profit and loss a/c			
– attributable profit	145,985	Balances c/f	
Balance c/f		– of raw materials	13,540
– accrued site		– costs to date plus at-	
expenses	5,495	tributable profits	1,372,940
	£1,386,480		£1,386,480

Certificates account

	£		£
		Customers' a/c	1,500,000
Balance c/f	1,500,000		
	£1,500,000		£1,500,000

Customers' account

	£		£
Certificates a/c	1,500,000	Retentions a/c	
		(*10% × £1,500,000*)	150,000
		Balance c/f	1,350,000
	£1,500,000		£1,500,000

Retentions account

	£		£
Customers' a/c	150,000	Balance c/f	150,000
	£150,000		£150,000

Extract from Balance sheet at 31 December 19X1

Current assets	£	£
Stocks		
Raw materials		13,540
Long-term contract work in progress		
Costs to date plus attributable profit	1,372,940	
Progress payments received and receivable		
(£1,500,000 – 150,000)	(1,350,000)	22,940
Debtors		1,350,000

27.4 COMPUTING THE PROFIT OR LOSS

1	Check total position of contract

		£
Contract price (*total value*)		
Estimated total costs		x
Estimated total profit (*loss*)		(x)
If loss, then provide in full. If profit, go to next step.		x

2	Can outcome be assessed with reasonable certainty?

There is no standard point at which outcome becomes certain. We are asking whether it is safe to take profit, or if it is still too risky.

If no, do not take any profit. If yes, go to next step.

3	Decide method of taking profit

Two methods are used:
A. By reference to work done only (*used where contract is divisible into stages*)
B. A proportion of estimated total profit (*used where contract is indivisible*)

A	B
Profit to date = Value of work done *less* cost of work done	Profit to date = Estimated profit × % complete The % complete may be by reference to value, or cost

4	Apply prudence factors

The profit to date may be reduced to allow for specific or general uncertainties.

Example 2

Constructors Plc are engaged in two long-term contracts. Details of the contracts together with transactions occurring in the year ended 31 December 19X6 are given below:

	Contract 1 £	Contract 2 £
Fixed contract price	2,000,000	3,000,000
Balances brought forward at 1 January 19X6 –		
Costs to date	830,000	1,625,950
Attributable profit taken	145,700	–
Costs incurred in the current year	295,600	329,640
Value of work certified to 31 December 19X6	1,400,400	–
Costs of remaining work (*estimate*)	481,900	1,196,710

Required:
(a) Calculate profits and losses to be taken in 19X6, assuming that profit is recognised as a proportion of estimated total profit, based on sales value;
(b) Recompute the profit taken on contract 1 if the basis is to take two-thirds of profit based on work certified.

(a) Profit on proportion basis	Contract 1 £	Contract 2 £
Total position:		
Selling price	2,000,000	3,000,000
Estimated total costs		
£830,000 + 295,600 + 481,900	(1,607,500)	–
£1,625,950 + 329,640 + 1,196,710	–	(3,152,300)
Estimated profit (loss)	£392,500	£(152,300)

	Contract 1 £	Contract 2 £
Profit taken: £392,500 × $\frac{1,400,400}{2,000,000}$	274,829	–
Loss in full	–	(152,300)
Taken in earlier years	145,700	
Profit (loss) taken in current year	£129,129	£(152,300)

(b) Profit on work certified	£
Value of work certified	1,400,400
Cost of work certified	
£830,000 + 295,600	1,125,600
	£274,800
Two-thirds thereof	183,200
Taken in earlier years	145,700
Profit taken in current year	£37,500

Exercises to Chapter 27

1. The following relates to contract X, which was commended during the current period:

	£
Direct labour paid	572,350
Materials purchased	321,570
Overheads allocated	142,960
Depreciation of site assets	52,420
Stock on site at year end	15,990
Labour earned not yet paid	24,960
Attributable profit taken	41,125

You are required to prepare a Contract account and identify the total amount of work-in-progress carried forward.

2. A business takes profits on contracts as a proportion of estimated total profit on a sales basis. Loss are provided in full. A particular contract has a fixed selling price of £1,000,000. Costs to date are £340,000. Work certified is £440,000. Progress payments received are £396,000.

You are required to compute the profit or loss taken in the first year, assuming respectively that:

(a) Estimated further costs are £520,000; and
(b) Estimated further costs are £720,000.

BILLS OF EXCHANGE

28.1 DEFINITION AND TERMINOLOGY

In essence a bill of exchange is a written acknowledgement of a debt.
The legal definition of a bill of exchange is contained in the Bill of Exchange Act 1883, Section 3, and is:

'An unconditional order in writing, addressed by one person to another, signed by the person giving it, requiring the person to whom it is addressed to pay on demand, or at a fixed or determinable future time, a sum certain in money to or to the order of a specified person or to bearer.'

The following terms arise in accounting for bills.

Term	Meaning
Acceptor or Drawee	The party owing the debt. That party accepts a bill drawn on them by their creditor.
Payee or Drawer	The party to whom the debt is owed. That party initiates the drawing of the bill upon their debtor.
Maturity date	The end of the term stated in the bill. On this date the acceptor is required to pay the amount specified on the bill.
Dishonouring	Failure of a debtor to make payment on maturity.
Negotiation	The drawer can 'sell' the bill to another person, or use it as payment for another debt. The recipient may renegotiate the bill to a third owner. At maturity date, the ultimate owner will present the bill to the

	drawee for payment. In the event that payment is not made, the ultimate owner has the right to reclaim money from previous owners.
Discounting	The drawer, or a person to whom the bill has been negotiated, may discount the bill with a bank, or some other financial institution. Discounting is a form of negotiating the bill. The bank will make a charge equivalent to interest on borrowed money. The charge will also take into account the risk borne by the bank. This depends on the identity of the drawee.
Retirement	The settlement of a bill before the maturity date. The drawer may agree to a small discount since payment is received sooner than expected.

28.2 ACCOUNTING IN THE DRAWEE'S BOOKS

The drawee's books are the more straightforward, since there can be no discounting.

The chain of events is thus from creditor to bill payable to cash payment.

Event	Debit	Credit
Goods are purchased (or creditor arises from some other source)	Purchases a/c	Creditor a/c
Bill of exchange, drawn by creditor is accepted	Creditor a/c	Bills payable a/c
Time passes	–	–
Maturity date, and bill is presented for payment	Bills payable a/c	Bank a/c

28.3 ACCOUNTING IN THE DRAWER'S BOOKS

The drawer's books are the more complex, since discounting, dishonouring and negotiating may all be included (although not usually all with the same bill!).

Event	Debit	Credit
Goods are sold (or debtor arises from some other source)	Debtor a/c	Sales a/c
Bill of exchange is drawn, and accepted by debtor	Bills receivable a/c	Debtor a/c
Bill discounted at bank	Bank a/c (sum received) Profit and loss a/c (discounting charges)	Bills received a/c
OR Bill negotiated as settlement for a creditor	Creditor a/c	Bills receivable a/c
OR Bill presented to drawee at maturity date	Bank a/c	Bills receivable a/c

When a bill has been discounted or negotiated, and the maturity date has not yet expired, then there is a risk that the bill may be dishonoured.

The person to whom the bill was negotiated or discounted would then reclaim the sum due from the drawer. This possibility of a future liability is a contingent liability (as defined by Statement of Standard Accounting Practice 18). The amount of the contingent liability, i.e. the face value of the bills discounted, would be shown as a note to the drawer's accounts.

The treatment of bills of exchange within a group, and their cancellation on consolidation was dealt with in Section 17.3.2.

Example

Trader Plc sells goods within the United Kingdom and also overseas, for which settlement is normally made by three month bills of exchange.

The following transactions occurred during 19X3:

10 Jan Sold goods to *A* for £500, to be settled by a three-months bill of exchange

20 Jan Sold goods to *B* for £450, to be settled by a three-month bill of exchange

30 Jan Sold goods to *C* for £625, to be settled by a three-months bill of exchange

8 Feb Sold further goods to *A* for £300, to be settled by a three-month bill of exchange

25 Feb Negotiated the first bill due from *A* for £500 to a supplier, *M* Plc, in settlement for goods supplied

1 Mar Discounted the bill due from *C* with the local bank, who charged £15 for the service

20 Apr   Bill for £450 was presented to B, who duly paid that sum
22 Apr   A requested early settlement of the bill for £300. Trader Plc
         accepted £295 in full settlement.

Required:
(a) The Bills receivable account as it appears in the books of Trader Plc;
     and
(b) The Bills payable account as it appears in the books of A.

(a) Books of Trader Plc

Bills receivable account

Date	£	Date	£
10 Jan Debtors' a/c – A	500	25 Feb Creditors' a/c – M Plc	
20 Jan Debtors' a/c – B	450	(*bill negotiated*)	500
30 Jan Debtors' a/c – C	625	1 Mar Bank a/c	610
8 Feb Debtors' a/c – A	300	Bank charges a/c –	
		(*bill discounted*)	15
		20 Apr Bank a/c	450
		(*bill matured*)	
		22 Apr Bank a/c	295
		Discounts allowed	
		(*bill retired*)	5
	£1,875		£1,875

(b) Books of A

Bills payable account

Date	£	Date	£
10 Apr Bank a/c (*bill matured, payment to M Plc*)	500	10 Jan Creditors' a/c – Traders Plc	500
22 Apr Bank a/c	295	8 Feb Creditors' a/c – Traders Plc	300
Discounts received (*bill retired*)	5		
	£800		£800

N.B. The negotiation of the £500 bill by Traders Plc to M Plc had no
effect in the books of A. The ultimate payment was made to M Plc.

Exercises to Chapter 28

A business has the following transactions involving bills of exchange:

1. Goods sold to X for £2,500, to be settled by a six-month bill of exchange.
2. Goods sold to Y for £3,200, to be settled by a six-month bill of exchange.
3. Goods sold to Z for £4,100, to be settled by a six-month bill of exchange.
4. Discounted bill due from Y to a bank, who charged £250.
5. Early settlement of bill from Z arranged, allowing a discount of 10 per cent.

You are required to prepare the bills receivable account and identify the balance carried forward.

PART VII

INTERPRETATION OF

ACCOUNTS

FUNDS STATEMENTS

29.1 PURPOSE AND CONTENT

29.1.1 Purpose of the statement

A funds statement, alias a statement of sources and applications of funds, is in essence a reconciliation of two Balance sheets. It covers the period between the two Balance sheets and lists the increases and decreases in the various Balance-sheet items with certain adjustments to enable a tie-up with the Profit and loss account to be made.

Its purposes may be described as:

(a) To identify movements in assets, liabilities and capital during a period, and the resulting effect on net liquid assets; and
(b) to explain the manner in which operations of a business have been financed, and in which its financial resources have been used.

29.1.2 Sources and applications of funds

The increase or decrease in any particular Balance-sheet item which affects the funds of the business is either a source of funds or an application of funds.

The following are examples of sources of funds and applications of funds.

(a) Sources of funds
Net profit before taxation and before depreciation
Proceeds of sale of assets
Cash received from shares issued/capital introduced by proprietor/ loans raised
Increase in balances due to creditors

(b) Applications of funds
   Purchase cost of new assets
   Cash paid to redeem or purchase shares/repay loans
   Dividends paid/Drawings of proprietor
   Taxation paid
   Increase in stock in hand
   Increase in balances due from debtors
   Increase in cash balances.

29.1.3 Presentation

The presentation adopted will depend on the reason for preparation. There are two basic reasons why a business prepares a funds statement:

(a) Limited company with turnover or gross income of £25,000 or more. Such a company is required by an accounting standard (SSAP 10) to include a funds statement within its audited accounts. Such statements tend to follow a standard format. This is dealt with in Section 29.2.
(b) Explanatory statement. A funds statement may be used to explain a change within a period, e.g. the relationship between profit and cash flow, the utilisation of a share issue, how a certain asset purchase was financed. Such statements are structured to highlight the movement to be explained. This is dealt with in Section 29.3.

29.2 STATEMENT OF STANDARD ACCOUNTING PRACTICE 10

29.2.1 Standard format

STATEMENT OF SOURCE AND APPLICATION OF FUNDS
SOURCES OF FUNDS

	£	£
Net profit before taxation		x
Adjustments for items not involving the movement of funds		
Depreciation		x
TOTAL GENERATED FROM OPERATIONS		x
OTHER SOURCES		
Issue of shares	x	
Loans raised	x	
Proceeds of fixed assets and investments sold	x	
		x
		x

APPLICATIONS OF FUNDS

Dividends paid	(x)
Tax paid	(x)
Fixed assets and investments purchases	(x)
Loans repaid	(x)
	(x)
	x

INCREASE/DECREASE IN WORKING CAPITAL

Increase in stock	(x)
Increase in debtors	(x)
Increase in creditors (*excluding tax and dividends*)	x
Increase in net liquid funds	(x)
	(x)

Although other formats may be used this format, which is taken from SSAP 10, is perfectly acceptable for examination purposes.

29.2.2 Technique for preparation

Step 1: Open pro-forma statement to enable entries to be made as they are computed.

Step 2: Open T accounts for:
   (a) Tax
   (b) Dividends
   (c) Fixed assets (*cost, accumulated depreciation, disposal*)
   (d) Profit and loss account.

Step 3: From opening and closing Balance sheets, enter relevant balances to T accounts and all other movements directly to funds statement.

Step 4: Enter double entry for tax charge, dividends appropriated, asset disposals.

Step 5: Identify balancing figures in T accounts to complete funds statement.

Example 1

The following are the draft accounts of Funflow Plc:

Balance sheets	31.12.X6		31.12.X5	
	£000	£000	£000	£000
Fixed assets				
Plant and machinery at cost		3,000		1,600
Accumulated depreciation		(1,200)		(850)
		1,800		750
Current assets				
Stock	950		690	
Trade debtors	700		580	
Cash at bank and in hand	20		30	
	£1,670		£1,300	
Creditors				
Trade creditors	(455)		(228)	
Taxation	(55)		(32)	
Proposed dividend	(50)		(40)	
	£(560)		£(300)	
Net current assets		1,110		1,000
Total assets *less* current liabilities		2,910		1,750
Debenture stock		(800)		
		£2,110		£1,750
Capital and reserves				
Ordinary shares of £1		1,700		1,500
Share premium account		100		
Profit and loss account		310		250
		£2,110		£1,750

Profit and loss account for year to 31.12.X6

	£	£000
Turnover		2,060
Operating costs (including depreciation £435,000)		(1,795)
Operating profit		265
Interest payable		(40)
Profit before tax		225
Taxation		(85)
Profit after tax		140
Dividends		
Paid		(30)
Proposed		(50)

Retained profit for year	60
Retained profit b/f	250
Retained profit c/f	310

The following information is relevant:

1 Depreciation of £435,000 includes £10,000 loss on sale of plant which had originally cost £100,000 and has accumulated depreciation at the date of sale of £75,000. The plant was sold for £15,000. The remaining £425,000 of depreciation represents the charge for the period.
2 Shares with a nominal value of £200,000 were issued at £1.50 each. The premium was credited to Share premium account.
3 Debenture stock was issued at par.

Required:
A statement of sources and applications of funds for the year for inclusion in the audited accounts.

FUNFLOW PLC

Statement of sources and applications of funds

Sources of funds	£000	£000
Net profit before taxation (*W1*) .		225
Adjustments for items not involving the movement of funds		
Depreciation (*and loss on sale of plant*) (*W5 + W6*)		435
Total generated from operations		660
Other sources		
Issue of shares (*200 + 100*)	300	
Issue of debentures	800	
Sale of plant (*W6*)	15	
		1,115
		1,775
Applications		
Purchase of plant (*W4*)	(1,500)	
Tax paid (*W2*)	(62)	
Dividends paid (*W3*)	(70)	

		(1,632)
Net sources (*applications of funds*)		143
Effect on net working capital		
Increase in stock	(260)	
Increase in debtors	(120)	
Increase in creditors	227	
Decrease in net liquid funds:		
Cash at bank	10	
		(143)

WORKINGS

(1) *Profit and loss account*

	£000		£000
Taxation a/c	85	b/f	250
Dividends a/c *(30 + 50)*	80	Profit before tax	225
c/f	310		
	£475		£475

(2) *Taxation account*

	£000		£000
Tax paid *(balance)*	62	b/f	32
c/f	55	Profit and loss a/c – charged	85
	£117		£117

(3) *Dividends account*

	£000		£000
Dividends paid *(balance)*	70	b/f	40
c/f	50	Profit and loss a/c – charged	80
	£120		£120

(4) *Plant and machinery at cost*

	£000		£000
b/f	1,600	Disposal a/c	100
Purchased *(balance)*	1,500	c/f	3,000
	£3,100		£3,100

(5) *Plant and machinery – accumulated deprciation*

	£000		£000
Disposal a/c	75	b/f	850
c/f	1,200	Charge for period	425
	£1,275		£1,275

(6) *Disposal account*

	£000		£000
Cost	100	Accumulated depreciation a/c	75
		Proceeds received	15
		Loss on sale	10
	£100		£100

Points arising:

1 All sources appear positive (including decrease in net liquid funds) and all applications negative.
2 Profit and loss account working was unnecessary, but ensured correct double entry in workings 2 and 3.
3 Tax paid, dividends paid and purchase of plant were all found as balancing figures in the workings.

29.3 EXPLANATORY FUNDS STATEMENTS

A funds statement can be used to explain particular movements between two Balance-sheet dates. The statement is presented to highlight the change that is to be explained, e.g. adverse movement in net liquid funds, purchase of fixed assets, cash received from a share issue.

The technique is exactly as before. The format of the final statement differs. This is best explained with an example.

Example 2

Simon Simple has traded successfully for many years, and is now expanding his business. However, despite healthy profits and minimal drawings, his Bank account has dipped into overdraft, much to the bank manager's alarm. The following accounts have been prepared:

Balance sheets at:

	30.6.X8		30.6.X7	
	£000	£000	£000	£000
Freehold property at valuation		21		11
Equipment at cost				
1 July 19X7	6		6	
Additions	15			
Disposals	(2)			
	19			
Accumulated depreciation	(4)		(2)	
		15		4
		36		15
Stock	23		11	
Debtors	15		7	
Cash at bank	___		2	
	38		20	
Trade creditors	(8)		(7)	
Overdraft	(11)		___	
		19		13
		55		28
Capital account				
1 July 19X7		28		28
Net profit for year		20		
Surplus on freehold		10		
Drawings		(3)		
		55		28

The equipment sold in the year had accumulated depreciation of
£1,000 at the date of sale, and was sold for £1,000. There was neither
profit nor loss on sale. The balance of depreciation changes represent the
charge for the period.

Required:
A Statement which explains to Simon Simple and the bank manager the
adverse cash movement.

SIMON SIMPLE

Statement to explain movement in bank balance

	£000	£000
Bank account		
At 1 July 19X7		2
At 30 June 19X8		(11)
Adverse movement		(13)
Explained by:		
Sources of funds		
Net profit for year	20	
Depreciation charged (W1)	3	
Total generated from operations		23
Sale of equipment		1
Increase in creditors		1
		25
Applications of funds:		
Purchase of equipment	(15)	
Drawings	(3)	
Increase in stocks	(12)	
Increase in debtors	(8)	
		(38)
Net application of funds		(13)

WORKINGS

(1) *Equipment – accumulated depreciation*

	£000		£000
Disposal a/c	1	b/f	2
c/f	4	Charged for year (*balance*)	3
	5		5

(2) *Disposal a/c*

	£000		£000
Cost a/c	2	Accumulated depreciation a/c	1
		Proceeds	1
	2		2

Points arising:

1 It is clear that Simon has increased equipment, stocks and debtors substantially. This is financed partly by profits, and partly by the overdraft. This situation is called OVERTRADING, and is remedied by Simon raising longer-term finance to offset the long-term increase in assets required by the expansion.
2 The revaluation of the freehold property did not appear on the funds statement. The Freehold account and Capital account increased by the same revaluation surplus which may be disregarded in the funds statement.

Exercises to Chapter 29

The following Balance sheets and Profit and loss account relate to a particular business:

	31.12.X5	31.12.X4
Fixed assets at cost	125,000	115,000
Accumulated depreciation	(62,000)	(51,000)
	63,000	64,000
Stock	51,000	43,000
Debtors	26,500	23,800
Cash at bank and in hand	11,250	10,300
	151,750	141,100
Trade creditors	(19,850)	(17,415)
Taxation payable	(8,420)	(7,130)
	£123,480	£116,555
Called-up share capital	50,000	50,000
Profit and loss account	73,480	66,555
	£123,480	£116,555

	£
Profit before taxation	26,600
Taxation charge	(9,175)
	17,425
Dividends paid	(10,500)
	£6,925

No fixed assets were sold in the year.

You are required to compute the following figures for inclusion in the funds statement:

    (a) tax paid;
    (b) total generated from operations;
    (c) total applications; and
    (d) effect on net working capital.

RATIO ANALYSIS

30.1 OBJECTIVE OF INTERPRETATION

30.1.1 The layman's problem

Financial statements may present understandable data to an accountant. To the layman, however, the conclusions to be drawn from the data may not be clear at all. There are two reasons:

(a) the layman may not understand the concepts of value and terminology on which the accounts are based, e.g. that assets are not stated at saleable value, but at historic cost less the proportion consumed as depreciation;

(b) the layman will not appreciate the significant relationships between the reported figures. The accountant as accounts preparer is best placed to explain the bases upon which the accounts are prepared to each particular user, be they clients, board of directors or shareholders. The major part of this book has concerned itself with such technical knowledge. This chapter addresses the second problem, by considering the various ratios which are in common use and which are relevant to an examination situation.

30.1.2 The accountant's objective

Interpretation of accounts, particularly in an exam setting, must take account of the following points:

(a) The answer given must address itself to the problem posed. Accountants should give an adequate explanation, using language that is understood. They should avoid giving too much information which may be confusing.

(b) Data must be presented (and if necessary represented) in a digestible format. A funds statement, for example, may give a useful explanation of changes.
(c) Ratios used should always be defined.
(d) Detailed workings should be relegated to supporting workings or appendices.
(e) Interpretation involves:

  - computing the ratio;
  - comparing the result with a norm, an earlier period, or a comparable business;
  - giving reasons for a change in the ratio;
  - noting the limitations of the ratio.

30.2 MANAGEMENT RATIOS

30.2.1 The pyramid system

Management require detail in order to properly assess a company's past performance and current position. At the same time the detail needs to be ordered and structured to be usable.

To this end a system called the PYRAMID ANALYSIS system is widely used. The pyramid is given below (Figure 30.1), and the ratios are then considered in turn. A full-worked example is given at the end of the chapter (p.431)

30.2.2 Return on capital employed

Return on capital employed (ROCE) compares a Profit and loss account statistic (return) with a Balance sheet statistic (capital employed).

There are many versions of ROCE, depending on which definition of profit and which definition of capital employed are used.

The version used here is:

$$\frac{\text{Operating profit}}{\text{Operating assets}} \text{ expressed as a percentage.}$$

Operating profit is profit after all operating costs but before interest payable, investment income, taxation and extraordinary items have been taken account of. For a consistent measure over time it may also be before exceptional items.

fig 30.1 *the pyramid system*

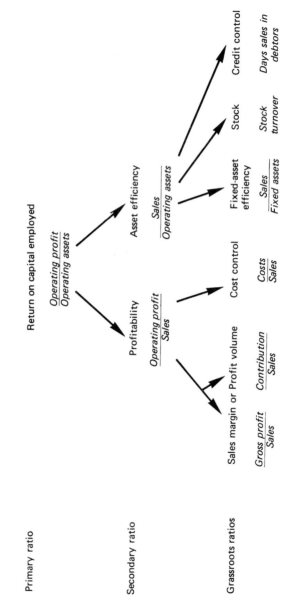

Primary ratio

Secondary ratio

Grassroots ratios

Operating assets are fixed assets (excluding investments other than subsidiaries and associates for which earnings or share of earnings are included in operating profit), stock and debtors. Cash is excluded, and no deduction is made for any liabilities so that we ignore the way in which a business is financed (which is considered separately). This enables the widest possible comparison between businesses. The definition of operating assets used is equal to:

'Share capital + reserves + liabilities − cash.'

The uses of ROCE are to give a measure of performance in relation to resources employed, and if compared over time, to give an indicator of growth in a business. When computed for a sole trader or partnership the ROCE measures the return on the combined proprietors and other funds invested in the business. In the case of a company the ratio is of limited use to shareholders, since capital employed in the Balance sheet bears no relationship to the price paid by a shareholder to acquire shares in the company.

The limitations of ROCE arise from using the historical cost convention. Assets which are old and stated at heavily depreciated historic cost will appear to give a better ROCE than a company with new assets that are regularly revalued. Revaluation is necessary to give a realistic measure of fixed asset value.

30.2.3 Profitability

By introducing one new statistic, sales, we can divide the primary ratio into two secondary ratios. The first gives a measure of net profitability, and is defined as

$$\frac{\text{Operating profit}}{\text{Sales}} \text{ expressed as a percentage}$$

The uses of this ratio are to show the profit earned per £1 of sales revenue. For further explanation it is necessary to examine the grass-roots ratios which include a subdivision of operating profit.

30.2.4 Sales margin

This ratio is relevant where costs can be divided into cost of sales (deducted from sales to find gross profit), administration, selling and distribution (which both separate gross profit from operating profit)

	£
Sales	x
Cost of sales	(x)
Gross profit	x
Administration expenses	(x)
Selling and distribution costs	(x)
Operating profit	£x

Sales margin ratio is:

$$\frac{\text{Gross profit}}{\text{Sales}} \text{ expressed as a percentage.}$$

The use of sales margin is to indicate the amount per £1 of sales revenue which is added to purchase or production costs to reach selling price. The ratio is expected to remain static. Movements may be due to:

- deliberate change in selling price (e.g. reduction to stimulate sales);
- increase in purchase costs or production costs not passed on to the customer;
- errors in stock counting, valuing or cut-off (stock cut-off means that paperwork such as purchase and sales invoices, and physical stock movements must be synchronised);
- sales mix (where there are two or more types of stock earning different margins).

30.2.5 Profit volume

Profit volume or P/V ratio is used in place of gross margin, where costs are divided between variable and fixed in relation to sales (known as 'marginal costing').

	£
Sales	x
Variable costs (cost of sales, administration, selling and distribution)	(x)
Contribution	x
Fixed costs (cost of sales, administration, selling and distribution)	(x)
Operating profit	£x

P/V ratio is:

$$\frac{\text{Contribution}}{\text{Sales}} \text{ expressed as a percentage.}$$

30.2.6 Cost control

Costs analysed by function (e.g. selling and distribution); cost centre (e.g. department *A*); or type (e.g. advertising) may be expressed as a percentage of sales.

The use of such ratios is to indicate whether costs have remained in line with changes in sales.

30.2.7 Asset efficiency

This secondary ratio is found by taking operating assets from the primary ratio and multiplying by sales.

$$\text{Asset efficiency} = \frac{\text{Sales}}{\text{Operating assets}}$$

The result represents the sales generated per £1 of investment in operating assets. The two secondary ratios complement each other.

Secondary ratio	Purpose
Asset efficiency	How often can we generate sales from the assets used?
Profitability	How profitable can we make the sales generated?

The two secondary ratios multiplied together will give the primary ratio.

Further analysis of asset efficiency is given by examining the related grassroots ratios.

30.2.8 Fixed-asset efficiency

Fixed asset efficiency is measured by:

$$\frac{\text{Sales}}{\text{Fixed assets}}.$$

The result measures the sales generated per £1 of investment in fixed assets.

The ratio can be further subdivided by taking each item within fixed assets in turn.

The main limitation, as with return on capital employed, is the use of historic cost depreciated assets rather than revalued amounts.

30.2.9 Stock control

There are two ratios in common use:

(a) Stock turnover

$$\frac{\text{Purchases}}{\text{Average stock}}.$$

Where purchases are not known, cost of sales may be used. The result measures the number of times that stock is sold and completely replaced in a period. It must be set against the business involved, e.g. a bakery or dairy would expect to sell and replace stock on a daily basis, whereas a shipyard may take over a year to produce one ship.

Within the context of the business a high stock turnover indicates efficient use of resources, but may indicate that the business is in danger of running out of stock in the event of a strike affecting supplies. A low stock turnover indicates that funds are being tied up in stock unnecessarily.

(b) Days sales in stock

$$\frac{\text{Closing stock}}{\text{Cost of sales}} \times 365$$

The result measures the number of days that the business could continue in the event that supplies were discontinued.

The main limitations of both ratios are inclusion of obsolete stock which has been given a value within the accounts, but which is unsaleable, and variations in stock valuation policy between businesses.

30.2.10 Credit control

Credit control entails the vetting of customers to whom credit is extended, collection of debts including the giving of settlement discounts.

The ratio used to test credit control is:

$$\text{Day sales in debtors} = \frac{\text{Trade debtors}}{\text{Credit sales}} \times 365.$$

The result measures the average number of days that debtors take to settle invoices. This must be set against the period offered by the business. A typical credit period is 30 days.

Days sales in debtors	Conclusion
0–30 days	Within normal period
30–45 days	Requires examination for general/specific late debts
45–60 days	Specific debts likely to be irrecoverable
Over 60 days	Serious problems

A business will generally produce an age analysis which subdivides debtors into age groups. This is used to identify late payers, and also to check the bad and doubtful debt provision.

An equivalent ratio may be produced for creditors:

$$\text{Days purchases in creditors} = \frac{\text{Trade creditors}}{\text{Credit purchases}} \times 365$$

If the business is to take advantage of credit from suppliers, then the result for this ratio should be similar to the days sales in debtors. If the days purchases in creditors were excessive, then there is a risk that suppliers may cease to extend credit.

30.3 LIQUIDITY RATIOS

30.3.1 Current ratio

The current ratio is defined as:

$$\frac{\text{Current assets}}{\text{Current liabilities}} \text{ expressed as a ratio.}$$

This measures the ability of a business to meets its liabilities as they fall due. It recognises that, in due course, stock will generate trade debtors,

428

trade debtors generate cash and that cash will meet payments to trade creditors for the replacement of stock. We call this process the 'working capital cycle'.

The ideal current ratio is 2:1. The major limitation is the inclusion of stock irrespective of how quickly it can be sold and turned into trade debtors, and to a lesser extent the various methods of valuation that may be applied to stock.

30.3.2 Quick-assets ratio

The quick-assets or liquidity ratio takes a more urgent view of liquidity than the current ratio, by examining the position over the immediate future, normally three months.

The quick-assets ratio is:

$$\frac{\text{Debtors + Realisable investments + Cash}}{\text{Current liabilities due within three months}}.$$

This measures the ability of a business to meet its immediate liabilites. Consequently it should always be at least 1:1 unless the business has arranged overdraft facilities.

The only limitation is the speed with which the business can generate debtors into cash.

30.4 GEARING RATIOS

30.4.1 Capital gearing

Gearing is the relationship between the long-term debt finance which a business uses in comparison with its equity capital.

(a) Debt capital is debenture and loan stock and other long-term loans on which interest is paid.

(b) Equity capital is share capital (ordinary and preference) and reserves.

The balance between equity and debt is important for two reasons:

(i) Interest paid on debt capital is allowable for tax purposes, whereas dividends on equity capital are paid from post-tax earnings. It is therefore more tax effective to pay interest rather than dividends.

(ii) On the other hand, dividends may be avoided in a poor year whereas interest must always be paid.

The capital-gearing ratio is:

$$\frac{\text{Debt capital}}{\text{Debt capital} + \text{equity capital}} \text{ expressed as a percentage.}$$

A high ratio indicates a high-risk factor in a business. In the United Kingdom 30 per cent is a typical capital-gearing ratio. For most companies debt may never exceed equity (a 50 per cent ratio). This limitation is set within the Articles of Association of each company.

30.4.2 Income gearing

Income gearing looks at the Profit and loss account aspect of gearing.

The income gearing ratio is:

$$\frac{\text{Interest charged}}{\text{Profit before tax and before interest}} \text{ expressed as a percentage.}$$

This represents the proportion of profits used to service the debt capital. It is quoted less frequently than the capital-gearing ratio.

30.5 INVESTOR RATIOS

Investors buying stocks and shares on the Stock Exchange will not have access to the detailed information available to management. They are limited to the published accounts and announcements made by the company. Nevertheless, investors are concerned with the return on their investment, future prospects and level of risk.

30.5.1 Dividend per share

Dividend per share represents the payment made by the company, net of basic rate income tax, for a full accounting period. It may be paid in two or more instalments (interim, final dividends).

30.5.2 Earnings per share

Earnings per share is the amount of profit after tax, before extraordinary items less preference dividends attributable to each ordinary shareholder.

The excess of earnings per share over dividend per share represents profits per share retained in the business and should be reflected in an increase in the value of the share.

30.5.3 Dividend yield

Dividend yield is:

$$\frac{\text{Dividend per share (grossed up for basic-rate income tax)}}{\text{Market value per share}}$$
– expressed as a percentage.

This represents a rate of return on the investment and is directly comparable with other investment returns.

30.5.4 Dividend cover

Dividend cover is the number of times that dividend per share divides into earnings per share (which may be after extraordinary items for this purpose).

A dividend cover of 1 indicates that earnings of the current period exactly covered the dividend leaving no retained profit for reinvestment.

A dividend cover of between 2 to 4 times would be comfortable. A smaller private company would require a higher cover, since it is more dependent on retained profits for reinvestment funds.

30.5.5 Price-earnings ratio

Price-earnings (or P/E) ratio is:

$$\frac{\text{Market value per share}}{\text{Earnings per share}}.$$

It represents the number of years' earnings which an investor will pay to acquire a share, and is thus a measure of market confidence in a company.

A low P/E ratio, 2 to 3, indicates that the purchase price is supported mainly by earnings, and not by demand for the share.

A high P/E ratio, 15 to 20, indicates a high demand for the share, quite beyond the earnings or dividends which will be attributed to the share. This may be because of anticipated growth in the capital value of the share.

Example

The following data relate to a large quoted company engaged primarily in the manufacture and wholesale selling of wines and spirits.

(1) Profit and loss account for year: £m.

Turnover	806.8
Cost of sales	(551.8)
Gross profit	255.0
Operating costs	(73.4)
Operating profit	181.6
Investment income	13.2
Interest payable	(11.3)
Profit before tax	183.5
Taxation	(63.3)
Profit after tax	120.2
Dividends	(49.5)
Retained profit	£70.7

(2) Market value per 50 p share is 293 p

(3) Basic rate of income tax is 30 per cent

(4) Balance sheet at end of period:

	£m.	£m.
Fixed assets		359.6
Current assets		
Stocks	813.1	
Debtors	237.8	
Investments	57.4	
Cash	19.8	
	£1,128.1	
Current liabilities		
Trade creditors	(91.4)	
Corporation tax (due in nine months)	(56.1)	
Other taxes and social security	(23.7)	
Proposed dividend	(33.2)	
	£(204.4)	

Net current assets	923.7
	1,283.3
Long-term liabilities	
Debentures and loan	(103.0)
	£1,180.3
Capital and reserves	
Ordinary shares of 50 p	181.6
Reserves	998.7
	£1,180.3

Required:
A brief analysis of results so far as the information permits.

(1) Management ratios – see facing page.
(2) Liquidity

Current ratio	5.5 times ($W9$)
Quick assets ratio	2.1 times ($W10$)

High current ratio is explained by the material stock maturing. Quick assets appear more than adequate despite the poor days sales in debtors.

(3) Gearing

Capital gearing	8.0 per cent ($W11$)
Income gearing	5.8 per cent ($W12$)

Both gearing ratios are very low.

(4) Investor ratios

Dividend per share	13.6p ($W13$)
Earnings per share	33.1p ($W14$)
Dividend yield	6.6 per cent ($W15$)
Dividend cover	2.43 times ($W16$)
Price-earnings ratio	8.9 ($W17$)

Dividend yield and P/E ratio appear marginally inferior to the average for brewers and distillers (5.11 per cent and 9.2 respectively), indicating that demand for the company's shares is below the average for that sector. Dividend cover appears reasonable.

WORKINGS

(1) Return on capital employed

$$\frac{\text{Operating profit}}{\text{Operating assets}} = \frac{181.6}{359.6 + 813.1 + 237.8} = 12.9 \text{ per cent}$$

433

(1) Management ratios
Pyramid of ratios
Primary

Return on capital employed
12.9 per cent (*W1*)

Secondary

Profitability
22.5 per cent (*W2*)

Asset efficiency
£0.57 sales per £1 operating assets (*W3*)

Grassroots

Gross profitability
31.6 per cent (*W4*)

Cost control
9.1 per cent (*W5*)

Fixed-asset efficiency
£2.24 in sales per
£1 fixed assets (*W6*)

Stock turnover
0.68 times
(*W7*)

Days sales in
debtors
108 days (*W8*)

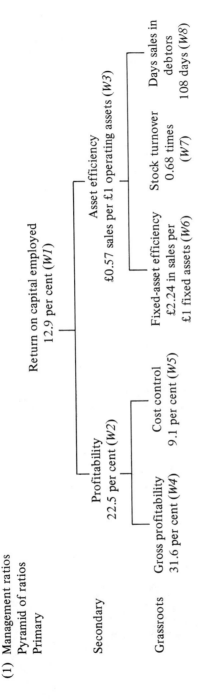

The overall position shows a profitable business, but one which uses assets, particularly stock, very inefficiently. This is understandable since the business is engaged in wines and spirits manufacture, and will hold substantial quantities of maturing stocks. The days sales in debtors appears to be very high.

(2) Profitability

$$\frac{\text{Operating profit}}{\text{Turnover}} = \frac{181.6}{806.8} = 22.5 \text{ per cent}$$

(3) Asset efficiency

$$\frac{\text{Turnover}}{\text{Operating assets}} = \frac{806.8}{359.6 + 813.1 + 237.8} = £0.57 \text{ in sales per } £1 \text{ operating assets}$$

(4) Gross profitability

$$\frac{\text{Gross profit}}{\text{Turnover}} = \frac{255.0}{806.8} = 31.6 \text{ per cent}$$

(5) Cost control

$$\frac{\text{Operating costs}}{806.8} = \frac{73.4}{806.8} = 9.1 \text{ per cent}$$

(6) Fixed asset efficiency

$$\frac{\text{Turnover}}{\text{Fixed assets}} = \frac{806.8}{359.6} = £2.24 \text{ in sales per } £1 \text{ fixed assets}$$

(7) Stock turnover

$$\frac{\text{Cost of sales}}{\text{Stock}} = \frac{551.8}{813.1} = 0.68 \text{ times per annum}$$

(8) Days sales in debtors

$$\frac{\text{Trade debtors}}{\text{Turnover}} \times 365 = \frac{237.8}{806.8} \times 365 = 108 \text{ days}$$

(9) Current ratio

$$\frac{\text{Current assets}}{\text{Current liabilities}} = \frac{1,128.1}{204.4} = 5.5 \text{ times}$$

(10) Quick-assets ratio

$$\frac{\text{Debtors} + \text{Investments} + \text{Cash}}{\text{Trade creditors} + \text{Other taxes} + \text{Proposed dividend}} = \frac{237.8 + 57.4 + 19.8}{91.4 + 23.7 + 33.2}$$
$$= 2.1 \text{ times}$$

(11) Capital gearing

$$\frac{\text{Debt capital}}{\text{Debt} + \text{equity capital}} = \frac{103.0}{103.0 + 1,180.3} = 8.0 \text{ per cent}$$

(12) Income gearing

$$\frac{\text{Interest charges}}{\text{Profit before tax and interest}} = \frac{11.3}{183.5 + 11.3} = 5.8 \text{ per cent}$$

(13) Dividend per share

$$\frac{\text{Net dividends}}{\text{Number of shares}} = \frac{49.5}{181.6 \times 2} = 13.6 \text{ p}$$

(14) Earnings per share

$$\frac{\text{Profit after tax}}{\text{Number of shares}} = \frac{120.2}{181.6 \times 2} = 33.1 \text{ p}$$

(15) Dividend yield

$$\frac{\text{Dividend per share grossed up}}{\text{Market value}} = \frac{13.6p \times \frac{100}{70}}{293p} = 6.6 \text{ per cent}$$

(16) Dividend cover

$$\frac{\text{Profit available for dividend}}{\text{Dividends}} = \frac{120.2}{49.5} = 2.43 \text{ times}$$

(17) Price-earnings ratio

$$\frac{\text{Market value}}{\text{Earnings per share}} = \frac{293p}{33.1p} = 8.9$$

Exercises to Chapter 30

The following Balance sheet extracts and Profit and loss account related to a particular business:

	31.12.X9 £	31.12.X8 £
Fixed assets at net book value	520,000	490,000
Stock	72,400	63,550
Trade debtors	42,130	39,600
Cash at bank and in hand	11,430	12,960
Trade creditors	(31,120)	(30,450)
Proposed dividends	(5,000)	(4,500)
Taxation due in nine months	(12,900)	(10,400)
	596,940	560,760
Unsecured loan stock	(100,000)	(150,000)
	£496,940	£410,760
Turnover	2,100,000	1,950,000
Cost of sales (all materials)	(1,450,000)	(1,375,000)
	650,000	575,000
Other operating costs	(478,500)	(453,690)
Operating profit	£171,500	£121,310
Earnings per share	82 p	79 p
Dividend per share (net)	25 p	20 p
Market value per share	800 p	750 p

You are required to compute for each period:

(a) primary ratio (%);
(b) gross profit to sales (%);
(c) Sales per £ of fixed assets;
(d) Stock turnover (19X9 only);
(e) Days sales in debtors;
(f) Current ratio;
(g) Quick-assets ratio;
(h) Price earnings ratio
(i) Dividend yield (assuming a 30% tax rate).

OUTLINE ANSWERS TO
EXERCISES

2.1 Cash account balance carried forward   £1,680
2.2 Rent account
      Credit balance carried forward   £300
      Profit and loss charge   £1,050
    Rates account
      Debit balance carried forward   £225
      Profit and loss charge   £875
2.3 Brown's account debit balance   £4,160
3.1 (a) £19
    (b) £27
    (c) £33
    (d) £32

3.2 Cash book balance   £1,423
3.3 Debtors' account balance   £42,880
    Provision for doubtful debts   £2,144
3.4 (a) Dr Suspense account   £40
       Cr Debtors' control account   £40
    (b) Dr Creditors' control account   £180
       Cr Suspense account   £180
    (c) Dr Purchases account   £110
       Cr Creditors' control account   £110
       (also credit personal account of supplier)
    (d) Dr Debtors control account   £65
       Cr Sales account   £65
4.1 (a) Loss on sale   £500
    (b) Loss on sale   £353
4.2 (a) Closing stock   £81,700
    (b) Closing stock   £72,600

4.3 (a) Finance charge £104 p.a.

    (b) Depreciation £280 p.a.

5.1 (a) Sales £10,400

    (b) Sales £10,250

    (c) Purchases £9,400

5.2 Gross profit £4,850

5.3 Net profit £39,690

6.1 Income and expenditure account credit £15,595

6.2 Bar profit £7,525

7.1 A: £6,000, B: £13,600, C: £19,600

7.2 A: £6,000, B: £8,600, C: £18,100

7.3 A: Loss £5,500, B: Profit £6,700, C: Profit £7,800

7.4 A: £9,000, B: £11,800, C: £18,400

7.5 A: £6,000, B: £13,200, C: £20,000

7.6 A: £16,600, B: £13,600, C: £10,800, Q: £5,000

7.7 B: £15,000, C: £10,000, Q: £4,200, A: (loan) £3,800

8.1 (a) Dividend £90,000

    (b) Dividend £18,000

8.2 (a) Dr Cash account £75,000

      Cr Share capital account £30,000

      Cr Share premium account £45,000

    (b) Dr Share premium account £26,000

      Cr Share capital account £26,000

    (c) Dr Cash account £21,600

      Cr Share capital account £12,000

      Cr Share premium account £9,600

    (d) Dr Land account £50,000

      Cr Revaluation account £50,000

10.1 (a) Dr Profit and loss account £300

      Cr Cash account – payment to Revenue £90

      Cr Cash account – payment to stockholder £210

    (b) Dr Cash account – receipt of interest £140

      Dr Income tax recoverable account £60

      Cr Profit and loss account £200

    (c) Dr Profit and loss account £5,000

      Cr Cash account £5,000

      Dr Corporation tax account £2,143

      Cr Cash account £2,143

    (d) Dr Cash account £4,200

      Cr Profit and loss account – investment income £6,000

      Dr Profit and loss account – tax charge £1,800

10.2 Profit and loss account charge £13,800

    Mainstream liability £6,800

11.1
Fees	£30,000
Other	313,000
Pension paid to former director	14,000
Total	£357,000

Emoluments (Excluding pension contributions)
Chairman   £95,000
Highest paid   100,000
Other directors in the bands:
  £0-£5,000   1
  £10,000-£15,000   2
  £45,001-£50,000   1

11.2 Staff costs
Wages and salaries	£424,600
Social security	32,600
Pension costs	32,900
	£490,100

12.1 (a) Dr Cash account   £6,000
    Cr Application and allotment account   £6,000
  (b) Dr Application and allotment account   £2,000
    Cr Cash account   £2,000
  (c) Dr Application and allotment account   £8,000
    Cr Ordinary share capital account   £5,000
    Cr Share premium account   £3,000
  (d) Dr Cash account   £3,800
    Cr Application and allotment account   £3,800
  (e) Dr Ordinary share capital account   £250
    Dr Share premium account   £150
    Cr Forfeited shares account   £400
    Cr Application and allotment account   £200
    Dr Forfeited shares account   £200
  (f) Cr Ordinary shares capital account   £250
    Dr Cash account   £250
    Dr Forfeited shares account   £200
    Cr Share premium account   £200

12.2 (a) Dr Ordinary share capital account   £10,000
    Dr Profit and loss account   £15,000
    Cr Cash account   £25,000
    Dr Profit and loss account   £10,000
    Cr Capital redemption reserve   £10,000
  (b) Dr Cash account   £11,250
    Cr Ordinary share capital account   £5,000
    Cr Share premium account   £6,250

Dr Ordinary share capital account £10,000
Dr Share premium account £5,000
Dr Profit and loss account £10,000
Cr Cash account £25,000

13.1 (a) 32%
(b) 15/125 or 12%

13.2 Balance carried forward (debit) £32,020

13.3 Net profit £1,923

14.1 Balance carried forward £2,820 due from A to B

14.2 Account is a mirror-image of 14.1. Balance is therefore the same.

15.1 Goodwill £28,100

15.2 Issue ordinary shares: X £15,000, Y £15,000, Z £7,500 Issue 10% cumulative preference shares: X £5,000, Z £2,500 Profit distribution: X £4,200, Y £3,700, Z £2,100

16 Balance carried forward – 500 shares, £1,073

17.1 (a) Goodwill on consolidation £12,000
(b) Minority interests £18,000
(c) Consolidated reserves £60,000

17.2 Consolidated balance sheet shows
Bills receivable £3,200
Bills payable £5,000

17.3 Dr Consolidated reserves account £2,500
Cr Stock account £2,500

17.4 (a) Group share pre-acquisition £10,750
(b) Group share post-acquisition £10,250
(c) Minority interest £7,000

18.1 Goodwill on consolidation £17,600

18.2 Dividends payable to minority shareholders £6,500

19.1 Turnover £86,080
Cost of sales £44,730

19.2 Total emoluments disclosed £70,000

20 Share of profit before tax £10,300
Share of taxation £4,200
Share of extraordinary item £1,900

21 Net assets £16,250
Share capital £8,000
Pre-acquisition reserves £2,000
Post-acquisition reserves £6,250
Reserve movements
Profit for year (at closing rate) £3,750
Exchange movement 2,500
                                 ———
                                 £6,250

22.1 (a) Finance profit   £80

      (b)   Profit in first year   £20

      (c)   Profit in first year (to nearest £)   £34

22.2 Loss on repossession   £13

24   (a)   Profit on consignment   £2,400

      (b)   Amount due from agent   £6,000

25   Payment in relation to first year   £50,000

      Payment in relation to second year   £65,000

26   (a)   Containers owned at depreciated value   £3,920

      (b)   Amount due to customers   £1,170

      (c)   Loss on container operations   £150

27.1 Work-in-progress (including profit)   £1,139,395

27.2 (a)   Profit taken   £61,600

      (b)   Loss provided   £60,000

28   Balance (bills receivable)   £2,500

29   (a)   Tax paid   £7,885

      (b)   Total generated from operations   £37,600

      (c)   Total applications   £28,385

      (d)   Effect on net working capital (increase)   £9,215

30

		19X9	*19X8*
(a)	Primary ratio	27.0%	20.5%
(b)	Gross profit to sales	31.0%	29.5%
(c)	Sales per £ of fixed assets	£4.04	£3.98
(d)	Stock turnover (based on cost of sales)	21.3 times	
(e)	Days sales in debtors	7.3	7.4
(f)	Current ratio	2.6:1	2.6:1
(g)	Quick assets ratio	1.5:1	1.5:1
(h)	Price earnings ratio	9.8	9.5
(i)	Dividend yield	4.5%	3.8%

INDEX

trade creditors 32
trade debtors 32
trading account 17
translation
   closing rate method 350
   temporal method 254
trial balance 14

U

unfranked investment income
   195

unrealised profit
   branch 250
   consolidation 307

V

value added tax 48–50
   SSAP 5 192
vendors' account 277

W

work certified, contracts 393